PATERNOSTER BIBLICAL AND THEOLOGICAL MONOGRAPHS

The Church and Deaf People:

A Study of Identity, Communication and Relationships with Special Reference to the Ecclesiology of Jürgen Moltmann

PATERNOSTER BIBLICAL AND THEOLOGICAL MONOGRAPHS

A full listing of titles in this series appears at the end of this book.

PATERNOSTER BIBLICAL AND THEOLOGICAL MONOGRAPHS

The Church and Deaf People:

A Study of Identity, Communication and Relationships with Special Reference to the Ecclesiology of Jürgen Moltmann

Roger Hitching

Foreword by Jürgen Moltmann

PATERNOSTER PRESS

Copyright © Roger Hitching 2003

First published 2003 by Paternoster Press
Paternoster Press is an imprint of Authentic Media
PO Box 300, Carlisle, Cumbria, CA3 OQS, U.K.
and PO Box 1047, Waynesboro, GA 30830-2047, USA

09 08 07 06 05 04 03   7 6 5 4 3 2 1

*The right of Roger Hitching to be identified as the Author
of this Work has been asserted by him in accordance with the
Copyright, Designs and Patents Act 1988*

*All rights reserved. No part of this publication may be
reproduced, stored in a retrieval system, or transmitted in any
form or by any means, electric, mechanical, photocopying,
recording or otherwise, without the prior permission of the
publisher or a licence permitting restricted copying. In the UK
such licences are issued by the Copyright Licencing Agency,
90 Tottenham Court Road, London W1P 9HE.*

British Library Cataloguing in Publication Data
A catalogue record for this book is available from the British Library.

ISBN 1-84227-222-5

Typeset by the author.
Published by Paternoster Press,
PO Box 300, Carlisle, Cumbria CA3 9AD.
Printed and bound in Great Britain
by Nottingham Alpha Graphics.

SERIES PREFACE

At the present time we are experiencing a veritable explosion in the field of biblical and theological research with more and more academic theses of high quality being produced by younger scholars from all over the world. One of the considerations taken into account by the examiners of doctoral theses is that, if they are to be worthy of the award of a degree, then they should contain material that needs to be read by other scholars; if so, it follows that the facilities must exist for them to be made accessible. In some cases (perhaps more often than is always realised) it will be most appropriate for the distinctive contribution of the thesis to be harvested in journal articles; in others there may be the possibility of a revision that will produce a book of wider appeal than simply to professional scholars. But many theses of outstanding quality can and should be published more or less as they stand for the benefit of other scholars and interested persons.

Hitherto it has not been easy for authors to find publishers willing to publish works that, while highly significant as works of scholarship, cannot be expected to become 'best-sellers' with a large circulation. Fortunately the development of printing technology now makes it relatively easy for publishers to produce specialist works without the commercial risks that would have prevented them doing so in the past.

The Paternoster Press is one of the first publishers to make use of this new technology. Its aim is quite simply to assist biblical and theological scholarship by the publication of theses and other monographs of high quality at affordable prices.

Different publishers serve different constituencies. The Paternoster Press stands in the tradition of evangelical Christianity and exists to serve that constituency, though not in any narrow way. What is offered, therefore, in this series, is the best of scholarship by evangelical Christians.

Contents

Foreword — xiii

Acknowledgements and Dedication — xv

Introduction — xvii

Chapter 1 — 1
Deaf People and the Church
    Introduction — 1
a. Choosing an Appropriate Ecclesiology — 1
b. Deaf People, Language, Culture, Difference, Suffering and Alienation — 4
c. Deaf People, Society and the Causes of Disability, Power and Politics and Confronting the Perspective of those who Dominate — 9
d. Deaf People, their History and the Causes of Oppression — 16
e. A Brief History of Ministry among Deaf People in the Church — 21
f. The History and Iconic Aspects of Sign Language — 23
g. The Place of Deaf People in the Church — 26
h. Self-image, Immediacy, Community, Self-Centredness — 31
i. Practical Concerns, Church Practice, Liturgy, Parish Organisation — 34
j. The Influence of Language in Understanding Identity, Communication and Relationships — 38
k. Perceptions of Language and Power — 43
l. The Processing of Theological Ideas in Sign Language — 46
m. The Dialectic of Spirit and Word and its Impact on the Interpreting and Understanding of Truth — 48

n. The Impact of Hope and the Changing of Interior Models
    of the World   50
    Summary and Conclusion   56

Chapter 2
Moltmann's Ecclesiology, his Theological Method,
Categories, Concepts and the Task of
Perceiving Reality   59
    Introduction   59
a. Eschatological Hope: The Power of God in the World   59
b. Eschatological Hope and our Understanding of God and
    Time   62
c. Eschatological Ontology, Language and the
    Conceptualising Process   65
d. Dialectical Encounter, Immediacy and Conceptualising
    Reality   67
e. Narrative and Storytelling   68
f. Scripted Reality and Rituals   70
g. Conceptualising Reality Using our Worldview and Model
    of the World   73
h. The Social, Suffering Trinity and Non-Hierarchical
    Relationships   75
i. Deaf People's Understanding of Self and their
    Interdependence   80
j. Moltmann's Cosmological and Ecological Understanding
    of Redemption and its Benefit for Deaf People   82
k. The Use of Biblical Categories in Viewing Reality   84
l. Openness to Others and the Function of Myths in
    Perceiving Reality   87
    Summary and Conclusion   89

Chapter 3
A Discussion with Moltmann Concerning his Theology
and Deaf People   93
    Introduction   93
a. The Tentativeness of Communication Using Metaphors
    and Signs and its Basis in Community   93

b.	The Impact of Social Forces on Views of Self and Relationships	96
c.	Identity of the Self through the Identity of God as Trinity	99
d.	Moltmann's Use of Trinitarian, Relational and Dialectical Processes to Define Being	101
e.	Openness in Moltmann's Ecclesiology	104
f.	How the Social Trinity, the Doctrine of God and the Kingdom of God in Moltmann's Ecclesiology can help Deaf People Gain Freedom from Oppression	109
g.	Dealing with Loss, Psychologically and Theologically	112
h.	Moltmann's Theology is Conducive to Developing Spiritual Maturity	114
	Summary and Conclusion	114

Chapter 4
Moltmann's Eschatological Ontology: The Identities of Man and God in Moltmann's Theology and their Relation to Deaf People 119

	Introduction	119
a.	Moltmann's Eschatological Ontology and its Centrality to his Doctrines of God and Man, and his Ecclesiology	119
b.	Moltmann's Eschatological Ontology and Immanent Transcendence as the Experience of God	122
c.	Christology and Eschatology and the Identity of Jesus	125
d.	Moltmann's Conceptions of God and Self and their Impact on Deaf People with Particular Reference to Wholeness and Impairment	127
e.	The Sources of Moltmann's Eschatological Ontology and his Epistemology	128
f.	Current Identity Crises: Falling into the Future	131
g.	Perspectives as the Link between Ideas and Matter The Need for an Open View and Moltmann's Concepts of Hope and Space	133
h.	Being and Doing and Existing in Praxis	138
	Summary and Conclusion	141

Chapter 5
The nature of Communication within Relationships in Moltmann's Ecclesiology and its Relevance to Deaf People — 145
    Introduction — 145
a. Methods used by Moltmann to Define Communication in Relationships — 146
b. The Effect of Symbols, Signs and Icons on the Formation of our Theological Concepts and Perception of Reality — 151
c. Moltmann's Linking of Ontology and Communication — 159
d. Effects of Translation on Immediacy and our Experience of God — 161
e. Boundaries and Communication — 164
f. Linguistic, Sociolinguistic and Neuropsychological Research — 166
g. Communication in the Church — 173
    Summary and Conclusion — 178

Chapter 6
The Concept of Relationship in Moltmann's Theology and its Appropriateness for Deaf People — 183
    Introduction — 183
a. Political, Economic, Cultural and Psychological Aspects of Being Church and how these Affect Relationships — 184
b. Openness in Relationships, Eschatological Hope, Promise and Fulfilment — 192
c. Moltmann's Use of Perspective and how Perceptions are Determined by Conceptions that come from Attributions and Attitudes — 196
d. Relationships Involving Interpreters and the Issue of Trust — 198
e. Defining the Difference between Hearing People and Deaf People — 201
f. The Effect of Society on Relationships — 202
g. The Value of 'Friendship Type' Relationships in the Deaf Context — 204
h. Trinitarian Relationships in Moltmann's Ecclesiology — 206

i. The Dialectic of Anxiety and Hope in Christian
   Relationships and Moltmann's Use of Process Thought   209
   Summary and Conclusion   213

Summary and Conclusion   **217**

Bibliography   **221**

Index   **229**

Foreword

I am delighted to have the opportunity to write a short foreword to this book by Roger Hitching. *The Church and Deaf People* came as a surprise to me: at first I had thought that it was just one more dissertation about my theology of which I should take note, but on reading it I discovered that it opened up quite new theological perspectives from the point of view of deaf people of which previously I had been quite unaware. So I read the book with growing fascination and felt enriched on every page.

This book is written out of personal experience and involvement in the life of deaf people and is therefore literally an eye-opener both for the deaf and for those who can hear. Sight is important for both these groups: it enables them to recognize one another and communicate with one another by visible signs and images. Our means of communication are always governed in a very one-sided way by the more powerful majorities in society. In our modern information society we are all programmed to see and hear. Without seeing and hearing we cannot drive a car or use television and radio. Sight and hearing are secondary developments in our senses: our primary senses are feeling, touching, tasting and smelling. Our fundamental sense is feeling, what in the mediaeval theory of senses was called the *sensus tactus,* and this operates through our skin: we are touched and feel the touch, and we develop feelings. Particular cells are then developed in the skin for smelling fragrances and tasting spices, seeing light and hearing sounds. But these are only specializations of the general sensitivity of the skin.

In the modern world, the primary senses of smelling and tasting are underdeveloped and atrophied, as is evidenced by the preference for fast food. If we are to develop our humanity as a whole, we need a new culture of the senses. We learn it from people who do not possess or cannot use the senses of hearing and sight and therefore have developed their other senses in a way that we no longer know. Those who cannot hear see far more than others. Those who can neither hear nor see feel far more than others.

The *Church and Deaf People* is not a book about compassion, care and help for deaf people, but first and foremost a book about the church as a healing community for all men and women, the deaf, the blind, those without feeling and taste. All of these can rediscover themselves in this healing fellowship. For God is present in this healing fellowship in such a way that he can be perceived by all the senses, and those who belong to it believe with all their senses. 'Behold and taste how gracious the Lord is,' runs the invitation to the eucharist in which Christ is present. All the senses open up to his healing presence in bread and wine. So in the church it is important to learn a great variety of forms of expression, in order to awaken all the human senses completely. This is not a matter of the method and organization of communication but an experience of the life-giving presence of the Spirit of God who awakens charismatic powers in everyone, those who are handicapped and those who are not, and brings about in everyone a new sensitivity to the miraculous gift of beloved life. As a German Pentecost hymn has it, 'You awaken all my senses.'

Roger Hitching is right: in Western theology a paradigm shift is at work which is leading from hierarchical thought to thought in terms of fellowship. In the concept of God the monotheistic 'Almighty' is being replaced by the trinitarian fellowship of the God who is rich in relationships, *perichoresis,* for God is love. This fellowship in God (John 17.21) is matched by the fellowship of God with his creation and finally the fellowship of human beings with one another in the worldwide fellowship of creation. A good expression for this human fellowship is 'friendship', because friendship combines commitment and respect.

At present we are seeing how the hierarchical Roman Catholic Church is becoming congregational and the Protestant Churches are becoming Pentecostal. The discovery of the community is new in the Catholic Church, and the discovery of the multiplicity of gifts and tasks in the charismatic fellowship of the community in the Protestant Church is a pointer for the future. In hierarchies the one ruler is the model for many; in fellowships each individual is respected for what he or she is. But even fellowships are not always ideal: they are threatened by group egotism. This can be overcome only when all together are seized by hope for the coming kingdom of God which is offered to all. Those who have this hope invest what they are and can do in this future. But those who cling to their possessions and attempt to preserve themselves have lost this hope. The law of the fellowship of Christ is: 'Whoever would save his life will lose it; and whoever loses his life for Christ's sake will save it for eternal life.'

I hope that this excellent book by Roger Hitching will help both deaf people and the church today. I hope that it will bring new sensitivity to others and to all members of the community and fill us all with courage and readiness for sacrifice, in hope of the eternal life of the world to come.

Jürgen Moltmann
Tübingen,
Good Friday, 2003

Acknowledgements and Dedication

I would like to acknowledge the support and encouragement of a number of colleagues, friends and family for their help in completing this research project.

I am grateful for the wisdom, advice and encouragement of my supervisor Tony Lane, his colleague Graham McFarlane and the other staff and post-graduate students at London Bible College. I am also indebted to my advisor on Deaf related matters, Alys Young, of the University of Salford, who helped me understand many aspects of the experience of Deaf people. My friends Ernie Abbott, Luke Raftery and Larry Bain have provoked me to persevere when thinking through theological issues as well as walking beside me during the darkest time of my life.

Funding of this research came from my first wife before her death; from her estate after her death; from my two friends in Singapore, Ernie and Kee-Tip Abbott and from my new wife Elisabeth – who also gave me the love, support and encouragement I needed to complete the project.

I dedicate this work to the memory of my first wife Jacqueline Margaret Hitching who died suddenly and unexpectedly 3 months after I started this research. She loved people, and Deaf people especially. My prayer is that it will be a fitting tribute to her life and work as a wife, mother and social worker. I trust that it will honour her commitment to hope in the delivering power of our faithful God. It was this hope that was so much a part of her personality and that enabled her to cheerfully persevere in the face of considerable adversity and 'get on with life'. Like so many Deaf people, she chose not to stand by and let the power of evil win.

I am convinced that the transforming power of the church and the gospel of Jesus Christ is the only answer to the power of evil and the problems of alienation in the world. My prayer is that this study on Moltmann's understanding of the church and Deaf people will bless Deaf people and hearing people. May it help us all gain a God centred perspective on all things.

INTRODUCTION

In this book,[1] our aim is to provide a practical understanding[2] of the ecclesiology of Jürgen Moltmann and to show its relevance for Deaf people.[3]

The theory we are advancing is that Moltmann's ecclesiology is especially appropriate for Deaf people because his theological method has similarities with their way of living and being. This includes how they understand their identity, the way they communicate and how they view their relationships.

Moltmann's theological concepts have an *eschatological focus* and he uses *dynamic, relational categories* and *perspectives* which function as hermeneutical tools for interpreting and understanding reality. His approach is to provoke thought and dialogue by the *suggestion* of *possibilities*. He often uses metaphor in a creative iconic way within a relational perspective to create theological concepts. This approach has parallels with the way Deaf people use *metaphorical iconicity* in sign language and in their conceptualisation process.[4] Some signs function as iconic metaphors for reality and Deaf people often creatively com-

---

[1] We should note at the outset that, although this research crosses the academic 'disciplines' of theology and Deaf studies, it is primarily *theological* in nature.

[2] The views of the writer are those of a hearing person and, whilst we are sympathetic to Deaf people and our points may be valid, our interpretation of the experience of Deaf people will inevitably be *one step removed* from the firsthand viewpoint of a Deaf person.

[3] In this research when we refer to 'Deaf people', spelt with a capital 'D', we mean people whose first or preferred language is Deaf sign language. There are over 50,000 Deaf people in the UK who use British Sign Language (BSL). Where deaf is spelt with a small 'd' in this text, authors cited have referred to Deaf people using 'deaf' with a small 'd' and we have not changed their spelling.

[4] Sign language is as able as any other language to convey complex abstract concepts as can be seen at Gallaudet College of Higher Education in the USA where it is the first language among the students studying there to degree level and beyond. Further details about the college can be found at the web site address http://www.gallaudet.edu/. Also, for an account of the positive effects of the successful protest in support of the appointment of a Deaf President at the University, that was very significant for Deaf people, and which occurred at the college in 1988 as a result of the *Deaf President Now* campaign, see I. King Jordan, 'The Roots of Equal Opportunity in Education' in *Deaf Worlds*, July, 1997, 13/2, 27-29.

bine iconic signs and sign-metaphors within a relational perspective to establish meaning, develop concepts and make sense of their lives.

The experience of Deaf people in a predominately hearing world is different from that of hearing people. Their perceptual boundary, that is the point at which they encounter '*the other*', appears to be closer than it is for hearing people.

Moltmann specifically addresses the fear of that which is '*other*' as he considers the issues of *alienation, anxiety* and *suffering* and how relationships involving *power* affect these. We will show that he is able to contribute positively to the situation of Deaf people as his ecclesiology emphasises a *tentativeness* concerning our own understanding of reality which encourages us to reach out towards that which is '*other*'. By stressing the *dialectical* and *interdependent* nature of our being he encourages us to have an *attitude of openness* towards other people and ideas.

Moltmann's ecclesiology can help Deaf people, who are a relatively small proportion of the population, to cross social and ecclesiastical boundaries and interact with other traditions because it stresses ecumenicity and the need for an approach that involves dialogue with those of different denominations and faiths. It also makes this approach possible by theologically addressing the fears of loss that normally hinder such approaches.

Moltmann is a theologian passionately concerned for all people, and has a particular affinity with oppressed and marginalized groups especially those who have suffered the disabling effects of the discriminatory practices of the church and society.[5] His emphasis on our need for 'openness' in our views and attitudes towards others leads to a liberating understanding of the church. He does not offer one fixed model[6] of the church, but asks us to view the church in the perspective of the kingdom of God as his intention is to provoke us to develop our own *holistic* understanding of what it is *to be* and *to be church.* By viewing all things in the perspective of *eschatological hope* he rede-

---

[5] Showing his personal concern and sense of responsibility towards disabled persons he has said 'I have been personally engaged in questions about the rehabilitation of the handicapped for a number of years. I have talked to many people who despair, and yet try to overcome that despair. I feel that this is my personal concern'. J. Moltmann, *The Power of the Powerless* (London: SCM Press, 1983) 136 (speaking at a conference that included disabled people entitled 'The Liberation and Acceptance of the Handicapped').

[6] Moltmann's *model* of the church is both explanatory and exploratory. See A. Dulles, *Models of the Church* (Dublin: Gill & Macmillan, 2nd edition, 1988) 24.

fines our perception of the relationship between past, present and future.

Moltmann's liberating eschatology incorporates a social understanding of the Trinity. His distinctive and dynamic doctrine of God is that 'God's Being is in his coming'.[7] God promises us that as we dialectically encounter the person of Jesus Christ we will live in anticipation of his coming kingdom. By the hope of redemption contained in his promise to come again, Christ can liberate us from our history. In the cross and resurrection of Jesus Christ, God has demonstrated his power over all that we fear and he experiences the history of the world within himself, suffering with those who suffer. The Bible records his dealings with all creation and how he fulfils his promises, which reveal his person.

Moltmann's ecclesiology challenges the view that the church needs a hierarchical structure of authority. For Moltmann, God reveals his love through his inner trinitarian relationships. These are non-hierarchical, characterised by openness and faithfulness and revealed by a process of promise and fulfilment. In his view, non-hierarchical relationships between Christians open to the possibilities of the future are one sign of the church and a demonstration of the kingdom of God.

Moltmann does not offer a 'system' in his distinctive approach to theology but suggests possibilities which provide theological *ways* and theological *forms*.[8] We will be drawing attention to significant parallels between his approach and the *forms* of sign language and the *ways* of Deaf people.

We want to emphasise that we are not suggesting Moltmann's ecclesiology is in some mysterious way 'custom-made' *just* for Deaf people or that they should adopt his approach completely and uncritically. We are suggesting that there are specific characteristics in Moltmann's methods and ecclesiology which could benefit Deaf people as they seek to understand themselves, their relationship to others and the church.

---

[7] J. Moltmann, *The Coming of God. Christian Eschatology* (London: SCM Press, 1996) 23.

[8] For Moltmann's description of his theological method, see his recent work, J. Moltmann, *Experiences in Theology. Ways and Forms of Christian Theology* (London: SCM Press, 2000).

Background to the research and brief summary of chapter contents

This research arises from our earlier academic work on Moltmann's ecclesiology,[9] the practical application of some of his ideas in the pastoral setting of our local church,[10] experiences of Deafness within our family[11] and work with Deaf people in the community.[12]

Starting with our knowledge of Deaf people and Moltmann's ecclesiology and recognising the unique experience of Deaf people in the church and society we began to explore the possibility that he could offer Deaf people a theoretical and practical way to view their identity, communication and relationships.

In chapter one, we will look at the history and present position of Deaf people and the church. We will carry out a preliminary examination of the way in which both Deaf and hearing people form and maintain views of self, God and the world and then indicate how we

---

[9] R. Hitching, 'Do we need Moltmann's radical church? – A critique of Jürgen Moltmann's ecclesiology in the pastoral context.' (MTh King's College, London, 1991). Our conclusion was that Moltmann has been successful in providing a very broad ecclesiology, with an exciting and challenging redefinition of the church. Our reservations were that his view of the institutional church, his use of one political ideology to analyse society's problems and his concentration on 'friendship type' relationships could limit the wider application of his ecclesiology.

[10] Which included providing Deaf people with interpreting facilities and pastoral care, (in an independent, charismatic, 'free' church that had been planted as part of the 'house church' movement) and developing friendships with Deaf people in other churches.

[11] The writer's grandfather, who was a sign language user, had been 'Deaf and Dumb' since early childhood (a term used in earlier times to describe Deaf sign language users who had no ability to speak verbally. Deaf people and others view it nowadays as offensive as it can convey another meaning for 'dumb', that is, stupid). The writer's wife lost 95% of her hearing ability over a 15 year period. It is common for the onset of deafness in adult life to produce feelings of loss similar to the feelings that occur in bereavement. She experienced the painful process involving feelings of denial and despair, depression and eventual acceptance and then qualified as a professional Social Worker, working in the London Borough of Bromley as the Social Worker for Deaf Adults.

[12] The writer also worked for local charities helping both hearing and Deaf people deal with homelessness, disability and mental health where we saw that Deaf people frequently lack basic background information about community services, lack access to adequate interpreting facilities and face communication difficulties because of the cultural and linguistic divide that exists between hearing and Deaf people.

Introduction xxi

will be developing the relationship between Moltmann's ideas and Deaf people.

In chapter two, we will develop an understanding of the way in which Moltmann approaches these matters to develop his distinctive ecclesiology, whilst continuing to consider the impact of this on Deaf people.

In chapter three, we will explore his key concepts of openness and tentativeness in the process of communication and how his emphasis on relationality affects our understandings of being.

Chapters four, five and six consider the areas of identity, communication and relationships respectively and we see how these are interlinked in Moltmann's thought and offer a way of understanding church which is radical and liberating.

Moltmann's theology addresses past and present oppressive practices, provides a means for developing strong personal and group identities, is readily adaptable to different contexts and emphasises self-determination, freedom and hope for the future.

Our conclusion will be that Moltmann's ecclesiology can provide Deaf people in the church with a liberating perspective. We will show that this perspective-changing approach to familiar church matters can provide Deaf people with a unique, safe and creative way of understanding their lives that can be a powerful tool for use in the pursuit of liberation from the forces of the dominant hearing culture, which has held them for too long in a position of subjection.

Chapter 1

Deaf People and the Church

Introduction

In this chapter, we start by explaining why we have chosen to concentrate on Moltmann's ecclesiology in preference to that of other theologians. Next, we will look at ways of defining Deaf people, language and culture and how they are affected by the concepts of difference, suffering, alienation and disability. We will then survey the history of Deaf people, ministry among them in the church and causes of their oppression.

We will examine how processes of perception and conceptualisation and the use of language affect the self-image and relationships of Deaf people. We will then examine the relationship between iconic aspects of sign language and Moltmann's ecclesiology. We will see that the way in which Deaf people process information, or 'know', is visual-spatial, non-static, emphasises relationality and demands involvement. This links with Moltmann's view that in order to 'know' we need a perspective that gives a view of the relational, socially involving and non-static nature of 'being'. For him, 'knowing' involves both linguistic and non-linguistic information, the latter sometimes taking the form of symbolic and iconic imagery.

We will explore Moltmann's dynamic biblical understanding of history and his focus on promise, fulfilment and eschatological hope and note how they affect our changing models of the world and understanding of reality. We will see how the normal process we use to filter unwanted incoming information can be affected by a more open attitude to that which is 'other'. We will see how Moltmann's stress on the eschaton can create a sense of anticipation which over-rides fear.

a. Choosing an Appropriate Ecclesiology

In this section, we will consider the appropriateness of other ecclesiologies for Deaf people. We should note, however, that the purpose of this research is not primarily to examine in detail and exclude other ecclesiologies but rather to show, from our specialist knowledge of Moltmann the particular aspects of his ecclesiology that can be applied to the situation of Deaf people.

Our view is that an appropriate ecclesiology must be one that addresses the current situation of Deaf people in society, confronts prejudice and challenges discrimination. It must provide Deaf people with a clear understanding of what it is *to be* and to *be church*. It must enable them to experience liberation from the past, protect against patronising attitudes in the present and empower them with realistic hope for the future.

Firstly, we will consider the ecclesiologies of the 'institutional' churches, including the Roman Catholic Church, the Church of England and other Episcopal churches. Deaf people can experience a form of stability through a strong emphasis on institutional aspects of church. These churches emphasise organisational systems that have a hierarchical structure and provide continuity through the generations. They often resemble state and public institutions in the secular world and they purposely use a patriarchal approach to ministry, emphasising the authority, power and status of the church and its ministers. They may encourage lay member involvement in the life of the church but they maintain a clear distinction between the ordained clerical ministry and lay people. Traditional structures can enable them to maintain doctrinal uniformity and safeguard the standards necessary for the selection and performance of the clergy. Although they may have 'failed' Deaf people in the past, these churches usually incorporate processes of reform into their structures and this could help them become more accessible in the future. The organisational structures and processes of these churches, which are their strength, can ensure that they protect and provide for vulnerable people. They have material resources in the form of buildings, equipment and staff, which are considerable in comparison with that of many other churches, and they could provide much for Deaf people.[1]

We cannot ignore the fact however that Deaf people have suffered oppressive practices in many of these institutional churches. Our view is that there may be a place for such churches in the lives of Deaf people but we must not ignore past problems particularly where they have been an unintended consequence of their ecclesiologies.

Problems can arise from the relative inflexibility of their organisational structures leaving them unable to respond to changes taking place in society. As a result they can fail to continue to provide adequate practical safeguards against the misuse of power and can unintentionally transmit discriminating attitudes and practices from one generation to the next. Moltmann considers that there may inevitably be a place for such churches but that they need other more flexible

---

[1] This is despite recent 'complaints' of insufficient resources for example in the Church of England.

and radical Christian groups to act as a reforming influence on their theologies and practices. As Deaf people are currently clearly engaged in a process of breaking free from the ties that have held them in the past, the theologies of institutions that have oppressed will not easily attract those who have suffered oppression. We consider that the situation of Deaf people requires a 'revolutionary' theology that can provide them with a fresh way of viewing themselves and what it is to *be church*.

We will next consider the theologies such as that of John Hick. In our view, these theologies often pay too high a price for their inclusiveness and their understanding of salvation viewed in a religious pluralist context is 'quite different from the traditional Christian one'.[2] Some Deaf people who do not see the need for an ecclesiology that affirms the exclusive claims of traditional Christianity may initially find these attractive, particularly because, in the past, Deaf people have frequently experienced exclusion from the church. We consider, however, that an appropriate ecclesiology for Deaf people needs to be able to re-envision Deaf people with Christian truths interpreted within a more distinctively Christian framework. Deaf people need to be open to those of different traditions and able to engage in ecumenical dialogue with other denominations but we believe that they can do this more effectively from a more orthodox Christian basis.

Similarly, we feel that the ecclesiologies of the predominantly existentialist theologians (such as Bultmann and those who have developed his ideas) have sometimes veered too far from traditional understandings of the faith and the Bible. As we shall show, there is a place for existentialist *influences* in a relevant ecclesiology but these theologians fail to provide sufficient continuity of experience, tradition and hope for the future.

The ecclesiologies of the newer Charismatic and Pentecostal churches have some potential for meeting the needs of Deaf people. We are including here groups of churches such as New Frontiers International whose theology has been influenced by Calvin and Pentecostal theologians, and the South East London group of congregations known as Ichthus, with their mainly Arminian emphasis.[3] These groups are often more innovative, flexible and radical in their approach than the institutional churches and their theologies have

---

[2] In this we are agreeing with L. Miller and S.J. Grenz (eds.), *Fortress Introduction to Contemporary Theologies* (Minneapolis: Fortress Press, 1998) 189.

[3] We have had personal experience and involvement with the Deaf ministry in such churches and have seen their strong practical love and ministry in the local church and at national gatherings of Christians such as Stoneleigh Bible Week and Spring Harvest.

potential for those Deaf people who are attracted to their charismatic style. Whilst we view them in a favourable light, we consider that they lack the strengths of the institutional churches that enable them to survive in similar form from one generation to the next and that an appropriate theology for Deaf people should appeal to Christians from a wider spectrum of church traditions.

The Brethren and other more traditional congregational churches also have the potential to accommodate an appropriate ministry among Deaf people. In their favour is their emphasis on a relational understanding of what it means *to be*, a trinitarian understanding of God and the practice of involving members more actively in church organisational matters. Traditional Brethren groups can offer advantages because they emphasise 'every member' participation in mission and encourage strong personal relationships. Their ability to reach a wide spectrum of Christians, however, could be limited. Any theology that seeks to offer alternative and practical ways forward for Deaf people must be able to adapt to a variety of existing church situations and theologies, perhaps by providing a different perspective on familiar matters, as well as offering an alternative view of the church.

Undoubtedly there is potential within the *liberation* theologies that have arisen since the 1960s for them to be adapted to the situation of Deaf people through a careful process of selection and reconstruction and some work is being done in this direction.[4] Moltmann's early work inspired some liberation theologians initially and he has recently asked some pertinent questions with the intention of helping them develop and 'gain a better hearing'.[5] Our view is that Moltmann's later theology, being more developed and holistic, offers greater potential for Deaf people.

We have examined these other ecclesiologies and although they may still be used successfully in the ministry of the church among Deaf people, in our opinion they are less appropriate, in many ways, than the ecclesiology of Moltmann.

b. Deaf People, Language, Culture, Difference, Suffering and Alienation

In this section, we will look at ways of defining Deaf people noting how the issues of language and culture affect this process. We will also

---

[4] See H. Lewis, 'The Deaf Challenge to the Churches', Paper presented to the Deafhood Conference, London 12 July 2001 (www.deafhood.org.uk) and the doctoral research currently being completed by Hannah Lewis at Birmingham University, email: lewis.griffin@virgin.net.

[5] Moltmann, *Experiences in Theology*, 293-299.

consider the issues of difference and suffering in the lives of Deaf people and link this with Moltmann's use of the concept of alienation. Defining the Deaf community is not easy.[6]

Doug Alker has given a useful broad definition of the Deaf community as '... a group of people whose common factor is that they are deaf, identify with being deaf and make some effort to come together regularly'.[7]

Ladd, who has been prominent in working for a change in the way Deaf people are treated by society, has noted that 'The deaf community can now be identified as a linguistic minority'.[8]

Kyle and Woll provide an excellent summary of what they believe constitutes the Deaf community.[9] They say that:

> ... there are severe difficulties in adequately characterising the deaf community. It involves a shared language; it involves hearing loss; it involves social interaction and political relations; but all of these interrelate and interact with attitudes towards other deaf people. The choice to communicate and share information with other people must be seen as a primary feature, and because of the language used by members of the community this communication will generally be restricted to other deaf people.[10]

Most hearing people in society view Deafness simply as a disability. For many Deaf people, however, the main issue is one of language. Others prefer to leave aside the language issue and concentrate on the view that Deaf people are a 'cultural' minority group and use this as the primary defining characteristic. Woodward, for example, says we should 'attempt to describe Deaf people from the point of view of Deaf cultural values. Thus differences between Deaf and Hearing people can be seen as cultural differences not as deviations from a Hearing

---

[6] J.G. Kyle and B. Woll, *Sign Language The Study of Deaf People and Their Language* (Cambridge: Cambridge University Press, 1988). See Chapter 1 for their excellent summary of the issues involved.

[7] D. Alker, 'The Changing Deaf Communities' in International Ecumenical Working Group (ed.), *The Place of Deaf People in the Church. The Canterbury 1994 Conference Papers* (Northampton: Visible Communications, 1996) 178.

[8] P. Ladd, 'The Modern Deaf Community' in D. Miles, *British Sign Language. A Beginner's Guide* (London: BBC Books) 41. We should note that unlike other linguistic minorities Deaf people are not (currently) so easily able to learn the language of the majority culture, although this does not take away from the importance of their need to redefine themselves in this way.

[9] Kyle and Woll, *Sign Language*, 5-23.

[10] Kyle and Woll, *Sign Language*, 22.

norm'.[11] Kyle and Woll stress that culture itself depends on language. 'Culture is distinct from community in that it includes the knowledge, belief, art, morals, and law as well as the practices of members of the community. These are mainly mediated by language, so deaf culture, like all cultures, is carried through the language'.[12]

In this research, we take the view that Deaf people '... should be primarily regarded as a cultural and language minority group rather than as individuals with an audiological disability. [Their] experiences often overlap with the experiences of hearing minority group members but at other times are unique'.[13] This socio-linguistic view of Deaf people is not yet universally accepted, but it 'is gathering support among educators, linguists, and researchers involved in the education of deaf people'.[14]

Although the view we are adopting can be a valuable tool in taking forward the cause of Deaf people, we should note that, in particular, the minority language emphasis is one shared by many minority groups and we agree with Kyle and Woll who say that '[t]he language dominance case should not be overplayed'.[15] They also recognize, however, and this is important for us in this research, that 'BSL is fundamental to the cognitive and linguistic representation which deaf people use'.[16] They conclude that some Deaf people using BSL 'appear to use a completely different form of coding' to hearing people.[17] The way in which the brain deals with sign language, because it is a spatial and visual, is different from the way in which the brain deals with spoken and written language. Later in this chapter we cover in more detail this important aspect of sign language.

We will now consider the issue of difference. The social processes of separating people according to their differences and treating them differently seems to be natural and inevitable. It is normal to use any defining characteristics such as disability, colour, language or ethnicity to categorise others, however, these defining characteristics can also

---

[11] J. Woodward, 'How You Gonna Get to Heaven if You Can't Talk With Jesus: The Educational Establishment vs. The Deaf Community' in *How You Gonna Get to Heaven if You Can't Talk With Jesus. On Depathologizing Deafness* (Silver Spring, Maryland: T.J. Publishers 1982) 11.
[12] Kyle and Woll, *Sign Language*, 9.
[13] I. Parasnis (ed.) *Cultural and Language Diversity and the Deaf Experience* (Cambridge: Cambridge University Press, 1996) inside front cover and frontispiece.
[14] Parasnis (ed.) *Cultural and Language*, inside front cover and frontispiece.
[15] Kyle and Woll, *Sign Language*, 259.
[16] Kyle and Woll, *Sign Language*, 258.
[17] Kyle and Woll, *Sign Language*, 261.

stigmatise. Language can be used powerfully to over-emphasise difference in other people, deny them equal status and create relationships based on fear and domination.

Deaf people have suffered in the past because they have been defined as 'different' and viewed as a problem in society. It is tempting, therefore, to avoid such classification. However, differences exist in every area of life and we should not avoid acknowledging them in this area, as long as we are conscious of the sensitivity needed when dealing with these matters.

Society and the church, in dealing with difference inappropriately, have deprived Deaf people of their dignity. Mistreatment of others will always be with us as part of our experience of a fallen world, but within the church, we should work towards a perspective of humanity that does not allow for institutionalised discrimination against minority groups such as Deaf people. It is necessary for us to differentiate ourselves from that which is 'other' in order to define ourselves. An appropriate ecclesiology for Deaf people, however, will protect them from the negative effects of such differentiation and the inevitable suffering and alienation this brings.

Having acknowledged that an over-emphasis of 'difference' can cause Deaf people suffering we will look now at how Moltmann's views can be helpful to Deaf people because of the way in which he views suffering and alienation and how his ecclesiology offers an alternative perspective.[18]

For Moltmann all of life, including suffering, has its basis in eschatological hope. This hope can help us as we seek to alleviate suffering, or accept its inevitability, by enabling us to challenge views of reality that incorrectly emphasise our relationship to the past. Our suffering, rather than being something to be feared, can become a means by which we may understand our relationships and can provide continuity for our 'life story'.

Moltmann invites us to explore the possibility that our presuppositions, that is, our existing perceptions of reality, *may not be correct*. These perceptions, which contribute towards our internal view of the world, act as a filter on our sensory input. They create a paradigm that constantly changes to reflect the reality of the world outside.[19] For Moltmann, it is essential that we have a right perspective with which to

---

[18] We should note that many Deaf people do not consider their *lack of hearing* causes them suffering. On the contrary, they frequently view those who do not use sign language as suffering because of their inability to appreciate the eloquence, beauty and power of Deaf sign language.

[19] The idea of paradigm shift used here follows that described by T. Kuhn, *The Structure of Scientific Revolutions* (Chicago: Chicago University Press, 1970).

understand the past, present and future and the relationship that exists between them. This perspective, which we might view sometimes as tentative or provisional, will enable us to understand the need to acknowledge difference but this does not cause suffering or alienation to others.

Moltmann sees alienation as the ultimate enemy against which creation struggles. In the light of the reality of our being, which we have through our faith in Christ and his completed work, we can view the power of alienation that we experience in this world as the illusion it really is.[20]

Salvation, for Moltmann, is a rescuing from alienation, personal, historical and cosmic. For him salvation must be viewed in the context of an *'Integrating Eschatology'*.[21] It is an eschatological event and something that we can experience, at least partly, now. Moltmann's theology provides a new metaphysical and theological framework with which we are to understand reality. Reality viewed in this way has its roots in a definite Christological historical event but also has its ground of being in the eschatological hope which this event inaugurated and made possible.

Moltmann takes the key biblical theme of Christ's coming again in power to judge and redeem the world and makes it the basic building block for an alternative understanding of reality. He provides an approach that is able to rescue the Christian faith from the historical determinism to which it appears to be subject.

The power of alienation can also show itself in the oppression we experience as we view ourselves as victims, emphasising our status as a victim over other aspects of our personhood.[22] The ultimate alienation that we face in life is death. Death seemingly renders life meaningless and appears to have the power to separate us from life. The ultimate purpose of hope must be to transform our view of death and its power over us. The uniqueness of the gospel is that it can challenge our wrong perceptions by calling us to view things differently.

Moltmann's theology is a perspective-changing theology. The placing of things by us in a particular perspective is an attributing of power by us to one thing or another. Bauckham has noted that Moltmann 'sees the eschatological future of messianic redemption as a radical alternative future, rupturing the endless prolongation of the present and

---

[20] The power of evil can be in its ability to alienate by deception.
[21] Moltmann, *The Coming of God*, xiv.
[22] All oppressed peoples face not only the problem of how to cope with or overcome oppression, but also of how to maintain a Christian response to their oppressors. Moltmann's view also offers liberation to the oppressors.

breaking the power of the perspective of the dominant [our italics]'.[23] We can see that it is a mystical vision, based on the love of God, which can provide a liberating perspective for all who will enter into that love relationship with him. He is the God who is beyond our understanding, yet reveals aspects of himself to us as we follow him in his way and these can lead us to liberating action. Thus, it is also a prophetic mysticism because it is active and leads others to action as they adopt its perspective.[24] For Moltmann it is that action, whether it is political, social or economic, which is a partial revelation of the kingdom of God. It is in that action that we find the person of Jesus Christ and his church. We will find that, for Moltmann, liberating action that flows from the breaking of the power of the perspective of the dominant will create space in which new relationships are possible.

c. Deaf People, Society and the Causes of Disability, Power and Politics and Confronting the Perspective of those who Dominate

Having looked earlier at how Deaf people can be defined, we will next consider the important matter of how they are affected by concepts of disability in society and the church. We will see how society and the church affect the lives of Deaf people and disabled people and how hierarchical relationships can result in the abuse of power. We will note that Moltmann's ecclesiology, through its alternative perspective, emphasises the value of political action that can challenge the perspective of those who dominate This enables us to confront and prevent oppressive practices that arise from some of the prevailing attitudes towards disability.

In our society and in everyday language the term 'disability' usually refers to a temporary or permanent physical, sensory or mental *impairment* present from birth or arising during our life by accident, illness or old age. It may result from the loss of, or loss of function of, a limb or other body part or the senses of hearing and sight, which are the main senses involved in everyday communication. Disability may affect a person's physical mobility, their ability to carry out everyday functions such as eating and drinking or their ability to communicate. Deaf people have a sensory impairment but usually do not want to be

---

[23] R. Bauckham, 'Eschatology in *The Coming of God*' in R. Bauckham (ed.), *God Will be All in All. The Eschatology of Jürgen Moltmann* (Edinburgh: T & T Clark, 1999) 28.

[24] Müller-Fahrenholz has said, rightly we believe, that Moltmann's 'theology of history is based in messianic mysticism'. G. Müller-Fahrenholz, *The Kingdom and the Power. The Theology of Jürgen Moltmann* (London: SCM Press, 2000) 241.

defined *primarily* as disabled. There are obvious, and sometimes tragic, results of bodily or sensory impairment but we must accept that the attitudes and practices of society can have a negative effect on the lives of impaired people. As we noted earlier, classifying people as 'Deaf' can alienate them from others, and similarly classifying them as 'disabled' can result in separation, stigmatisation and patronising attitudes.[25] We take the view that people with impairments are sometimes further disabled by the non-inclusive processes of society.[26]

It is important to emphasise that the critique of the activities of Christians that follows is written from the context of our time. We now have the 'luxury' of being able to address some of the 'second order' causes of problems that Deaf people face today. These are the institutional roots of oppression that exist in the attitudes and beliefs of people in the institutions that act on their behalf.

Churches and religious people have often been at the forefront of seeking to help ill or disadvantaged persons including Deaf people. When Christians seek to follow Jesus' command to 'love your neighbour' they express their Christian love by caring for those less fortunate than themselves. Undoubtedly, many caring Christians have provided much in the way of practical help for Deaf people. When we see great need, our Christian love will impel us to act.[27] Help for Deaf people has been directed towards education, employment and religious welfare. Though much good has been done by the church and society their overall record of dealing with disabled people, including Deaf people, is poor. Well-meaning people have sometimes acted in unhelpful ways.[28] Inappropriate practices have often resulted in oppressive relationships. This oppression of Deaf people has occurred as much in the church as in society generally.[29]

---

[25] In this section, much of what we note about the situation of disabled people in general applies to the situation of Deaf people.

[26] See M. Oliver, *Understanding Disability* (London: MacMillan Press, 1996) Chapter 1.

[27] This writer's Grandfather, for example, received much in the way of practical help through the Deaf Welfare workers in the early decades of the last century, and through the activity of the Salvation Army. In the context of the poverty that many 'working class' families like his experienced in the 1920s and 1930s, where there was sometimes no money for the day's food or shoes for children, practical Christian loving care often made a significant difference to people's lives.

[28] Sometimes they have wanted to compensate for past injustices, perhaps out of feelings of guilt.

[29] Deaf people were not alone in suffering in the past. Among others who suffered stigmatisation, mistreatment and sometimes incarceration were orphans, mentally ill people, physically handicapped people and, prior to the abolition

Our society and the church often recognise the *direct* causes of problems associated with physical, sensory or mental impairment, and then help by direct intervention and assistance. Our normal human response to disability, based on Christian values, includes a sense of compassion and a motivation towards helping or healing. We rightly consider that disabled people may need assistance if they are to exist and function in the same way as other people. Life is made easier through medicine, surgery and by providing appliances and aids, for example, artificial limbs, wheelchairs, hearing aids and spectacles or through therapies, such as teaching an injured person how to walk again. All this can enable disabled people to experience a better quality of life.[30] Recent legislation has also helped by raising awareness of the way the physical environment can be changed to help disabled people, for example by requiring new or refurbished publicly accessible buildings to incorporate such things as ramps and lifts for wheelchair users or people who have reduced mobility. Similarly, in banks and other public places we now more often find lower counters for wheelchair users or electronic aids for hearing impaired people. There is also now more training in disability awareness and availability of information on the issues faced by disabled people.

Society and the church have become more aware in recent years of the *indirect* causes of problems associated with disability. Society and the church have begun to encourage actions and attitudes that 'include' rather than 'exclude' disabled people.[31] Legal and educational processes have been used in an attempt to establish appropriate norms and attitudes but the process is complex and difficult, however, and time will be needed for these remedies to take effect. More awareness of the way in which wrong responses to the idea of 'difference', which is inherent in the concept of disability, will lead us to more compassionate action and provision of resources to help if we can. Disabled people may be 'different' but this should not cause non-disabled people to feel superior to them or fear their presence.

---

of the Workhouse laws, 'ordinary' poor people. We view it as a Christian responsibility not only to provide an 'ambulance service' type of caring action for the relief of people's immediate needs but also to look at the structures of societies' institutions to see where they could be improved to help those who are viewed as the less well off in society.

[30] At the time of writing in the UK the state also provides financial assistance to disabled people in the form of 'living allowances' so that they can meet some of the additional costs they encounter because of their disability.

[31] For example, Health and Safety and Environmental Health laws, regulations and inspectors work to create safer working and living environments to prevent accidents and disabling injuries occurring.

Without adequate sensitivity, however, it is still very easy to stigmatise disabled people and diminish their sense of self-worth. The church, in particular, has a duty to respond morally and practically to the situation of disabled people, either at the individual or local church level or as it influences society's social norms and practices. In the Gospels we see Christ not only healing and helping disabled people but also accepting all people as 'persons in their own right'.

We can only deal with many of the effects of disability if we have the financial and material resources and the will to do so, however, much can be done if we have a right view of how problems associated with disability are caused.

We turn now to the further contributions that Moltmann can make in this area. His ecclesiology emphasises the personal dignity of all persons, disabled or non-disabled and their right to self-determination. Moltmann has spoken of the effect society has on people with a disability and what our attitude should be towards this. He tells of how there is

> ... the unjust disabling of people already handicapped by nature. These unjust handicaps are those imposed by other people, and by the laws determining public life in this society of non-handicapped people. None of us must rest content with this handicapping of the already handicapped.[32]

He has also spoken of the defining of self which society carries out on behalf of disabled people.

> The final and most important point of all, however, is the liberation of handicapped people from despondency and sadness. Where does this inward burden come from? It comes from the prejudices of the capable and strong, which convey to the handicapped the paralysing feeling that they are judged as being of inferior value.[33]

Moltmann challenges and confronts the common view of disabled people that simply categorises them as lacking something.[34] He does not deny the fact that people with impairments may not have all the abilities of able people but focuses instead on the incompleteness of all humanity. He stresses the value that all people, disabled or otherwise, bring to the church. He emphasises that linguistic and cultural differ-

---

[32] Moltmann, *Power*, 139.
[33] Moltmann, *Power*, 141.
[34] An example of this view is a definition which describes deafness as 'Partial or total deficit of hearing in either ear', *Hutchinson Encyclopaedia* (Oxford: Helicon Publishing, 1996). This is adequate at the medical level but inadequate when considering what is meant by Deafness in social and political terms.

Deaf People and the Church

ences require particular practical responses from the church, and that we should view no person as being any less human than any other.

As we consider the ways in which church and society affect the lives of Deaf people and people with physical or sensory impairments we should note that an important issue is that of power, and particularly the power that comes from certain types of relationship. Moltmann views relationships within the Trinity as being non-hierarchical and considers that these are a model for all relationships. He views people in hierarchical relationships as being particularly vulnerable to the abuse of power. He sees status as a way of acknowledging difference rather than a measure of superiority that can result in domination. Churches, in common with other organisations in society, often give status and power to people in authority who may then have the opportunity to dominate others. They may also influence church members to consider certain people, including disabled people and others who are different, as 'outsiders'. For Moltmann, 'outsiders' deserve our care and attention, as much as 'insiders'. He says we should not judge another person as being of less value because they appear to be poor or seem to be lacking something that makes them different. We may even be surprised to find that they are actually able to enrich us. The gospel involves an inversion of worldly values so we may view the weak and vulnerable as blessed in the sight of God. In his approach, Moltmann encourages us to recognise our God-given responsibility to be open to the 'other' person who appears to be different to us, even if this makes us vulnerable. In the light of the status of us all before God, we must view one another as equals. He does not do this, however, through a simple dogmatic emphasis on, for example, the teaching of 'the sermon on the mount'. Rather he has developed a doctrine of God in which the face of God confronts us through the face of the poor. When we encounter them, we encounter him.

For Moltmann, the power which exceeds all others is the power which comes from the cross and resurrection of Jesus. This power grounds Christian faith in that historical event which inaugurates the expected eschaton. Jesus dying and being raised from the dead is the one *new thing* in the history of the world that heralds the future restoration of all things.[35] It is hope generated by this eschatological future which liberates all creation from the slavery of history in which there

---

[35] For an interesting critique of Moltmann's view of heaven, see C. Deane-Drummond, 'Jürgen Moltmann on Heaven' in A.N.S. Lane (ed.), *The Unseen World* (Carlisle and Grand Rapids: Paternoster and Baker Book House, 1996) pp. 49-64.

can only be cause and effect and in which there can be no place for any *new thing*.

Moltmann's eschatological ontology sees God as the power of the future coming towards us, and as the source of our being. We can view all worldly experiences of power in the anticipation of the eschaton. Through the power demonstrated in the cross and resurrection of Jesus, God will transform us. God will be 'all in all' and all things will be reconciled with one another as all of history is renewed. By viewing our lives from the *perspective* provided by an awareness of the eschaton, the fear that arises from people misusing and abusing power will be recognised by us as only temporary and therefore limited in its power to affect us.[36]

Disability is a political matter, for it is through politics, as well as religion that the norms and standards of our society are established and maintained. To be active in working for the improvement of the lives of disabled people will also mean that we will be politically active, at one level or another, and we will see that Moltmann's theology encourages political action as a necessary responsibility attached to the Christian faith.

Moltmann often views *power* as a political matter and he sees it as important that Christians involve themselves in the political process. Liberation can occur in this life as well as in the life to come. Oppressed people are often afraid that they might suffer the use of force. It is a *perspective* of fear of force that oppresses them. This can be more powerful than the actual use of force. The oppressed remain oppressed because they adopt a perspective that considers the use of force against them a real possibility. Moltmann's alternative perspective enables Christian to challenge this perspective of the oppressor.

Mike Oliver persuasively argues that social and political action or inaction actually causes disability. We certainly cannot separate disability from politics if the situation of disabled people is to be improved. He says,

> [D]isability has been redefined by many disabled people and their representative organisations as the social barriers, restrictions and/or oppressions they face and professional interventions have come to be

---

[36] Here we can note how Moltmann's understanding of eschatology differs from the traditional view which emphasises the chronological series of events that will occur in 'the last days'.

seen as often adding to these problems rather than seeking to deal with them.[37]

There is a constraining power in the fear of confronting and challenging accepted, and defective, views of reality, that those who are oppressed most need to overcome. Jenny Morris makes this point when speaking of disability in Western culture.

> The way that the general culture either ignores or misrepresents our experience is part of our oppression ... It is fear and denial of the frailty, vulnerability, mortality and *arbitrariness* of human experience that deters us from confronting such realities. Fear and denial prompt the isolation of those who are disabled, ill or old as 'other', as 'not like us'.[38]

We should note that there is a specific danger to be aware of when we are considering the subject of liberation. Moltmann suggests that modern Western society often seems to operate at an ideological level with a false, secular model of messianism. We may believe that 'liberation' will occur when we acquire certain material goods, when we have achieved a certain goal, or when a certain special date has arrived. We are promised a future liberation from our present situation. This is a deception however and contrasts dramatically with Moltmann's messianic ecclesiology. In this, our lives are affected positively as we become aware that our *being* is determined in part by the fact that Christ is coming. As minority groups, including Deaf people, consider the possibility of achieving political and social liberation they might be tempted to believe the promises of this false messianism that once they have achieved certain objectives, 'all will be well'. This is unrealistic, however, because once they have won certain battles in dealing with oppression and discrimination, other problems will take their place. Ignorance and misrepresentation will always be with us, like 'the poor'.[39] Confronting fear and encouraging hope, in the midst of this process, will be a task to which the church must continually apply itself.

---

[37] Oliver, *Disability*, 10. For a further introduction to this important new viewpoint see also M. Oliver, *Politics of Disablement* (Basingstoke: Macmillan and St Martins Press, 1990).

[38] J. Morris, *Pride against Prejudice. A Personal Politics of Disability* (London: Women's Press, 1991) 85.

[39] In spiritual terms we are all 'the poor' for we all lack something outside of our transformed being that comes with being 'in Christ'.

We have seen that social, political and economic circumstances can contribute to the problems people with impairments face[40] and that serious problems can occur when society makes well intentioned but inappropriate interventions in the lives of disabled people. We will next look at how society has believed, in the past, that certain approaches to education were in Deaf people's best interests and how it has subsequently been shown that those approaches have been the main cause of Deaf people's under-achievement, abuse and oppression.

d. Deaf People, their History and the Causes of Oppression

In this section, we will note how judgements by 'professionals' significantly influence our attitudes and beliefs concerning Deaf people. We will see how this has occurred in the fields of education, psychology and other medical areas and how it has contributed to the oppression of Deaf people.

In the field of education, Lane notes how the decision of a small group of hearing people negatively affected the lives of tens of thousands of Deaf people for almost a hundred years. At the notorious Milan Congress of 1880, a small group of paternalistic hearing instructors opposed to the use of sign language decided that it would be in the best interests of Deaf people if teachers adopted the approach of oralism. This is communication by voice and lip-reading only, without the use of sign language. The consequence of their decision was that the use of sign language in education thereafter was dramatically restricted. Lane comments that,

> [d]espite its devastating impact on deaf children and adults for over a century, the Milan meeting was merely a brief rally conducted by hearing opponents of sign language. The congress amounted to two dozen hours, in which three or four audists reassured the rest of the rightness of their actions in the face of troubling difficulties.
>
> Nevertheless, the meeting at Milan was the single most critical event in driving the languages of deaf communities beneath the sur-

---

[40] This may be at the practical level of access to buildings for the physically impaired, where a wheelchair user might as well be facing a ten-foot high wall because a six-inch high step has stopped his or her wheelchair from entering a building. For hearing impaired people, the common 'entry-phone' which produces electronically reproduced speech of such a poor quality that they cannot understand it, may as well be a sign that says 'Keep Out'!

face; I believe it is the single most important cause of the limited educational achievements of modern deaf men and women.[41]

After the Congress, oralism was the official method of communication used in education in many countries.

In the UK, Deaf children were usually educated at special residential schools for the Deaf where sign language use was strongly discouraged. Deaf pupils were punished if they were found communicating in this way. Since the 1960s, there have been considerable changes in Deaf children's education. Most are now educated in Hearing Impaired Units within mainstream hearing schools where sign language use is encouraged. Teachers of the Deaf often now have qualifications in sign language use. Interpreters and communication support workers also have their respective qualifications to help ensure that the quality of their work is sufficient for the task and now work alongside Deaf people in schools and colleges.[42] The education process has also benefited from rapid advances in audio technology. Communication aids for Deaf children in schools are now commonplace. All of these developments have empowered Deaf children considerably by enabling them to receive their education in their own language and to make their own choices in other areas of their lives.

In spite of all these improvements, it is sad to note that the potential of Deaf children is still not being realised. Although they normally have the capacity to reach the same levels of achievement as hearing children, the average reading age of a Deaf person leaving full-time education at 16 (18 in the USA) is approximately that of an 8-year-old hearing child.[43]

In the field of psychology, the attitudes towards Deaf people have often been paternalistic. Within clinical psychology in the 1960s and 1970s psychologists suggested that deafness had a negative influence on personality development. They also described Deaf people in nega-

---

[41] H. Lane, *The Mask of Benevolence. Disabling the Deaf Community* (New York: Vintage Books, 1993) 113.

[42] Corker says the role of sign language interpreters as service providers needs to be 'led by and responsive to a range of user concerns and preferences, rather than by the whims of elitist practitioners working within narrowly defined linguistic frameworks'. M. Corker, 'Deaf people and interpreting – the struggle in language' in *Deaf Worlds* 13 Number 3 (November 1997) 13.

[43] Kyle and Woll, *Sign Language*, 235. For the situation in the USA see I. King Jordan, 'The Roots of Equal Opportunity in Education' in *Deaf Worlds* 13 Number 2 (July 1997) 30.

tive terms such as 'egocentric, rigid, impulsive and lacking in insight'.[44]

In other medical areas, professionals have often worked with an oppressive model of deafness. This 'medical model' emphasises the need to be 'normal'. Dr Mary Weir argues that the medical model 'rests on a theological assumption that the image of God equals the "normal" or the "usual" or the "dominant"'.[45] She says the medical model tends to define deafness as '"unhealthy" or "undesirable"'.[46] Those who use it want to make all people conform to the dominant social norm. It despises difference instead of celebrating it. She says that,

> [i]t also devalues people for whom deafness is a central and unchangeable element in their existence by insisting that the goal of healing is restoring the sound, thus ignoring the rather different gifts of vision and sensitivity that are equally part of deafness.[47]

She has called for change. 'I would suggest that we need a paradigm shift to the way of thinking and actively believing that considers all human beings as having the possibility of perfection—each in the wholeness in their uniqueness'.[48]

Lane has argued that the *perspective* of the dominant hearing group, such as that of educationalists, psychologists and other medical professionals, produced stereotypes that other people then adopted. Hearing professionals have often negatively interpreted any characteristic that indicates difference in Deaf people.[49]

Commenting on the restricting nature of paternalism, Lane says, 'Paternalism places its beneficiaries in a dependent relation and keeps them dependent for its own psychological and economic interest. Paternalism deprives its beneficiaries of their history and therefore of the possible lives they can envision'. Commenting on how domination occurs over time through the power to attribute values and determine beliefs, he says, '[a]llowed to endure, paternalism instills (sic) the benefactor's values in the beneficiary'.[50] He makes comparisons be-

---

[44] S. Gregory and G.M. Hartley (eds.), *Constructing Deafness* (London: Pinter Publishers, 1991) 53 (referring to the approach of J.D. Rainer and K.Z. Altshuler 'Psychiatry and the Deaf' [New York: Grune and Stratton, 1967]). For another list of traits attributed to Deaf people in the professional literature of psychologists see Lane, *Mask*, 36.
[45] M. Weir, 'Made Deaf in God's Image' in International Ecumenical Working Group (ed.), *The Place of Deaf People in the Church*, 6.
[46] Weir, 'Made Deaf', 7.
[47] Weir, 'Made Deaf', 7.
[48] Weir, 'Made Deaf', 7.
[49] Lane, *Mask*, 31-49.
[50] Lane, *Mask*, 39.

tween the situation of Deaf people and the colonization of Africa and shows similarities between the ways in which certain traits attributed to the natives of Africa by the colonizers mirror the attributing of traits to Deaf people.[51]

We can see from Lane's analysis that it is the unintended effect of caring as a father might for his young child that is the problem. The intention may be to relieve suffering, and this may be achieved in the short term, but the long-term effect is the construction of a relationship in which one person has dominance over the other. Dominance occurs as the benevolent person decides what is given and when and attributes traits to the beneficiary. The *perspective* of the dominant can then become the *perspective* of the oppressed.

These views can surprise hearing people who are only familiar with viewing deafness through the lens of the medical model. It is no wonder that Deaf people experience so much marginalization, oppression and prejudice, or that church organisation and settings can sometimes actually cause these things.

Our attitudes and actions towards Deaf people are therefore significant for the type of relationships they will experience. Hearing people often see Deaf people as a problem. 'Dealing with' the problem can take the form of seemingly benevolent action intended to benefit Deaf people whom hearing people believe to be in need of help. We may want to help by providing things for Deaf people, which is a valid response and we are not suggesting that we should not respond according to our conscience but we need to draw attention to the frequently neglected need to examine, and if necessary change, our attitudes towards Deaf people.

The experiences of Deaf people in a hearing church can be surprisingly illuminating for hearing people and often involve humour. Misunderstanding the meaning of words can be a source of amusement. One Deaf lady, who used lip-reading to understand the hearing preacher, once asked why the preacher kept talking about people's knees (needs!).

There is a serious side though. Vera Hunt tells of how difficult it was for her to first receive the gospel message in hearing churches, and later to train for ordination.[52] She highlights the lack of understanding existing in church settings. She did not find in churches a special consideration for others who are different. She writes of her experience as a Deaf child in a hearing church.

---

[51] Lane, *Mask*, 37.
[52] V. Hunt 'My Story' in International Ecumenical Working Group (ed.), *The Place of Deaf People in the Church*, 20-34.

> There was no place for deaf people in either of the churches I have mentioned — no place for understanding — no place for deaf people to participate in the worship. The only place for me within the church in those days was to sit quietly like an ornament and receive the sacrament without understanding exactly what it was all about or understanding the Eucharist prayers. Was the eye saying to the ear, "I don't need you"?[53]

She indicates that the problem lies both in the different conception of deafness held by hearing people and the lack of practical knowledge of the needs of Deaf people.[54]

Weir and Hunt both refer to the passage in 1 Corinthians 12 and in particular v16 where the diversity of the members of the 'Body of Christ' is acknowledged. Weir in her discussion on the image of God in humanity refers to the Genesis picture which, like 1 Corinthians, shows 'people-in-cooperative-and-coordinative relationship as an image of what God is like'.[55] She argues that God has created some people Deaf, and that means different, not lacking in their God-given humanity. 'Human differences are not accidents, but rather a significant part of God's very good intentions for the world. Accordingly, deafness is to be understood as created goodness, not primarily as the lack of something essential to being human'.[56] We consider it simplistic only to view deafness as being God created. Deafness may be due to negligence, accident or genetic defects that require us to view it in the light of God's sovereign ability to redeem any human situation. It is quite possible to view it as something that he has not willed but allowed to happen.

Weir has called for 'a deaf theological perspective [to] expand contemporary ways of thinking about God' and 'a move away from a concept of God that is so purely verbal'. She suggests considering 'approaching God in terms of vision and touch, image and drama'. We can speak of 'a God who gives visions and dreams, who touches us

---

[53] Hunt, 'My Story', 23.

[54] For example, at the very least, when we use an interpreter in a hearing service, we should seat Deaf people so that they can clearly see the interpreter without strain. Providing sermons in written form beforehand may help so that the interpreter can consider how to convey difficult or unusual words or ideas. There may be a need to slow the pace of delivery of the sermon and have breaks for Deaf people to rest to help them avoid eyestrain through continued concentration on the signed message. For practical information on matters like this see, for example, information provided by 'Hands Together', website address, http://www.jireh.demon.co.uk/.

[55] Weir, 'Made Deaf', 6.

[56] Weir, 'Made Deaf', 6.

and in putting our hip out of joint makes us truly God's own. I believe we need a theology of Vision, probably a theology of Touch too. Yes, and also a new respect for silence and story as the places where God becomes known — for we who are deaf know well the depth of this language'.[57] Church members, especially those in positions of authority, have for too long treated Deaf people as if they lacked a full humanity.

Moltmann considers 'openness' a defining characteristic of the church and its members. This could be a very useful tool for Deaf people as they seek liberation from the oppression of the past and try to develop a new understanding of their identity. It could also enable others to view Deaf people as full human beings. This will involve new perspectives and attitudes by Deaf people and hearing people, arising from a theology that encourages us to view all people, including Deaf people, as worthy of respect.

e. A Brief History of Ministry among Deaf People in the Church

In this section, we will look at some of the ways in which ministry to Deaf people has been carried out in the past. As we have already noted, the approach to helping the less fortunate in society has varied in the past according to prevailing views on the role of the carer and the perceived needs of the recipient. A paternalistic approach has often characterised ministry to Deaf people up until the present time and still exists in many churches.

Ministry among Deaf people in the church has taken a number of forms but most prominent in the past has been the work of the Deaf Missioners.[58] They initially acted as missionaries and pastors to Deaf people. Arthur Dimmock notes that between 1840 'when the first institution was opened for deaf people to gather socially and for spiritual enlightenment ... and 1939 62 societies and missions were established for deaf people's benefit'.[59] He describes the missioners as 'clergymen or educated deaf men of strong religious principles'. They provided activities, the main ones being 'church services and Bible reading' and encouraged the 'practice [of] temperance'. The missioners also worked hard helping the unemployed Deaf people find work as well as attending to other spiritual and practical welfare needs. They were however autocratic and had considerable power over the lives of

---

[57] Weir, 'Made Deaf', 9.
[58] A misleading description as these people were almost always hearing.
[59] Dimmock, A. 'Sport and Leisure' *Gallaudet Encyclopedia of Deaf People and Deafness* (New York: McGraw-Hill Book Company, 1987) 330.

Deaf people, being the only linguistic and cultural link with the hearing world.

A dominant paternalism also occurred in other organisations set up to help Deaf people. Kyle and Woll note with reference to the origins of the British Deaf Association which 'had its origins in a charity funded by hearing persons to aid poor and sick aged deaf people' that '[p]erhaps, inevitably, and as can be seen in the other national bodies concerned with deafness, the role of hearing people quickly became a dominant one'.[60]

Dimmock notes that 'From 1900 there was a notable change. Missions became clubs and the management of them was taken up by a committee formed of deaf members'.[61] Increasingly the powers of the missioner were limited by the committee and the social aspect of the club took over from the spiritual in importance in many cases. Welfare workers with limited hours of availability took over from the missioner. Indoor games and the selling of alcoholic drinks caused the transition to a club where social activities were the main benefit to Deaf people.

We need to question whether the church mission based type of social service was less effective because it was provided by religious people. We also need to ask whether the religious aspect of the missioners' work took priority over the giving of practical help.

Parratt and Tipping say that to suggest that 'deaf work is degraded by having its origins in religion ... is both unrealistic and unfair'. They point out that religious bodies founded most of the caring services in this country and that along with 'missionary zeal', a very strong force was the Victorian commitment to dealing with poverty. They point out that 'the church ... can also be an important force for social change as is evident in South Africa today'. They ask, about the missionary model, 'Does it suggest the location of welfare services in church based centres, or does it mean a particular type of relationship with deaf people?'[62]

Parratt and Tipping[63] say that in 'the two major works on the history of the provision of services to deaf people' – Lysons (1977/79) and Stephens (1982) – a negative view of the missioner as a 'hearing policymaker' is given. They also implied that evangelism took priority over practical care. Taylor (1986), who relied on the works of Lysons, later reinforced this view.

---

[60] Kyle and Woll, *Sign Language*, 11.
[61] Dimmock, 'Sport', 330.
[62] D. Parratt and B. Tipping, 'The State, Social Work and Deafness' in *Journal of the National Council of Social Workers with the Deaf* 2 Number 4 (1986) 8.
[63] Parratt and Tipping, 'State', 8-9.

This negative view of the role of the missioner and his work can be usefully compared to the missionary work of churches and missionary organisations in the last century in undeveloped nations.[64] These are often viewed in missionary circles today as misconceived and inappropriate by today's standards. The main objection is that they seemed to be carrying out a form of cultural imperialism as much as they were spreading the gospel.

With hindsight it is easy to see how the missioners used language and practices that were appropriate and in accordance with the values and beliefs of their time but which by today's standards were oppressive. These practices had the long-term effect of contributing to the oppression of Deaf people rather than liberating them. Against this, we can note that, as Parratt and Tipping point out rightly, 'Deaf people have always striven to resist oppression and to use services to their own advantage'.[65]

Speaking of social work in the early 1960s Denmark says this of welfare work for Deaf people.

> Welfare Officers for the deaf were often hearing children of deaf parents. Some were ordained and were called 'missioners'. They were employed by societies and missions for deaf people, which were charitable organisations. They were inevitably fluent in sign language but did not have any training in social work. Perhaps understandably, they were often paternalistic.[66]

The practical care for Deaf people, which previously was given by the missioners, was later provided through Local Authority Social Service departments. The ministry to the spiritual needs of Deaf people is today provided by chaplains and we will be looking at this provision in more detail later.

f. The History and Iconic Aspects of Sign Language

We will now provide a brief overview of the main areas of the history and iconic aspects of sign language that affect our research.[67]

---

[64] For his pertinent comments concerning 'benevolent paternalism' see D.J. Bosch, *Transforming Mission. Paradigm Shifts in Theology of Mission* (Maryknoll, New York: Orbis Books, 1991) 295-96.

[65] Parratt and Tipping, 'State' 247.

[66] J. Denmark, 'Back to the future' in C. Laurenzi and S. Ridgeway (eds.), *Progress through Equality* (London: BSMHD Publications, 1996) 6.

[67] For an excellent initial and detailed introduction to sign language and BSL see Kyle and Woll, *Sign Language,* and R. Sutton-Spence and B. Woll, *The Linguistics of British Sign Language. An Introduction* (Cambridge: Cambridge University Press, 1999).

Crystal notes 'Very little information is available about the early history of sign languages. References to Deaf signing are found in Greek and Roman writings, but there are no details'.[68] We can trace modern study of signing from

> Abbé Charles Michel de l'Epée ... who in 1775 developed a sign language for use in a school for the deaf in Paris. ... Several foreign educators studied at this school, and the influence of this system spread to many parts of the world.[69]

Local sign languages exist in countries throughout the world and there is an 'Esperanto' of sign language known as 'International Sign'. Even without this, many Deaf people find they are able to communicate more easily with people from other countries. This may be because meaning is conveyed in non-verbal ways and because sign language uses some signs that show symbolically the visual characteristic of that to which they refer.

Concerning this matter, Kyle and Woll say that 'BSL is made up of images and arbitrary symbols. It exists in a visual special mode, with iconic signs ... but there are also [other] signs ... which have no clear iconic origins'.[70] Crystal notes that 'A clear distinction must be drawn, first of all, between sign language and gesture'.[71] Gestures are very limited in number and sign is far more comprehensive in its ability to convey meaning. Crystal refers to the iconic nature of some signs.

> Some of the hand movements of sign language can be plausibly interpreted by non-signers because they reflect properties of the external world (they are *iconic*) ... It is possible that many of the signs were iconic when they were first devised, but little information is available about this point in the past, which some have speculated may be as early as the origins of human language ... the iconicity has been lost in most instances because of the influence of linguistic change, which affects sign as it does spoken language.[72]

It is possible that this iconicity, could explain why, on occasions, hearing people are sometimes emotionally moved by sign language. In churches, where we have interpreted into sign language hearing people have frequently said they were moved emotionally by watching the sign interpretation. Sometimes hearing people claimed that they could understand the message better because they had watched the signs as

---

[68] D. Crystal (ed.), *The Cambridge Encyclopedia of Language* (Cambridge: Cambridge University Press, 1990) 221.
[69] Crystal, *Language,* 221.
[70] Kyle and Woll, *Sign Language,* 26.
[71] Crystal, *Language,* 220.
[72] Crystal, *Language,* 220.

well. This could be because they were recognising iconic signs that connected with images stored in their mind. Alternatively, it could be because sign language often graphically conveys emotional content in visual form. Another possibility is that religious emotional images might communicate more effectively when signs are added to words. Hearing people may also be pre-disposed to being affected by what they see because of the compassion they feel for Deaf people.

Sutton-Spence and Woll suggest that 'visually motivated' is a better term than iconic, but they argue for this from a position that '"Icon" just means "picture"',[73] however in theological understanding it has much greater depth than this, so we will retain our terminology during this research. They are clear on their view that 'the meanings of gestures are based upon cultural norms, and these vary'.[74]

Sign languages have developed different vocabularies in different countries, but there may be more similarities between some than others. An example is Australian Sign Language, which is closer to British Sign Language, than Singapore Sign Language. The latter uses a mixture of American Sign Language, some Shanghai (Chinese) signs, and local Singaporean signs. The sign hand formations are sometimes familiar but they have different meanings. We have found when travelling abroad that not knowing the local sign language can generate the same feelings that accompany a visit to a foreign country when we do not know the spoken language. A sense of fear and confusion accompanies not being able to communicate. This can be a daily experience for Deaf people in a hearing world.

It would also seem that, because of the iconic nature of some signs and the dynamic, visual and spatial nature of the language, it has the potential to communicate, sometimes more effectively, concepts which are difficult to put into spoken words. Deaf people use sign language to convey ideas and concepts with a subtlety and directness that often exceeds the ability of hearing people using only voice.

---

[73] Sutton-Spence and Woll, *Linguistics*, 168.
[74] Sutton-Spence and Woll, *Linguistics*, 168.

g. The Place of Deaf People in the Church[75]

We will look at some further aspects of the ways in which Deaf people experience church in the United Kingdom. This will provide some helpful background information against which to view our research. We will give examples from the Church of England, the Roman Catholic Church and the worldwide situation, and then look at some aspects of ministry that those involved with Deaf people must carefully consider.

It is important at the outset to acknowledge the relatively small number of Deaf sign language users in the church, and therefore the relative size of ministry to Deaf people. In the Church of England, each Diocese may have a chaplain to Deaf people, possibly part-time, who may provide services in British Sign Language. These may be monthly at one place in the Diocese. Some have services that are more frequent but this is not the norm. Some have relatively small numbers attending, perhaps a handful, whilst others may have up to 20 or 30 Deaf people. The chaplain is more often than not a hearing person and the signing will often be in Sign Supported English as opposed to the Deaf person's natural language of British Sign Language. Chaplains may not have had any previous experience with Deaf people before their appointment and so their fluency and use of sign language is often elementary. It was only in 1996 that the church agreed that ordained clergy who were proposed for the role of Deaf chaplain be allowed a period during which they might begin to learn sign language. There are plans to increase the number of Deaf lay chaplains and this will improve matters, but progress is slow.

As an example we can note the situation in the writer's diocese, the diocese of Rochester. At the time this research was started a group of Deaf people averaging between 5 and 10 in number met monthly in the lounge of a local sheltered housing unit for disabled people. Communion was celebrated. The chaplain to the Deaf at the time had a level of signing that was approximately CACDP[76] Stage 1, which is a very basic level of communication. Despite this, there was a great sense of

---

[75] This was also the title of a conference held at The University of Kent, Canterbury by 'The International Ecumenical Working Group' and the papers presented provide some insight into the theoretical and practical matters affecting Deaf people in the church, and especially the Church of England. See International Ecumenical Working Group (ed.), *The Place of Deaf People in the Church*.

[76] CACDP (Council for the Advancement of Communication with Deaf People) provide qualifications with professional standards for sign language users, including interpreters. For information on services provided by them see their website address, http://www.cacdp.demon.co.uk/.

importance attached to the meeting by the Deaf people who attended. Good relationships flourished and there was much humour in evidence, which is not unusual when Deaf people meet together. Similar meetings were held monthly at two other venues in the diocese.

Despite the limitations, Deaf people often very much appreciate the services provided. Their situation is somewhat similar to that of missionaries in a foreign country who meet together for fellowship and church services. They are a small group who are separated from their own culture and language. They may feel quite isolated and are grateful for any ministry provided for them.

Shrine, who is Deaf, and a Church of England chaplain to the Deaf, believes that the future for the Deaf church 'requires the development of a variety of ways of being church that are appropriate for deaf people. This could include sign language congregations in parish churches, sign-based home groups, or deaf groups in mainstream churches with interpreters …'.[77]

He sees three main problems with the deaf church.

1 Its members are ageing, which implies that many deaf churches will die out in the next twenty years or so. Younger people are not joining.
2 It has a poor image in the deaf community, where it is often regarded as irrelevant, old fashioned and stuck on English and hearing ways of doing things.
3 It is generally ignored and marginalized by the wider church.[78]

Another problem Shrine identifies is that of 'tokenism' in the appointment of Deaf chaplains. By this he means that in order to appear to be giving responsibility to Deaf people the church may appoint them to positions of authority but not adequately empower them to minister. Giving an example of this, he says 'Of the eight deaf chaplains we now have only three have responsibility for a diocese'.[79]

Within the Roman Catholic Church, Deaf ordained people are also rare. The Deaf priest Father Peter McDonnough made the comment in 1994 that 'In the British Catholic population, there are only one deaf Jesuit and myself, very often situated at more than two hundred miles apart'.[80]

---

[77] R. Shrine, 'Interview', *Signs, Magazine of the National Deaf Church Conference* (Spring 2001) 9.
[78] Shrine, 'Interview', 9.
[79] Shrine, 'Interview', 9. By this he means that the other 5, whilst having the status and title of 'chaplain', have only a limited authority to minister.
[80] P. McDonnough, 'A Deaf Priest's View' in International Ecumenical Working Group (ed.), *The Place of Deaf People in the Church*, 42.

Worldwide the figures are equally astoundingly small. 'In 1993, the first world-wide Gathering for Catholic deaf priests and Religious were (sic) attended by thirty one deaf people ... from ten different countries'.[81]

There are two main alternatives for ministry among Deaf people. These are integrated services where Deaf people meet with hearing people and separate services for Deaf people. Integrated services may involve the use of an interpreter, lip speaker or note taker so that one or more Deaf people can participate. Separate services are conducted in sign language.

One possible danger of integrated situations is that Deaf people may fear that hearing people may somehow 'take' their sign language from them. As Deaf people closely link sign language with their sense of identity this is an understandable fear.

Hearing pastors working with Deaf people need to be aware of the difficulties that can arise if they are not sensitive to the special situation of Deaf people. Leila Monaghan, a hearing anthropologist, gives a graphic example that occurred in a church in Washington, DC. The hearing pastor wanted to emphasise the 'oneness' of the church. He arbitrarily informed the Deaf congregation, which had been meeting separately for some years, that they were, in future, to meet with the main hearing congregation on Sunday mornings. As a result, the Deaf group split away from the main church. Monaghan reports the response of the Deaf deacon who said

> The Deaf were surprised and reluctant to agree with [the decision] ... because of our historical experience of being oppressed by hearing society at home, work, school, and even church. ... We repeatedly expressed our feelings about the whole thing: language, barriers, culture, discrimination. ... [The old church] has failed to recognize that the growth of the Deaf ministry was not done by the church but from the Deaf to the Deaf by the Deaf.[82]

The wider church can be enriched by involvement with Deaf people and sign language. Kerwin, in describing how he introduced his hearing colleagues in his seminary to sign language in liturgical celebrations, says he was aware of the risk involved but successful acceptance meant that the risk paid off. He concludes:

> I took the courage to bring a native Deaf language into the public. The risk seems to have paid off. Our liturgical celebrations have

---

[81] McDonnough, 'View', 43.
[82] L. Monaghan, 'From Strength to Strength: The Future of Deaf Communities', Paper presented to The Deaf Futures Conference, University of Central Lancashire, June 1996, 1.

taken on a new dimension with the signing from the seminary community. This is a great challenge for our Church: to make liturgy accessible for the Deaf, with Deaf and hearing people worshipping together inclusively.[83]

In considering the question "Deaf church, or alternative church?" Father Peter McDonnough acknowledges that 'There have been arguments which say that we shouldn't have separate congregations and a separate liturgy for deaf people because we are all members of the whole Body of Christ, and that we should all celebrate and worship together'.[84]

He is forced to conclude however that it is only when Deaf people have the same access to ministry as hearing people, as a right, that they have any hope of being part of the church to the same extent. This would mean both hearing and Deaf people being suitably qualified before ministering to Deaf people. They would need language ability and knowledge of cultural and linguistic differences. His conclusion is that a suitably trained Deaf person using British Sign Language would almost certainly provide a better ministry to Deaf people.

Elsewhere, McDonnough provides an understanding of the implications of deafness for our doctrine of God and Man and how this affects church life in varying ways. He usefully draws attention to the story of the healing of the Deaf man in Mark 7, noting that

> The word Jesus used when he cured the Deaf man was 'Ephphatha' meaning 'Be opened' (Mk. 7:34), this occurred at the moment the Deaf man was re-introduced into the community of the society that had rejected him. It is not merely a coincidence that the Deaf man in question was now opened to the mystery of other human beings surrounding him when he was no longer in isolation and ignorant of his own personhood.[85]

By noting this aspect of 'opening' that has occurred, McDonnough points out that this release from the closed world in which the Deaf man lived is, for him, also the gaining of a new horizon in his understanding. McDonnough's own view of deafness is that 'it is still a handicap, a curse'.[86] Self-transcendence will come as self-awareness is achieved through a process of developing the conscience and reflecting

---

[83] Kerwin, J., *Building Bridges...Between the Deaf and Hearing Cultures* (Dutton Park, Australia: Brisbane Catholic Education, 1996) 24.

[84] McDonnough, 'View', 52.

[85] P. McDonnough, 'Deaf and Made in the Image and Likeness of God. Deaf and Made Like God: Deaf People Communicating the Gospel'. Swanwick Conference Paper, June 1998, 2.

[86] McDonnough, 'Deaf and Made', 8.

on our nature. Then '[s]elf –transcendence leads to accepting our ordinary story as sacred rather than trying to deny it – namely, deafness – and avoid the danger of idealizing deafness'.[87] His reminder is useful, for it is sometimes tempting for Deaf people to avoid the reality of their impairment, in order to avoid the pain necessarily associated with acknowledging it. As he reminds us, 'To be fully conscious of oneself is to acknowledge we have a need for God and others. Being Deaf often leads us into a situation where we are forced to ask for help and support'.[88]

Concerning liturgy and the responsibility of Deaf people he says

> Even if we have eliminated oppression, increased deaf awareness in the church, and promoted "Deaf liturgy" etc., we often find ourselves facing the last hurdle which appears to be almost insurmountable and this comes from the Deaf people themselves. They still have the attitude that liturgy is in the realm of the spiritual and therefore it belongs to priests and ministers …[89]

Shrine also speaks significantly concerning the potential contribution of Deaf people to church life.

> It is no longer, "How can the church help Deaf people?" but, "What contribution can Deaf people make to the church?" Deaf people can contribute in many ways: signing enhances worship and adds a new dimension; storytelling and drama present new ways of conveying the Gospel; the need for visual access can encourage the creative use of space; Deaf spirituality and Deaf theology can give the whole church new perspectives.[90]

A significant factor that leaders of hearing churches must address is the impact that the presence of a sign language interpreter can have on the hearing people in the church. Sign language often involves communicating by using facial expressions, which for hearing people seem exaggerated. They can cause people to focus more on the interpreter than on the preacher. This can be disruptive. The overall impact of any interpreting provision needs careful thought.

Leaders need to be careful to ensure that potential interpreters have sufficient ability to communicate the relevant concepts and ideas in sign language. Care needs to be taken to ensure that the language and signs common to the denomination of the church are used as these vary

---

[87] McDonnough, 'Deaf and Made', 8.
[88] McDonnough, 'Deaf and Made', 8.
[89] McDonnough, 'Deaf and Made', 12.
[90] R. Shrine, 'Challenge and Opportunity. What are the Deaf Ways of Being Church?', unpublished paper, undated, 13.

Deaf People and the Church

considerably even within denominations. For example, the meaning of salvation and accompanying sign may be quite different in a Church of England evangelical church from that with a high church tradition. Another common problem is that signers are very prominent in most settings and there may be more desire for prominence than willingness to serve Deaf people with humility. As with all regular ministry in the church there needs to be a considerable commitment on the part of those providing ministry interpretation to ensure continuity in the event of holidays, sickness, etc.

h. Self-Image, Immediacy, Community, Self-Centredness

In this section, we will consider these four matters and how they connect Deaf people with emphases that we find in Moltmann's theology. In practice, his theology can enhance the sense of well-being of Deaf people, by providing an improved self-image and helping them understand their place in the church. From this comes the possibility of freedom from domination. Moltmann in addressing power issues has a particular concern to enable vulnerable persons to avoid exploitation, alienation or abuse and he analyses society with an approach which has the aim of increasing self-awareness and knowledge of the way in which society develops.

Research has shown that, among Deaf people, the compound effects of a number of factors have served to produce a situation whereby concepts of self are poor when compared to the hearing population generally.[91] If we add this to the imbalance of power that exists between Deaf sign language users and hearing people, we can see the potential for abuse and exploitation.

One shocking result of society's oppression of this vulnerable group is the extent of child sexual abuse (defined as assault, rape and attempted rape). In one survey conducted in 1992 in the North West of England 81%, of the 102 Deaf adults interviewed, reported being abused in this way. Ridgeway says, 'The comparative figures for the non-deaf population, using a broader definition (which includes exhibitionism and pornographic exposure), are on average, 12% for girls and 8% for boys'.[92]

Ridgeway says 'We know that most deaf people grow up to develop poor self concepts'.[93] She is concerned with the way in which poor

---

[91] See S. Ridgeway, 'Deaf People and Psychological Health – Some Preliminary Findings' in *Deaf Worlds* 13 Number 1 (March, 1997) 9.

[92] S. Ridgeway, 'Teddy Bear...Teddy Bear...' in Laurenzi and Ridgeway (eds.), *Progress Through Equality*, 28.

[93] Ridgeway, 'Teddy', 30.

self-concepts and other factors increase the likelihood of abuse. She identifies some of these in the following list:

- Deprivation of language development and communication skills.
- Lack of exposure to other deaf people and a lack of a deaf peer group.
- Rejection of deaf identity and lack of deaf consciousness and deaf awareness.
- Conflict in the family over deaf issues.

She then notes,

> [a]ll of these factors might give rise to feelings of rejection and abandonment as their deaf "sense of being" is rejected in favour of an attempt to integrate into an alien state of being [hearing culture]. Disintegration of self easily results. This state of disintegration can lead to negative self-image, poor self concept, social isolation and poorly developed sense of identity. The resulting isolation reinforces the lack of a sense of belonging which is essential for good positive mental health and psychological development.[94]

Acquired attitudes can contribute to distorted perceptions of reality for Deaf people. We can note similarities with the experiences of black people. Giddens states, 'Attitudes learned in early childhood probably continue as important underlying orientations in later life. Blacks often acquire an early sense of their own inferiority that may prove very difficult to dispel later'.[95] Economic self-interest can also determine attitudes. As an example Lane argues that the economic and career interests of hearing people involved in 'helping' Deaf people reveals a vested interest in the continuation of the belief that Deaf people are inferior in the sense that they need help to cope with the hearing world. 'This market is controlled by hearing people'.[96]

Amongst users of sign language there is often a sense of immediacy of communication. Compared to the experience of hearing people there is a greater sense of being directly involved in an un-mediated way. This can be due to the way in which the signs used sometimes convey almost instantaneously, the meaning inherent in them. This may be because they iconically communicate that to which they refer. It may also be to do with the linguistic structure of sign language and its way of constructing and using propositions. Kyle and Woll say:

---

[94] Ridgeway, 'Teddy', 29.
[95] See A. Giddens, *Sociology* (Cambridge: Polity Press and Blackwell Publishers, 2nd edition, 1993) 263.
[96] Lane, *Mask,* 49.

[s]ince BSL is visual, then the feeling of being in the story must be more pronounced ... The focus of this [the language surface structure] is the language itself and, in particular, the use of 'verbs' within it.[97]

When dealing with hearing society, the Deaf person will often be reliant on another person to mediate speech and the context in which it is occurring. This occurs automatically when Deaf people use interpreters, lip speakers or note takers. In a church situation, unless the church is using an established written liturgy, these intermediaries will mediate the content and meaning of the spoken message. A significant cultural difference we can note here is that Deaf people are used to working hard at establishing what something means if they do not understand it. They will not normally hesitate to interrupt and ask the interpreter the meaning of something if they do not understand! Unfortunately, some interpreters may not be able to fulfil this mediating role adequately.

The type and quality of the relationships that Deaf people build is also an important consideration. It affects the balance of power in relationships and can influence their lives considerably. Some people believe that this tendency to be less skilful in making effective relationships derives from poor educational provision. Phoenix notes that

[d]eaf adults often illustrate significant contrasts in identification processes with significant others in their lives. In fact, deaf and hearing mental health workers alike will remark upon the 'erratic' relationships exhibited within the deaf community.[98]

The Montgomerys[99] suggest that difficulties in forming effective relationships is thought to be the result 'of lack of integration of abilities to read, write and converse, the deliberate separation of sign language from written language in the educational process, and the lack in Deaf people's lives of access to secondary, background information informally picked up by overhearing conversations and sounds'. All this can contribute to '[t]he instability of affiliation, loyalty and conviction of Deaf people educated along purely oralist lines in the pressure tank residential schools of England, [which] we have personally found on

---

[97] Kyle and Woll, *Sign Language*, 212.
[98] S. Phoenix, 'Identification Processes and Staff Training in Family Intervention Using Total Communication' in Laurenzi and Ridgeway (eds.), *Progress Through Equality*, 44.
[99] Whilst the basis for their comments may be sound, they can be criticised rightly for the rather extreme language in which they express them and their pathologising approach.

occasions to be breath taking'. The Montgomerys refer to their research.

> The specialisation of language and non-language hemispheres of the brain facilitates the development of separable personalities in an individual [so that] the external communication difficulties of deaf children are internalised and the brain is compartmentalised with no very efficient communication between compartments [and this can lead to] deaf children with poor mental cohesion who are thereby more vulnerable to the more serious forms of multiple personality.[100]

The result can be a seemingly self-centred personality, more intent on exploiting relationships than building and maintaining them. The Montgomerys say it 'seemed significant that we could find no sign for "loyalty" in BSL – in fact one interpreter suggested the nearest, was the sign for "myself"'. However they are quick to stress that 'The majority of deaf people of our acquaintance are sociable, generous and unselfish in many ways', but that 'the long-term effects of reduced information input from outside, may leave them open to experience which is self-referencing and not sensitive to or even aware of the views of others'.[101]

These factors, affecting relationships entered into by Deaf people, dramatically illustrate the disadvantages that they experience when trying to exist as users of a minority language. Within a culture where the dominant language provides hearing people with more information that can support their relationships, Deaf people face a barrier that is difficult to overcome.

i. Practical Concerns, Church Practice, Liturgy, Parish Organisation

We will now look in more detail at the major ministry among Deaf people in this country, that of the Church of England. It is important to keep in mind that the hierarchical structure of that church itself will affect the nature of the ministry among Deaf people.

In the 'Report to the Synod of the Church of England', only five of the 64 pages that form the body of the report concern themselves directly with theological reflections.[102] None of the report's recom-

---

[100] J. and G. Montgomery, *No Lesser God* (Edinburgh: Scottish Workshop Publications, 1997) 48.

[101] Montgomery, *No Lesser God*, 49.

[102] Church of England, Advisory Board of Ministry Working Party (eds.), *Ministry Paper No. 14. The Church Among Deaf People, A Report prepared by a Working Party of the Committee for Ministry among Deaf People for the Gen-*

mendations contains specific theological content. This may reflect the nature of the report itself that is concerned to practically improve the provision of ministry to Deaf people and their overall experience of church. These concerns are mainly to improve training and support, access to resources and activities for Deaf people. The Church of England's approach allows for either integrated congregations with interpreting provision or separate groups where sign language is the main language used.

From Moltmann's perspective, orthopraxis is an important part of good theology. Reform of church organisational structures will clearly have some effect on the experience of the church by Deaf people. The view of Deaf people in the report is that of a group of people for whom things should be provided. Improving provision is therefore seen to be the important issue. Although acknowledgement is made that Deaf people have suffered from oppression in the church they are not viewed as equals nor are they given a rightful place in the decision-making processes of the organisation.

Perhaps the most significant move in this direction was the recommendation to 'recognise the National Deaf Church Conference as the national organisation representing deaf people in the Church of England and provide adequate funding to extend its work throughout the country'.[103] As the NDCC is an organisation led by, and consisting mainly of, Deaf people, this is a trend towards an acknowledgement that Deaf people ought to be involved in considering their own needs in the church.

The model of change that the report seems to adopt continues to be one that follows trends in the provision of services by Local Authority Social Service departments, in which the needs and choices of the 'service user' are now considered to be an important part of service provision. There seems to be a division between 'service provider' and 'service user'. There is what appears to be a move towards making structures more democratic, but the reformed structures still leave power in the hands of those 'providing'.

For the Church of England to become more like Moltmann's model there would need to be a change in the understanding of the status of 'lay' members. In Moltmann's ecclesiology there is a fellowship of friends interrelating and serving within what are primarily informal structures and networks. The organisational structure of the Church of England is one of hierarchy, with ordained clergy and other office

---

eral Synod of the Church of England's Advisory Board of Ministry (London: Church House Publishing, 1997) 58–62.

[103] Church of England, Advisory Board of Ministry Working Party (eds.), *The Church Among Deaf People*, 64.

holders (for example, pastoral workers and readers) exercising authority over others within the church.[104] Some people might argue that this is merely a form of service and that really the office holders are subservient to those they serve, in a Christ-like way. In practice, however, those who bear the title are privileged and this gives them power. This is partly because of legal requirements concerning responsibility for property and the fabric of the church and the right to access material and spiritual resources.

The report in its theological reflections acknowledges the need for the church to recognise that the church community will be incomplete unless Deaf people play their full part. It acknowledges that '[i]n practice, a church without Ministry among Deaf People, or with a ministry offered by people not thoroughly competent in sign language, is maintaining "fallen humanity's alienation from the intentions of our loving God"'.[105] Communicating in a language that can be understood is seen to be central to the fulfilment of God's intentions. We can also note here the Church of England 'Articles of Religion', Article 24,[106] which concerns the need for ministry to be conducted in a language that is understood by the people.

The stated aim of the report is to see Deaf people proclaiming the 'Good News', sharing fellowship, leading worship, developing liturgies, and serving alongside hearing members of the church. It views the gifts of Deaf people as special. It notes that everyone can experience the drama and excitement of liturgy afresh in the company of Deaf people. The report says '[t]he graceful nature of sign language can provide beauty that matches the beauty of the sounds of music in worship, thus providing another dimension to refresh and stimulate the vision of God'.[107] It acknowledges that Deaf people's experience can bring a different perspective to the life of the church. It says '[b]ecause of the way society and the Church tend to behave, deaf people are often pushed to the margin and made to feel excluded from many

---

[104] Note Moltmann's strong words of criticism concerning the 'holy rule' that developed from the distinction between lay people and clergy and exhibits itself in the 'monarchical episcopate' in the Roman Catholic church and the 'Protestant pastoral aristocracy, or its somewhat more modern variation in the form of a theological and pastoral expertocracy'. Moltmann, *Experiences in Theology*, 265-266.

[105] Church of England, Advisory Board of Ministry Working Party (eds.), *The Church Among Deaf People*, 59.

[106] *The Book of Common Prayer*, (Glasgow: Collins, undated) 568.

[107] Church of England, Advisory Board of Ministry Working Party (eds.), *The Church Among Deaf People*, 60.

things. Yet this is the very place that Jesus chose to be in his life and ministry'.[108]

Sadly, however, as an example of what can easily be viewed as 'the patronising paternalistic language of colonialism'[109] we can note the following quote from the report that speaks of the 'nature of the faith of Deaf people'.

> Their relationship with God, and his with them, is often untrammelled by detail or the complexities of knowledge or understanding. Often their faith is direct, clear and simple, but very powerful because it feels, to those who know them, like the faith Jesus calls for – the faith that is childlike in its openness and trust.[110]

We will next look at an alternative approach in the Roman Catholic Church. James Kerwin, a Roman Catholic priest in training, said that

> [t]o appreciate the diversity of the Church and at the same time incorporate that very diversity into unification, is to appreciate the true catholicity of the Church. The Deaf and Hearing are different to each other, but also there are sub-cultures within the Deaf and Hearing worlds. Not all Deaf are the same.[111]

Noting the parish system that exists within the Roman Catholic Church he says that one model is for there to be a 'Deaf parish' operating alongside the normal parishes, with a central parish 'home base' to which Deaf people would relate and which would provide, say, monthly services. For weddings and other special services Deaf people may use the local parish with a suitable interpreter and attend hearing services there at other times. This system is used with other ethnic groups successfully 'such as the Spanish community who may gather once a month too, to experience a Spanish speaking liturgy, but also attend their own parish services at other times'.[112] This model allows '[Deaf people] to be equal in the ecclesial sense of the Catholic com-

---

[108] Church of England, Advisory Board of Ministry Working Party (eds.), *The Church Among Deaf People*, 60.

[109] See Lane, *Mask*, 34, for a list of '[t]raits attributed to the Africans in the literature of colonialism'. Lane rightly sees many similarities between Deaf people's experience of oppression and the colonization of African communities. Both involved 'the imposition of alien language and mores, and the regulation of education in behalf of the colonizer's goals' (*Mask*, 31).

[110] Church of England, Advisory Board of Ministry Working Party (eds.), *The Church Among Deaf People*, 60.

[111] Kerwin, *Bridges*, 45.

[112] Kerwin, *Bridges*, 45.

munity while retaining their special needs and wants'.[113] This is a good practical model.

The main church services for Deaf people in the UK are those provided by the Anglicans and the Roman Catholics. Unless a radical transformation of their view of ministry occurs the hierarchical nature of these churches makes it improbable that Moltmann's suggestions will be adopted in full but aspects of his approach could positively influence future attitudes and practice.

Moltmann views the members of the Trinity as existing in a relationship that is non-hierarchical. He then uses this view to define the being of man and his relationships. He argues that this non-hierarchical view can eliminate the power-based exploitative relationships, which exist in our society. Mutual respect and acknowledgement of the rights and responsibilities of the individual will follow. These rights will include the right to use a different language and have a different set of values and beliefs to those of the dominant culture. There will be less likelihood of institutional exploitation and people will have a better understanding of their self-identity and how to form relationships.

Moltmann views the church primarily as a relational entity, a community of believers, as opposed to an institution. This places emphasis on the quality of relationships within it, and the responsibilities of people to others. Peer reinforcement of views of the self will follow from the interaction involved in meeting together. People will focus on the tasks of creating and maintaining good relationships through the acknowledgement that suffering, and the suffering of God in particular, is a central part of the Christian faith. People will see that the alleviation of that suffering comes through the proclamation of the coming kingdom of God. Moltmann's model here requires the acceptance of a creative dialectical tension which exists in the acknowledgement that conflict can be viewed as potentially constructive and will enable persons experiencing conflict to gain a perspective of hope.

j. The Influence of Language on our Understanding of Identity, Communication and Relationships

In this section we look at the influence of language from a number of aspects. We look at 'political correctness', how social values are inherent in language and how words express intention and incorporate attitude. We look at how attitude is vital in defining the nature of relationships and how it is necessary for the development of holistic concepts of knowledge. We look at how the storytelling approach in

---

[113] Kerwin, *Bridges*, 44.

Scripture is mirrored in sign language and how both describe relationships and convey attitudes and intentions by appealing to visual and spatial imagery.

We use language to understand our experience and we often use abstract concepts in this process. Alongside our language are a whole host of non-verbal signifiers that supplement language or provide us with separate autonomous input. Certain words or phrases can also carry additional meaning.

Within recent years, terms such as 'disabled people' have replaced 'the handicapped'.[114] The inclusion of the word people into the description is intended to transfer the emphasis from a state of being to the condition of a 'person' who may require special help. We acknowledge that there is in this practice of changing terminology, a 'repackaging' process. The intention is to separate people's images of disabled people from the words with which they were identified in the past, and so improve attitudes towards them. However, there often seems to be a simple transferring to the new terminology the concepts that were attached to the old names. It is clear that some attempts by people to impose a 'politically correct' way of describing reality are as oppressive as the attitudes of people that oppressed others in the past. Laughable though some of these attempts are, attitudes have needed changing, and this 're-naming' process sometimes helps. Disabled people have in the past appeared to be a group of people who are separate from normal humanity. Some disabled people cannot forget the eugenics experiments of the Nazis before and during the Second World War. Large numbers of disabled and mentally ill people were 'treated' for being sub-human initially by sterilisation programmes so that they would not procreate. Later they were killed in State run institutions. Many Deaf people died then and the memory of this is a legacy that still exists among them. Some fear that eugenics will again be used to 'eliminate' Deaf people.[115]

---

[114] On a personal and partly humorous note, and to illustrate the practical difficulties of changing terminology, the executive committee of an organisation for which I worked ten years ago, (rightly) struggled to convince some members that its name should be changed from Bromley Association for The Handicapped, (known locally by its initials BATH) to Bromley Association for Disabled People. This, they said, emphasised the fact that it existed for the benefit of 'people' and 'disabled' was a more appropriate term than 'handicap'. Ironically, it has had to retain the initials BATH in its publicity, probably because it has over 30 years history of being recognised by these! The local Deaf sign is to sign 'bath' (as in bathing) for BATH and it seems unlikely that this can easily change to suit the new initials!

[115] See Lane, *Mask,* 213–216, and the following section on 'the Risks and Limitations of Childhood Cochlear Implants' for the way in which medical science

We can note that language is a carrier of socially constructed judgements concerning the value of individual members of society. The subtlety with which it is used can influence the nature of identities and relationships. There is ability in any language to convey complex notions of faith related issues and belief and value systems. A Deaf person living partly in a hearing world will experience the influence and power of both sign language and the spoken word. We can see another demonstration of the power of language in relationships in the example of hearing professionals meeting Deaf people. They will occasionally use British Sign Language but more often than not, the language used will be Sign Supported English. If the professionals were truly concerned about the interests of the Deaf people for whom they were providing services, they would be required to learn and use their language. As it is, hearing people retain control through the dominant culture, using language to perpetuate dominance in relationships, even if this is not overtly intentional.

For hearing Christians ministering to Deaf people, similar cross cultural considerations might apply, as it might when a white Christian Englishman goes to Muslim Pakistan on a missionary venture. Whilst the proclamation of the gospel will confront and challenge through its content, the language used in proclaiming it will need to have sufficiently recognisable and appropriately used symbols within it, and alongside it, if it is to act as an adequate communicator which builds bridges to understanding.

David Braine has provided a cleverly constructed argument for viewing language as the specific defining feature of human nature. He describes what he sees as the difference between human beings and animals.

> [W]hat matters is our capacity to initiate and respond to new types of enquiry and to handle new situations in thought. This is where the unlimitedness or potential infinity of what the human being can do with finite resources arises, and it is a result of the open-endedness and flexibility of words, the result of the leeway between word and sentence and of the many-track character of the kind of disposition or skill which is called 'knowing the meaning of a word'.[116]

---

sees deafness in certain periods of history mainly as something that can be 'cured' or eliminated. Also for an account of 'attrocities and sufferings experienced by Deaf people under the rule of the Third Reich', see H. Biesold, *Crying Hands. Eugenics and Deaf People in Nazi Germany* (Washington, DC: Gallaudet University Press, 1999).

[116] D. Braine, *The Human Person, Animal and Spirit* (London: Duckworth, 1993) 354.

Braine argues that human beings express their intentions in action. Language provides us with an efficient tool for expressing our thoughts and judgements. The 'meaning' of our communication exists only in our words and not in the mind as a symbol or picture. It is the infinite capacity of words to change their meaning according to the context within which they are used, that allows for such a wide variety of meaning as is possible at any one time. Thus he says '... that the words of the sentence or speech-unit do not merely identify its meaning but express it'.[117] He also says:

> We may rightly speak of models, images or representations as having a role in connection with thinking. But propositions statements and senses are not such models, pictures or representations: rather they incorporate force or attitude.[118]

This incorporation of 'force or attitude' is an important aspect that we will return to later. Noting the processes involved in perception, and the understanding that follows from it, he argues that the empiricists have replaced Plato's 'Forms' with 'ideas' known by imagination and derived from experience. Arguing from 'Aquinas' account of abstraction and judgement'[119] he shows that:

> ... in the act of judging itself there had to be a presentation of material objects, whether through perception or through imagination, and so, in the typical case, there has to be what Aquinas refers to as a *conversio ad phantasmata*, a turning to *phantasmata* or images.[120]

His goal is to show from a phenomenological viewpoint a unity of being which human beings have contrasted to dualist understandings of soul and body. He says:

> The effect of regarding the material as self-contained for purposes of the consideration of causation, prediction of behaviour, and identity is to make belief in the subsistence of the soul or in the after-life into the superstition called dualism. And this is what happened in 17th century thought—and this is why the return to the Aristotelian perspective, whether or not it be stated in terms of a doctrine of the soul as form, is absolutely crucial.[121]

It is the body as it exists in the world that is one with the spirit and it is this unity that transcends this world. He says,

---

[117] Braine, *Person*, 370.
[118] Braine, *Person*, 410.
[119] Braine, *Person*, 420.
[120] Braine, *Person*, 421.
[121] Braine, *Person*, 526.

> ... we give the phenomenological in the human case an explanatory and ontological status and thus avoid the evil in dualistic and materialistic explanations which has always included the inventing of a gap between how we 'experience ourselves' and 'the realities as they are in themselves'.[122]

Braine's ideas are similar to Moltmann's in places. Moltmann has a holistic understanding of being. He also sees 'being' as 'being there', as 'being within acting', and as 'becoming'. Braine uses language ability as the basis for human uniqueness. Perception of our being occurs as we use our linguistic ability to express our intentions. He effectively 'externalises' what we sometimes believe to be internal models of reality. What is particularly impressive are his thoughts on the way in which thinking *about* things differs from thinking *of* things. Braine carefully concentrates on language in its complexity as being the key to our understanding of the holistic identity of self.

When considering the way in which understanding occurs we should ask to what extent are signs (used by Deaf people) analogous to words (used by hearing people)? In their research, Kyle and Woll note that:

> If Chafe (1977) is correct, then BSL would represent a language which tends to emphasise the storage and recall of events, whereas English requires much more superficial specificity in recall. BSL therefore stores story information and re-tells it in a way which would occur for all languages, but spoken language surface structure (reflecting only a specific point in time and context) would tend to hide this in its effort for reconstruction of meaning.[123]

Significantly, they quote De Matteo (1977) whose research into ASL (American Sign Language) found that 'the richness of aspectual information comes from their visual-spatial characteristics and that there is an appeal to the visual imagery of the receiver in telling the stories'.[124]

Kyle and Woll were concerned to go 'deeply into the structure of BSL from a cognitive psychological perspective'.[125] They concluded that 'The fears that BSL consists of a limited, concrete visual language localised in the right hemisphere, can be discounted'[126] and that 'BSL processing involves sequential and spatial codes, uses direct visual

---

[122] Braine, *Person,* 527.
[123] Kyle and Woll, *Sign Language,* 214.
[124] Kyle and Woll, *Sign Language,* 214.
[125] Kyle and Woll, *Sign Language,* 214.
[126] Kyle and Woll, *Sign Language,* 214.

representation for its syntax while displaying the same complexity of meaning as English'.[127]

Their research seems to indicate that sign language uses the right hemisphere for the visual spatial aspect of sign language and the left hemisphere for the linguistic aspect. Sign language seeks to involve the person being signed to in the re-living of the story, which is the container for the information being conveyed.[128]

We can draw interesting parallels with the way in which, traditionally, storytelling was the mode used by Old Testament Jews and the early Christians for preserving and passing on theological understandings of God's dealing with the world. The nature of Scripture also, with its dialectical confronting of our experience of reality through the variety of literary schemes, including historical, poetic and prophetic approaches, also seeks to draw the listener or reader into the reality conveyed.

k. Perceptions of Language and Power

In this section, we wish to look further at the way in which our perception is dependent on the language we use, our identity, our relationship to others, and the attitudes arising from societal and organisational structures within which we live.

Democratic and representative organisations of disabled people, including Deaf people, claim that there is a need to change the perspective of our society.[129] This will involve a political process that will move disabled people from a position where they are viewed primarily as recipients of benefit or charity to one where they are seen as people with impairments. The task of a democratic society is to enable them to contribute to it as fully as possible and to the same extent as non-disabled people. The issue is one of authority and power.

---

[127] Kyle and Woll, *Sign Language*, 215.
[128] For details of research currently being undertaken in this and associated areas, see Ursula Bellugi, website address, http://www.salk.edu/faculty/bellugi.html.
[129] For an example of the campaigning work being done by four of the major UK organisations, see the following organisations:
British Deaf Association, website address,
http://www.britishdeafassociation.org.uk/
National Deaf Children's Society, website address, http://www.ndcs.org.uk/
Royal National Institute for the Deaf, website address, http://www.rnid.org.uk/
United Kingdom Council on Deafness, website address,
http://www.ukcod.freeserve.co.uk/ .

The question is one of who decides the fate of others and under what terms.[130]

We have noted previously that in the past, our society viewed people that it considers different, or who speak a different language, with much less tolerance than it does today. We will only tolerate or accept difference when the difference does not appear to constitute a threat to our existence or to the values and structure of our society. Perceptions of reality change over time and the dominant forces in society determine our values and beliefs. People in positions of power create the dominant value system of our society. This occurs through their conscious actions, or through the institutions they form that have their own values, framework for understanding the world, and related vocabulary. They establish the perspective.

In Britain, the class structure pervades all of society. The upper classes, more than the lower classes, have traditionally sought to protect their interests through use of the legal system. The legal system emphasises the value of property and civil rights and can work in the interests of all members of society, but access to it is usually expensive. Within British society, language is a means of identifying the social class of the speaker and it can thus be a subtle means of restricting access to power. In some parts of society, for example, 'Standard English' and 'Received Pronunciation' are seen as being superior to other linguistic expressions of the English language. Only people who speak in a certain way will be allowed into certain situations, and that can include situations where power is exercised.[131] Language is routinely used to discriminate against and form barriers between people. Steven Pinker points out that '[l]inguists repeatedly run up against the myth that working-class people and the less educated members of the middle class speak a simpler or coarser language ... The myth that non-standard dialects of English are grammatically deficient is widespread'.[132]

---

[130] Woodward notes the difficulty of challenging the views of those who hold the reigns of power. '[N]o matter what amount of research in the Deaf community and comparative research in other communities can be presented at this time to demonstrate that Deaf people form a minority group with language varieties quite different from English, the Hearing controlled educational establishment generally still rejects the idea of a Deaf minority group' (Woodward, *Heaven*, 13).

[131] Another process of discrimination we can note, within the Deaf community, is when some Deaf people view those who are 'born Deaf' as being at the core of the Deaf community, and others as having a lesser standing.

[132] S. Pinker, *The Language Instinct* (Harmondsworth: Penguin, 1995) 28.

Moltmann's analysis of power in relationships supports his belief that the proclamation of the gospel exists to liberate 'the poor'. Liberation will be from oppressive relationships. Deaf people, rightly, may feel an immediate indignant response to any suggestion that they should be viewed as 'the poor'. In Moltmann's understanding of the gospel, however, belonging to the category of 'the poor' does not make a person a lesser being, deserving of paternalistic 'good works'. It includes an acknowledgement of the fact that Christians believe *all* people are 'the poor' in that they are in need of the gospel message. For Moltmann 'the poor' are the people that have a privileged position in the eyes of God and they play a prominent part in how he understands the church to be constituted. One manifestation of the church is amongst 'the poor' of society. He says, '... the true church is to be found where Christ is present'[133] and this means 'in its missionary presence among the poor'. Moltmann's view is also that the presence of God is experienced as we reach out to 'the poor' and that this is promised in Mt. 25:40 '[a]s you did to one of the least, you did it to me'. Moltmann says, 'What is new about the option for the poor is that the poor are no longer the object of Christian charity. They are taken seriously as determining subjects among Christ's people'.[134] Sugden has helpfully described the poor as the Bible sees them. 'The Bible gives attention, not to wealth and poverty as the accumulation or lack of riches as a commodity, but to the relationships between people which poverty and wealth express'.[135] To be 'poor' is not a permanent classification but a description of a person's state of being that is transitory. We consider that the meaning of the poor that Sugden uses is a powerful way of illustrating the need to use the right terminology when referring to disabled people. It also leads us towards an understanding of 'being' that is defined by the relationships within which we exist.

We should note how effectively language is able to provide the power for us to include or exclude people. Hearing people observing Deaf people using sign language can feel excluded from the conversation. This sense of exclusion is similar to that felt by Deaf people when watching hearing people speak. The experience is also similar to Eng-

---

[133] J. Moltmann, *The Church in the Power of the Spirit. A Contribution to Messianic Ecclesiology* (London: SCM Press, 1977) 122 .

[134] J. Moltmann, 'The Liberation of the future and its anticipations in history' in Bauckham (ed.), *All in All*, 287. See also a clear explanation of Moltmann's position on this subject in R. Bauckham, *The Theology of Jürgen Moltmann* (Edinburgh: T & T Clark, 1995) 130.

[135] C.M.N. Sugden, 'Poverty and Wealth' in S.B. Ferguson and D.F. Wright (eds.), *New Dictionary of Theology* (Leicester and Downers Grove, Illinois: IVP, 1988) 523.

lish speakers encountering foreign language speakers. When this happens to us we can experience a profound sense of encountering something that is 'other'. Our language and how we use it are fundamental parts of the expression of our identity.

An important issue to note is that when Deaf people deal with hearing people in positions of authority there may be a reaction by hearing people to some of the component parts of sign language. There are facial expressions and gestures used in sign language that symbolise different things in spoken English. For example, 'a puffing out of both cheeks with air' like a trumpet player or 'the thrusting forward and exposing of the tongue through open lips' are both used as grammatically significant markers by Deaf people. These are part of sign language but hearing people can sometimes interpret these wrongly in the context of their own language and norms of cultural expression. Another example is when a hearing person in a position of authority, such as a police officer, encounters a Deaf person who has become distressed. The hearing person may see a very 'animated' use of signs with arms and hands seemingly 'thrashing' around. For the Deaf person it is merely the equivalent of a hearing person raising their voice to emphasise a point, but from a hearing person's perspective it could appear that the person was losing control or threatening violence.

When looking at ministry with Deaf people, it is important to acknowledge these differences in perception. There can be initial goodwill towards those who are different but defensive attitudes can easily develop if our dominant values are seen to be threatened. Those ministering among Deaf people need to be aware of existing social and ecclesial power structures, unacknowledged prejudices and differing uses of symbolic communication. To ignore these important forces is to court misunderstanding and undermine efforts to minister a gospel of grace.

Moltmann's theology combines openness to the outsider and the rejected, and a reaching out, that is not just a benevolent action but is the source of the very being of God. A model of church that is enabling for physically impaired people must adopt these inclusive attitudes, and will be aware of the power inherent in linguistic terms.

1. The Processing of Theological Ideas in Sign Language

We will now consider the process associated with understanding theological ideas and the non-linguistic components of language.

For Moltmann, the processing of theological ideas involves non-linguistic as well as linguistic material and it is particularly effective for a number of reasons. We will examine these in more detail later in the book. We can note now that they include an emphasis on intuitive and holistic understandings of what it means to 'know' and the importance of viewing communication as only being possible as we are in relationship with others. Moltmann also includes a concept of the need to overcome social barriers and attitudes that constrain. The Deaf community's corporate memory includes experiences of the past that form a strong part of its self-understanding and act as constraints. As Deaf people process Moltmann's theological ideas they will find that the power of these constraints exists in the view they have of them and they have the power to be liberated from them as they adopt a new perspective.

Some research has indicated that there is a language processing area in the left side of the brain that processes sign language. Steven Pinker has drawn on the research work of Ursula Bellugi and her colleagues.

> Deaf signers with damage to their left hemispheres suffer from forms of sign aphasia that are virtually identical to the aphasia of hearing victims with similar lesions ... [they are] unimpaired at non-linguistic tasks that place similar demands on the eyes and hands, such as gesturing, pantomiming, recognising faces and copying designs. The right hemisphere is known to specialise in visuospatial abilities, so one might have expected that sign-language, which depends on visuospatial abilities, would be computed in the right hemisphere [but] language, whether by ear and mouth or by eye and hand, is controlled by the left hemisphere. The left hemisphere must be handling the abstract rules and tree underlying language, the grammar and the dictionary and the anatomy of words, and not merely the sounds and the mouthings at the surface.[136]

The key thought here is to do with what Pinker describes as 'non-linguistic tasks'. We can say that an observer of sign language who does not understand it does not process it as language and therefore processes it in the right hemisphere. It is non-linguistic material. The non sign language user processes the signs not as language but as 'gesturing, pantomime' and other non-verbal items. It is similar to the experience of the non-French speaker hearing a stream of sounds, which are in fact normal French speech.

It would seem that we are pre-programmed to decode more efficiently the messages conveyed by hands and faces than those conveyed by spoken language.[137] In spoken language non-verbal signals exist

---

[136] Pinker, *Language,* 302.

[137] It is not within our scope to explore in depth the considerable research done by neuroscientists recently, but Michael Persinger has made a relevant comment. Quoted by Ian Cotton, who was exploring the simulating of religious experi-

alongside spoken words. These non-linguistic components have meaning in themselves and when we process them with words or signs that have a linguistic meaning they can reinforce this meaning.

For Moltmann, processing theological ideas includes a dynamic understanding of being. Attitudes that help our understanding will include those that allow for movement. Moltmann's idea of the way in which the eschaton 'draws' us towards it is an illustration of this. He also emphasises the need, in processing theological ideas, for an attitude of respect.[138] Respect will extend to all of creation. Moltmann maintains that the response required from us by God to creation should be one of enjoying it and being responsible for treating it well. Deaf people can help to dispel myths that hearing people may have about them, as mutual trust and respect develop during the communication process.

m. The Dialectic of Spirit and Word and its Impact on the Interpreting and Understanding of Truth

The issues connected with the processing of theological ideas by Deaf people have similarities with hermeneutical issues in biblical interpretation. The process of interpreting and understanding truth is not a straightforward one.

Clark Pinnock helpfully points us towards the need for understanding to occur within the community. He says:

> [t]here is a spiritual dimension in the recognition, interpretation, and application of the biblical text as the Word of God that does not easily fit into scholarly technique and comes more naturally to those 'uncorrupted' by it. For this reason, in my own approach I consider it essential to listen to the Spirit, not only in scholarly circles, but in the community of faith, which tends to keep a healthier balance in the dialectic of mind and spirit.[139]

---

ences through electrical stimulation by means of the insertion of electrodes, into the brain, Persinger said: 'we were using a strobe and ... generating ... temporal lobe spikes ... the subject who, after a sharp spike in the right temporal region, saw this gnarled hand thrust into her left visual field. Now we know from monkey studies, and indirectly from human studies, that there are neurons that actually code for complex shapes like hands'. I. Cotton, *The Hallelujah Revolution* (London: Warner Books, 1996) 212.

[138] 1 Pet. 2:17 'Because every human being bears the image of God', Donald W. Burdick and John H. Skilton in *The NIV Study Bible* (London: Hodder & Stoughton 1987) 1851 footnote.

[139] C.H. Pinnock, *The Scripture Principle* (London: Hodder & Stoughton, 1985) vi.

As we seek meaning in a communication we may be able to understand it clearly or we may not. If we develop a tentative approach that involves an attitude of humility we can acknowledge that perceptions of truth may at times be unclear. This does not mean that they are unknowable in a clear way but it allows us to acknowledge that lack of clarity initially exists in our perception of them. In Christian personal relationships attitudes of humility and respect, friendliness and a serving spirit can make use of such tentativeness. They can help us be more tentative and less judgmental as we acknowledge that our understanding may not be complete. We can also apply this principle to our relationships with non-personal entities such as doctrinal truths and the church.

The goal for Pinnock is a method of interpretation that takes as full account as possible of what the text meant to the original writers and a transfer of the equivalent of that into words for today's hearers. He is keen to retain the moderating influence of tradition, reason, experience and other sources in his proposals but wants to maintain a position where we do not rewrite doctrine to the extent that the result is a non-Christian product. Skill is called for. 'Good interpretation is a skill, like swimming and horseback riding'.[140] As a critical realist Pinnock acknowledges that the biblical text has a surplus of meaning through its use of symbol and metaphor. This enables it to be understood both in its original context in one way and then in a variety of ways to subsequent generations of interpreters provided that the central tenets of the faith remain as overarching judges of what may or may not be inferred from the text.

> When Jesus says, 'I am the door,' and when he claims that God's kingdom is like leaven he is making assertions that transcend the strictly literal and point us in the direction of profound understanding. There is a splendid versatility to such a mode of expression that sets up a range of possible meanings that can scarcely be exhausted. Although the general point is usually plain enough, other possibilities will always exist.[141]

Pointing to the 'primacy of narrative in Scripture' he says that

> ... revelatory knowledge is imparted in Scripture, not normally through propositional discourse, but through the symbolic patterns which are carried on by liturgy. Symbols ... contain a plenitude of

---

[140] Pinnock, *Scripture*, 220.
[141] Pinnock, *Scripture*, 189.

meaning that surpasses discursive speech and draws us into whole worlds of meaning.[142]

Following a similar line to Moltmann, who makes theological suggestions and invites dialogue, Pinnock says that 'Scripture may grasp us more by its suggestive power than by logic and in this way speak to the believer's situation here and now'.[143] He wants to pursue a method that will avoid evangelicals 'using philosophies which lack revelational status and poorly express the dynamic biblical portrait of God'.[144] He proposes a paradigm which appears to have similarities to Moltmann's scheme and which he calls 'the trinitarian openness of God'[145] which allows for the 'idea of God's not knowing the future exhaustively' and which can appeal to 'scriptural intimations that the future is open for God to some degree'.[146]

From both Moltmann and Pinnock we can learn to look beyond static closed models for understanding our process of perception. We derive meaning from dynamic interaction with the person communicating as well as internally processing the sounds, signs and symbols. Our worldview will have a hermeneutically filtering effect.[147] There will be a range of possible meanings to what we perceive and we establish these by a number of means. We use reason and apply rules derived from our worldview. An optimistic or pessimistic view of the world and the future will affect our attribution of meaning. We may censor our perceptions sub-consciously so that we avoid taking into account some 'unacceptable' information. Much of the meaning of a communication appears to be in the hands of the beholder. For Christians it is liberating to know that ultimate meaning is held by the community of believers interacting with God, each other and Scripture.

n. The Impact of Hope and the Changing of Interior Models of the World

Moltmann's ecclesiology is dependent on an eschatological ontological understanding of self and God. He has a view of church as community in which symbolic and iconic imagery can express the whole range of

---

[142] C.H. Pinnock, 'Evangelical Theologians Facing the Future: An Ancient and a Future Paradigm', Keynote Address for the 33rd Annual Meeting of the Wesleyan Theological Society Nov 7-8, 1997, 7.
[143] Pinnock, *Evangelical*, 8.
[144] Pinnock, *Evangelical*, 9.
[145] Pinnock, *Evangelical*, 13.
[146] Pinnock, *Evangelical*, 15.
[147] We should note that some Deaf people may have a different worldview to that of hearing people, but some may have a similar one.

experiences of God that the community consider important. Hope may exist at the conscious level, but also at a sub-conscious, or pre-conscious level, where it is a primary constituent within the belief system. Members of the church will exhibit, and are defined by, optimism and thankfulness deriving from this hope. His dialectical model of self incorporates interior models of the world of our past. These can include the biblical narratives of the events of the cross and resurrection as well as our memories of actual life experiences. These co-exist and interact with our understanding of the future in the shape of the hope of the eschaton.

Viewing the world is an intrinsic part of a person's life experience. Our interior model of the world changes as we process information, including language information. Our belief and value systems are included in that interior model. We receive information in linguistic and non-linguistic forms. There are symbolic and iconic elements in sign language and we have already noted that research indicates that we deal with the linguistic component in the left hemisphere of the brain and deal with the visuospatial part in the right hemisphere.

In order to help us to understand some of the processes involved when looking at our interior models of the world we will next consider the research of John Bowlby.[148] We are particularly interested in his work as it throws some light on the way in which internal models of reality may exist and function. This is significant for our understanding of how Deaf and hearing people process information they gain through experience.

Christian religious experience includes loss in the process of dying to self and the consequent redefining of the self. We feel positively about our emotional attachments and experience pain on separation. We also experience the pain of loss in all new encounters as we gain knowledge of anything that is 'other'.

> In my perception of others I subject myself to the pains and joys of my own alteration, not in order to adapt myself to the other, but in order to enter into it. ... Together with the other I enter into a process of reciprocal change. These pains of alteration and the joys of new insights are inherent in every learning process.[149]

Bowlby writes:

> It is ... redefinition of self and situation [that] is no mere release of affect but a cognitive act on which all else turns. It is a process of 'realization' (Parkes 1972), of reshaping internal representational

---

[148] Bowlby developed his theories of human attachment and loss whilst working in the sphere of clinical psychology on the results of bereavement.

[149] J. Moltmann, *God for a Secular Society* (London: SCM Press, 1999) 145.

models so as to align them with the changes that have occurred in a bereaved's life situation.[150]

Bowlby draws important conclusions about the way in which this takes place and in particular has observed and tested clinically the hermeneutical filtering and blocking function of the mind as it is faced with what it believes to be unacceptable sensory input. This could have relevance when looking at the dialectical process of development of knowledge and faith where we may assume that the mind will be able to cope with the task.

There are occasions when something we perceive is so at odds with the existing internal model of the world that denial is the response. A person who has just lost a leg in a train accident for example may refuse to accept the reality of it for a time. Messages from the severed nerve endings may in fact signal that it is still there and that it is causing pain. Similarly, a person newly diagnosed as being Deaf may deny the reality of the new situation. They may 'explain' the problem as being caused by others. They may say 'its because they mumble and do not speak clearly or loudly enough'. Such experiences are also common in the loss accompanying bereavement. A person receiving initial news of a death may go through a time when they do not accept the truth of what they have heard. Bowlby shows that a 'pathological' outcome to the bereavement process can occur. This is when we have not fully accepted the new situation as 'real' because we have not relocated the deceased person in our mind.

Moltmann emphasises the place of eschatological hope in our understanding of ourselves the world and God and it is important for us to consider the way in which that hope exists and functions. It exists at an ontological level in the life of the believer. This hope affects all information we store, process and receive into our interior model of our self. A belief system that emphasises the centrality of eschatological hope in a person's understanding of their being will produce optimistic attitudes. Hope involves openness towards the future and may therefore act in the interests of Deaf people as a powerful liberating tool. It may cause people to move towards a more accurate appreciation of themselves and others. It could provide an antidote to hearing people's mistaken attempts to try and make Deaf people more 'normal'.

We can use Bowlby's model to understand what is happening when our experience meets our internal world. Bowlby says '[a]fter some decades of controversy and steadily improving experimental tech-

---

[150] J. Bowlby, *Attachment and Loss, Volume III. Loss: Sadness and Depression* (Harmondsworth: Penguin, 1981) 94.

niques a multi-stage theory of perception is now widely accepted'. In developing a theory of what he calls 'perceptual defence' he proposes that:

> [t]he recognition of pattern as it occurs during perception proceeds in two directions simultaneously. On the one hand, the arrival of a sensory stimulus triggers an automatic series of analyses that start at the sense organs and continue centrally far up the chain of processing stages. On the other hand and simultaneously, the situation in which the sensory events are occurring triggers expectations based on past experience and general knowledge. These expectations produce conceptually driven processing in which guesses are made about what the input probably means. As the two forms of processing merge the guesses are checked against the data and the task completed.[151]

In Moltmann's scheme the category of *anticipation* that accompanies eschatological hope mediates in the process of evaluating what incoming perceptual data is to be counted as acceptable. The openness to the other that he encourages enables us to have a broader range of acceptance of possible future conditions of our self. We give less importance to the defence of our self because we can more easily accept the possibility of loss. We have less fear of pain as we encounter thoughts of potential loss. Our model of reality includes faith and trust in a coming God who will carry us safely through the process of adapting to the changes that may occur.

Additionally Bowlby considers the absorption of non-verbal sensory input and his clinical tests have shown that it is quite possible unconsciously to absorb values and beliefs that we encounter at a subliminal level.

> A second feature of a modern theory of perception is that sensory inflow can be processed outside a person's awareness to a stage sufficient for much of its meaning to be determined. Thereafter it can influence his subsequent behaviour, including his verbal responses, without his being aware of it.[152]

This has implications for theological understandings of reality and for our understanding of the way in which sign language communication works.

We can see connections with this information-processing model, which Bowlby has used to understand situations of loss, with the theories of inherited and internally held and communally transmitted

---

[151] Bowlby, *Loss,* 47.
[152] Bowlby, *Loss,* 47.

psychological archetypes of the type which Jung[153] proposed and Hillman[154] developed.

The way in which actors use a form of 'shorthand' to convey meaning can also help us to understand how our minds process non-linguistic forms and movements. One explanation of the effectiveness of this process is that the actors are able to communicate by connecting with internally held imagery that is common to all people. There could be implications from this for Deaf people in understanding the ways in which they process information. In addition there could be implications for the hearing church and preachers who may need to consider more carefully the effect of their non-linguistic communication.

It will help us now to briefly consider the internal model of the world in the experience of the person with a dysfunctional mental process. We will use as an example a psychotic person who appears to have no contact with our perception of the world. The point of the example is to illustrate how our mental processes involve imagery that is sometimes *ill-defined*, in this case because definitions of the mental images were not produced in the normal way during childhood. These images link us with reality, and are part of the internal processes that we use to understand the outside world. They provide the means by which we 'know' the difference between ourselves and the world. The 'primal psychic experiences' referred to could correspond to archetypal images, pregnant with meaning, used by us all in the conceptualising process.[155]

Maffei's example looks at how we may understand the experience of a psychotic person.[156] We are to establish contact with them, and acknowledge the nature of their experience and provide accompanying messages of feeling associated with that recognition. This will provide a framework for the patient to interpret what Maffei describes as 'primal psychic experiences'. These exist in the mental processes of the patient but they have no definition or meaning. They cause confusion in the psychotic person at the pre-conscious level and prevent the establishing of relationships with others on normal terms. He maintains

---

[153] See for example C. Jung, 'Approaching the Unconscious' in C. Jung (ed.), *Man and his Symbols* (London: Picador/Pan Books, 1978) 58.
[154] J. Hillman, *Archetypal Psychology. A Brief Account* (Dallas: Spring Publications, 1983).
[155] We are referring here to the concepts used in 'archetypal psychology'. For an introduction to the subject, see Hillman, *Archetypal*.
[156] G. Maffei, 'Archetypal Structures, Primal Repression and the Therapeutic Relationship with Psychotics' in R.K. Papadopoulos and G.S. Saayman (eds.), *Jung in Modern Perspective. The Master and his Legacy* (Bridport, Dorset: Prism Press, 1991) Chapter 7.

that our relationships in early life provide us with a way of interpreting these primal forces. We then attribute images appropriate to them that function in our sub-conscious or conscious mind. This process enables us to discriminate between our own feelings of omnipotence and the reality of our existence.

This suggests that we may know with a 'knowledge' that is not only based on linguistic formulations and concepts that can be defined in linguistic terms. As we experience life in community, our understanding of ourselves can be gained through the total experience we have of that community and in response to the relationships in which we exist. Our internal model of the world is formed by the totality of our experience, and may be represented by symbolic understandings, or symbols and imagery that have no immediate apparent meaning on their own. When viewed together with others that we hold they produce a working understanding of reality for us. Meaning for us may then be socially produced as will our understanding of our 'being'.

In Moltmann's theology he provides a social basis for understanding being but emphasises that we should view our relationships in the light of the eschaton. This future hope that is in Christ's coming will determine the shape of our understanding. For Moltmann our understanding of this future hope involves viewing '… reality in the context of promissory history'.[157] This is because *'[p]romise opens up history in the possibilities of God'* and by using a language of *promise*, which leads us to new possibilities, we avoid concepts which tend to freeze and objectify. Moltmann says, '[t]he historical present and the eschatological future can only be bridged in *the language of promise*, not in *the language of concepts'*.[158] We can also enhance our understanding by making use of his view that suggests we need to encounter and interpret reality from a God centred perspective.

Summary and Conclusion

In this chapter we surveyed the main issues affecting Deaf people and the church including language, culture, disability, power, politics and history and the resulting problems such as exclusion and oppression. We linked Moltmann's theological method with the visual-spatial and iconic nature of sign language which affects the way that Deaf people conceptualise. We saw that Moltmann's ecclesiology has advantages for Deaf people because his ideas can be adopted by them however they experience church, whether it be through integration with the hearing church, a separate ministry or a combination of both of these.

---

[157] Moltmann, *Experiences in Theology*, 103.
[158] Moltmann, *Experiences in Theology*, 102.

It can address some of the problems facing the Deaf church which include a poor self image and marginalization by the wider church. It encourages open attitudes and actions towards those who are considered different, encourages dialogue and includes rather than excludes. It challenges institutionally based prejudice and discrimination. It confronts paternalism and oppression that arise from the power that 'helping' gives to the care-giver. It encourages us to see people who are different or impaired as being fully human. It makes us aware of problems such as stigma and isolation that arise from Deaf people being defined as 'different' and reminds us of our duty to challenge the social, economic and political causes and effects of oppression.

We looked at how the linguistic structure of sign language is distinctive. We saw that Deaf people are often reliant on hearing people for their view of the world and that there was more information available to hearing people than Deaf people about the hearing world within hearing culture. Evidence suggested that Deaf people were more self-centred when forming and maintaining relationships. We noted that some steps towards Deaf self-determination were being taken in the Church of England and that it acknowledges the church would be incomplete without Deaf people.

We saw that knowledge can come from linguistic and non-linguistic sources. We also saw that we can use language to subtly maintain our power over others by conveying socially constructed judgements and that our use of language can subtly affect attitudes. From Braine we saw that intentions can be expressed in action and language and that propositions that are pictures, or images, of reality can incorporate force or attitude, although in Braine's scheme he externalises what we view in this work as internal matters. Like Moltmann, Braine has a holistic understanding of being.

We saw how sign language differed from spoken language in that it emphasised the storage and recall of events. It uses story telling as a distinctive feature and being visual-spatial it stores rich aspectual information and appeals to the visual imagery of the receiver in telling the stories. We drew connections with the scriptural method of using storytelling to communicate and can note the importance Moltmann places on this and how we can gain knowledge about the nature of God by the fulfilment of his promises recorded in the stories of Scripture. Research by Kyle and Woll showed that BSL processing involves sequential and spatial codes and direct visual representation for its syntax while displaying the same complexity of meaning as English. We saw that the visual-spatial aspects of sign language are stored and processed *separately* by the brain in the right hemisphere and linguistic aspects in the left.

Deaf People and the Church

We next looked at the way in which perceptions of language and power are dependent on the language we use, our identity, our relationships and the attitudes arising from the societal and organisational structures within which we live. Our values and beliefs and the views we have on authority and power mainly come to us from the perspective of the dominant ideology of the society in which we live. Deaf people gain their perspective from the dominant hearing ideology in society. We saw that different perceptions affect our views on matters involving the use and abuse of power such as class differences and poor people. We saw how language has the power to classify and so cause us to include or exclude certain people or groups in our thinking. Deaf people can suffer because culturally and linguistically distinctive ways can be misinterpreted by hearing people.

We saw that non-linguistic information could help form theological ideas and our understanding of them. We noted how attitudes were important in Moltmann's ecclesiology and how he allowed for a non-linguistic, intuitive and holistic understanding of the basis of knowledge and that these characteristics had within them liberating power which Deaf people could access. We saw that the issues connected with the processing of theological ideas by Deaf people have similarities with hermeneutical issues in biblical interpretation. We noted that the process of interpreting and understanding truth could benefit from the tentative approach suggested by Moltmann which would be distinguished by an attitude of humility, that allowed for the fact that there were other possible meanings besides the one we saw.

We noted how the biblical text has a surplus of meaning through its use of symbol and metaphor and that these images contain whole worlds of meaning. For Moltmann, processing theological ideas includes a dynamic understanding of being. He incorporates ideas of movement in his ecclesiology and we link this with the movement inherent in sign language.

We saw that both Moltmann and Deaf people attribute importance to the way in which we derive meaning from dynamic interaction with others. We saw that our worldview has a filtering effect on the range of possible meanings that we consider when faced with new information and that an 'open' and optimistic attitude, as Moltmann suggests, can come from eschatological hope and can help us be less self-defensive or fearful of change. We noted that Christians see meaning as deriving from the beliefs, values and interactions of the community and our world view derives from linguistic and non-linguistic sources.

Using research carried out by Bowlby we saw that our interior model of the world determined our response to the outside world and that information we viewed as not compatible with it could be filtered and not accepted. From Bowlby's work we also saw that we can absorb non-verbal information unconsciously, so that meaning may be gained by us through absorbing socially produced symbolic forms or representations. These may be communally transmitted archetypes that can provide us with meaning and knowledge without us being initially consciously aware that we have absorbed them. This idea is supported by the possibility that primal experiences may also exist in us and we may, or may not, understand them. We linked these findings with the way in which Moltmann works with a social understanding of being and a view of the future that shapes our understanding of the present. We saw that, for him we need to encounter and interpret reality from a God centred perspective.

To summarise then, in this chapter, we considered definitions of our subject matter and some current and historical views of what it means to be Deaf and to be 'the church'. We have also looked at how theological perception and conceptualising may occur in Deaf and hearing people. We have explored how we interpret both Scripture and reality through words and symbols. We have considered the possibility that we can have a limited personal understanding of reality and this does not detract from the possibility of clear and unambiguous truths existing beyond our perception. We have also considered the influence of sub-conscious perception and pre-conscious blocking of unwanted incoming data.

We have considered a view of ourselves consisting of an internal prevailing world model coupled with a worldview. This worldview will include an understanding of the doctrine of God and the way in which being exists in a dynamic dialectic of movement towards the future. This will result in attitudes and ontological understandings of self that transcend the static and evolutionary models that pervade present common understandings. The future can also be a constituent of self, the presence of which will determine perceptions of reality in the form of identity, communication and relationships.

Chapter 2

Moltmann's Ecclesiology, his Theological Method, Categories, Concepts and the Task of Perceiving Reality

Introduction

In his ecclesiology, Moltmann uses a dialectical and eschatological[1] Christology. He sees our understanding of the cross and the resurrection as the basis for all Christian belief and experience. The church is Christ's church, radical, missionary, ecumenical, political and non-hierarchical. He sees it as a fellowship of people who are in friendship type relationships. He has a social understanding of the Trinity. The Trinity is the model for, and basis of, all relations in creation. It incorporates willing suffering within the Godhead. He views all creation and salvation as occurring within God's history with the world. When we view the church as an institution it often detracts from the emphasis we should be placing on the kingdom of God in our lives. Status in the church is less important than personal relationships within which the gifts and fruits of the Spirit may be experienced.

a. Eschatological Hope: The Power of God in the World

Moltmann employs dynamic conceptualities. His theological concepts are always intended to be mediated through the category of hope.

> For our knowledge and comprehension of reality, and our reflections on it, that means at least this: that in the medium of hope our theological concepts become not judgments which nail reality down to what it is, but anticipations which show reality its prospects and its future possibilities. Theological concepts do not give a fixed form to reality, but they are explained by hope and anticipate future being ... they illuminate reality by displaying its future.[2]

---

[1] For a fascinating survey of current theological views concerning eschatology, see D. Fergusson and M. Sarot (eds.), *The Future as God's Gift. Explorations in Christian Eschatology* (Edinburgh: T & T Clark, 2000).

[2] J. Moltmann, *Theology of Hope. On the Ground and the Implications of a Christian Eschatology* (London: SCM Press, 1967) 35-36. Hope also motivates

Moltmann emphasises that God is the 'coming God'. He also stresses the importance of being wholly involved in the fullness of life, the interdependence of creature and creation, their incompleteness and the hope that salvation will redeem all. In Moltmann's theology, we can trace the intermixing of the dominance of Rationalist thought after the Enlightenment and the similarly strong influence of the reaction of the European Romantics.[3] Neill comments that 'German theology has perhaps never quite freed itself from the influence of this judgement of Lessing that "the contingent truths of history can never serve as the demonstration of eternal truths of reason"... He [Lessing] leaves no doubt as to his judgement that the eternal truths of reason are the important thing and that history necessarily belongs to a provisional and inferior order'.[4]

Albert Schweitzer's theology as a whole is vastly different to that of Moltmann, although Moltmann appears to have been influenced by his view that the key to theological understanding is eschatological. The holistic approach Schweitzer had in his 'reverence for life' principle that extended to embrace all life forms, including plants and insects, has echoes in Moltmann's all encompassing vision of salvation and the kingdom of God.[5]

Moltmann's origins and his theological predecessors influence his work. We find reactions by him to the importance of hierarchical authority and obedience to it as these are experienced in many German churches. There is also his reaction to the nation's post-war experience of trying to come to terms with the Nazi era and the holocaust, and the rise of anarchist movements in the 1960s.

---

by producing discontent. It has the power to change because it makes suffering more difficult to endure. T. Hart, 'Imagination for the kingdom of God' in Bauckham (ed.), *All in All*, 49-76, says that it works through imagination. He quotes Steiner who has shown that imagination works with our language, which uses future tenses of verbs to allow us to mentally construct possible futures.

[3] S. Neill has succinctly summarised the tremendous influence of the relatively small group of German Romantics – philosophers, historians, poets and theologians – on European thought in the 18th century starting perhaps with Immanuel Kant. (Neill rightly suggests he 'has perhaps a stronger claim than Descartes to be the founder and creator of modern philosophy') S. Neill, *The Interpretation of the New Testament, 1861-1961* (London: Oxford University Press, 1973) 2.

[4] Neill, *Interpretation*, 280.

[5] See J. Moltmann, *The Source of Life. The Holy Spirit and the Theology of Life* (London: SCM Press, 1997) 49, and J. Moltmann, *The Trinity and the Kingdom of God* (London: SCM Press, 1981).

Central to Moltmann's theology is eschatological hope. With 'Theology of Hope' Moltmann's purpose, noted by Bauckham, is that of 're-orientating theological work'.[6] Moltmann refers to the change he is hoping for which is '... a liberation of eschatological hope from the forms of thought and modes of conduct belonging to the traditional syntheses of the West'[7] and how 'Christian eschatology in the language of promise will then be an essential key to the unlocking of Christian truth'.[8]

Moltmann's work on ecclesiology seeks to challenge existing power structures within churches and the response to it by churches has therefore been less than might otherwise be expected. Bauckham helpfully comments that:

> *The Church in the Power of the Spirit* seems to have attracted less interest and has certainly provoked far less theological discussion than Moltmann's other major works ... it may be because, though rooted in theological argument, they are controversial in their practical thrust towards reforming the life and structure of the church.[9]

Moltmann sees the power of God in the world showing itself in the action of believers, acting in love by faith to bring liberation *to particular groups of people*. He says,

> Faith which is active in love is always 1. contextual, 2. determined by its *kairos*, and 3. related to its own community. That means that Christian theology which reflects critically about this praxis in the light of the gospel must be consciously contextual, determined by its *kairos*, and have its sights set on particular groups of people.[10]

His theology is praxis centred. It provides a prophetic voice to the church to accept the need for change. He believes that without change there is no life. The message of the gospel is one of turning to God and trusting in him and this means the church abandoning some of the ways of the past. In particular, the hierarchical structures of the church come in for strong criticism by Moltmann. His theology is controversial for it threatens the basis of human power structures that exist in churches and other organisations. Criticising Moltmann, Grenz and

---

[6] Bauckham, *Theology*, 29. Bauckham rightly comments that Moltmann's early theology the core of which is in *Theology of Hope* and *The Crucified God* both has 'a certain polemical extremeness' and a 'dialectical and prophetic style of theology'.

[7] Moltmann, *Theology of Hope*, 42.

[8] Moltmann, *Theology of Hope*, 41.

[9] Bauckham, *Theology*, 119.

[10] Moltmann, *Experiences in Theology*, 59, quoting W. Dilthey, *Gesammelte Schriften*, Vol.V, Stuttgart 1965, 332.

Olson conclude that his 'social and political antipathy to hierarchy distorted his otherwise creative and insightful approach to theology'.[11] Moltmann has also been criticised for implying the need for a form of pantheism. Grenz and Olson pointed to the pantheistic implications of Moltmann's *The Crucified God* but noted that he attempted to redress these implications as he 'developed his trinitarian panentheism farther' in his book *The Trinity and the Kingdom*.[12]

Moltmann's panentheistic and anti-hierarchical views of the church provide a *new perspective* that seeks to replace the perspective of those who dominate others through hierarchical structures.

b. Eschatological Hope and our Understanding of God and Time

The relationships of God within his trinitarian being are, in Moltmann's scheme, pictured as constitutive of his being. The cross denotes the suffering experience of God the Father who suffers because of the loss of his Son. God experiences separation within Himself as he takes death up into the Godhead making it a community action of sacrifice. We can view the cross as 'the principle constitutive event in the relationship between the Father, the Son, and the Holy Spirit'.[13] God's experience of the world, past and the future and including the cross are constitutive of his being.

Eschatological hope provides us with a messianic understanding of our experience of reality. 'The messianic interpretation of the experience of the moment that ends and gathers up time is the *redemption of the future* from the power of history'.[14] It also allows for a dynamic perception of the being of God that enables Moltmann to state categorically that

> *The God of Hope* is himself *the coming God* (Isa.35.4; 40.5). When God comes in his glory, he will fill the universe with his radiance, everyone will see him, and he will swallow up death forever. This future is God's mode of being in history. The power of the future is his power in time.[15]

As we reflect on how hope affects our perception of what it is 'to be', and 'to be in relationships', we are able to acknowledge the function of

---

[11] S.J. Grenz and R.E. Olson, *20th Century, Theology* (Carlisle: Paternoster Press, 1992) 182.
[12] Grenz and Olson, *20th Century*, 184.
[13] M.D. Meeks, 'Foreword' in J. Moltmann, *The Experiment Hope* (London: SCM Press, 1975) xvi.
[14] Moltmann, *The Coming of God*, 45.
[15] Moltmann, *The Coming of God*, 24.

the category of 'not yet' which Moltmann has developed from Bloch's 'Philosophy of Hope'. With Moltmann, we can ask ourselves: '[c]an there be such a thing as harmony and contemporaneity on man's part in the moment of today, unless hope reconciles him with what is non-contemporaneous and disharmonious?'[16] '... [H]ope is not something which one man has and the other does not have, but is a primal mode of existing or the most important constituent of human life'.[17] Moltmann acknowledges how he draws on Barth[18] when he uses his categories. He says, '[i]n all sectors of life there are conditions which are in contradiction to the kingdom of God and his righteousness, and conditions which are in harmony with it. The correspondences and harmonies in the conditions of history are our concern'.[19] He says that Barth views these correspondences as 'parables of the kingdom of God' but Moltmann calls them 'real promises of God's coming kingdom'. Openness is possible in human life through the divine promise. 'The *word* of the promise itself already creates something new'.[20] The category of promise is used by Moltmann to show how a person is led to expect fulfilment. The type of fulfilment to come is unknown and so it is best understood as being similar to a surprise. The scriptural record shows that of the many promises given many were fulfilled. Some promises were partially fulfilled and others seemingly not. Others were reinterpreted.

These interpretations of the nature of God and our relationship to him enable us to recognise our participation in his life through faith. For our being we rely on our relationship with God, the transforming power of eschatological hope and a messianic understanding of Jesus Christ. This nullifies the power of the past and the future, which we experience as guilt and fear respectively. God calls Christians to embrace that which they might fear. Moltmann says:

> [i]nstead of eliminating the categories of risk and danger, of the new and of historical transformation, as has most of modern theology, Christian hope is called to embrace them in its missionary search for the concrete possibilities of new obedience to God's rule.[21]

Within the community of faith, the time eternity-dialectic brings believers into an experience of the transcendent God. Moltmann develops Ernst Bloch's understanding of God who dynamically affects us, as we

---

[16] Moltmann, *Theology of Hope*, 31.
[17] Moltmann, *Experiment*, 20.
[18] Moltmann, *Secular Society*, 282.
[19] Moltmann, *Secular Society*, 254.
[20] Moltmann, *Experiment*, 49.
[21] Foreword by Meeks to Moltmann, *Experiment*, xii.

perceive him coming to us through the hope we have in his promised future. 'Experiences of this God are experiences of a remembered past and an expected future'.[22] These experiences of God draw us into a relationship with him. This relationship transforms our perceptions of this life. 'The eschatology of the coming God calls to life the history of new human becoming, which is a becoming without any passing away, a becoming into lasting being in the coming presence of God'.[23] God enters our present experience through our anticipation of what he will bring to pass according to his promises. This is a dialectical process similar to 'Hegel's dynamic dialectic of love which creates unity in division and division in unity, because it itself is the union of division and unity'.[24] In the Christian tradition all things exist in God. Moltmann's model maintains God's *creatio ex nihilo*. God has created a space within his being, and all creation exists in this.

The dimension of time in Moltmann's scheme is important. It helps us understand the forces determining development in a historical context. By a dialectical process of encountering 'the other', that which is not, we see experience proceeding on a linear time line. The possibility of 'the new thing' is a central concept and we are able to experience this through experiencing the power of the future eschaton. This is the finite future point at which all things will be reconciled to God and to one another. As we accept this as a certain future event and it becomes part of our belief system, it exerts on us a strong and dynamic pulling power. It introduces 'the other' into the present. Our being and acting are both affected dramatically.

In our belief system, strength is given to the future event of the eschaton by basing it on the past events of the cross and resurrection. We experience the forming and reforming of our self as we allow our awareness of future and past events to influence us. The past comes to us by written and oral means and our knowledge of it exerts forces on our current life. We know how to conform socially by acceptance of the norms of behaviour that our community communicates. We find ourselves partially controlled by our knowledge of the past and our current experience of community pressure. Our actions are dependent on our interpretation of these factors.

Eschatological hope is for us the power of God coming into the present. Future hope then becomes for us that which determines the outcome of all possible future developments. It is therefore constitutive of present existence and self, and all creation, can therefore be viewed as having an eschatological ontology.

---

[22] Moltmann, *The Coming of God*, 23.
[23] Moltmann, *The Coming of God*, 24.
[24] Moltmann, *Secular Society*, 145.

c. Eschatological Ontology, Language and the Conceptualising Process

In considering Moltmann's eschatological ontology we need to consider how he views both terms.

Ontology can be defined as 'department of metaphysics concerned with the essence of things or being in the abstract'.[25] Ontology, for Moltmann, is concerned with the processes surrounding things in addition to their essence or substance and concrete reality as well as abstract reality. As we shall see, Moltmann's theological method uses eschatological hope as a constant focus and the over-riding interpretative principle to which he makes all other theological categories subject. With this dynamic way of viewing reality, we have a process that is adaptable to different contexts.[26]

The classical understanding of eschatology, according to Moltmann is 'generally held to be the doctrine of "the Last Things", or of "the end of all things"'.[27] He says of this understanding, '[t]o think this is to think in good apocalyptic terms, but it is not understanding eschatology in the Christian sense.'[28]

Moltmann's understanding of eschatology is radically different from this. Rather than viewing eschatology as referring to the events of our world history *within* linear time or eternal events *outside* time, he says the 'eschaton means a change in the transcendental conditions of time. With the coming of God's glory, future time ends and eternal time begins. Without a transformation of time like this, eschatology cannot be thought'.[29]

In describing his own early understanding of eschatology at the time of writing *Theology of Hope* he says he 'had a revolutionary Christianity ... which would turn the wretched condition of the world into what was good, just and living by virtue of its hope'. His thinking about eschatology has developed from that time. He then viewed the cross and resurrection of Jesus Christ as a 'paradigm for the relation between old and new, history and eschatology, the result was a rigid *dialectic of*

---

[25] H.W. and F.G. Fowler (eds.), *The Concise Oxford Dictionary of Current English* (London: Oxford Univ Press, 5th edition, 1964).

[26] For a vigorous review of Moltmann's work which recognises the substantial contribution he has made to theology whilst seriously questioning many aspects of it, cf. D.B. Farrow, 'In the end is the beginning: a review of Jürgen Moltmann's systematic contributions,' *Modern Theology* 14 (1998) 425-447.

[27] Moltmann, *The Coming of God*, x.

[28] Moltmann, *The Coming of God*, x.

[29] Moltmann, *The Coming of God*, 26.

contrarieties.[30] Later he says he 'used less inflexible, more living forms of dialectic'.[31] In *The Coming of God* Moltmann considers eschatology from personal, historic, cosmic and divine perspectives. He uses 'broad and unifying characteristics'.[32] Moltmann's eschatology is '(1) christological, (2) integrative, (3) redemptive, (4) processive, (5) theocentric, (6) contextual, (7) politically and pastorally responsible'.[33]

The view of reality that proceeds from an eschatological ontology as Moltmann presents it affects how we understand the conceptualising process. This process differs in Deaf culture where *sign based concepts* take the place of *written and word based concepts* in hearing culture. Deaf people's sense of being comes less from an abstract conceptualising of their identity and more from their understanding of their relationships. Hearing people are less able to experience this relational understanding of identity as they are more likely to conceptualise their sense of being in an abstracted way. We agree with Sacks who prefers not to view language as being the sole determinant of the world that we construct in an abstract way but an important and indispensable influence. He views the propositions by which language decodes life as existing independently of the words themselves. Deaf people still need to convert experience and discourse into propositions in order to make sense of ideas and engage with others logically, and gaining this skill comes with language acquisition, a point made by Sacks. The pre-lingually Deaf, that is Deaf people who do not have hearing, or lose it, before language is acquired, do not have the ability to 'propositionize' until language is developed and Sacks compares their position with that of people with the condition of aphasia (loss of speech). 'The languageless deaf ...[suffer] and in a particularly cruel way, in that intelligence, though present and perhaps abundant, is locked up so long as the lack of language lasts'.[34]

In his later discussion of how Deaf people can progress from a perceptual to a conceptual world as language ability develops through sign language, either in childhood or later, he draws heavily on Vygotsky. The passage from perception, which is a more limited world in an intellectual sense, to conception, is reliant on a complex dialogue. This is 'a dialogue that first occurs with the parents, but is then internalised as "talking to oneself," as thought'. Citing Vygotsky, Sacks' argument

---

[30] J. Moltmann, 'Hope and Reality: Contradiction and Correspondence' in Bauckham (ed.), *All in All*, 81.
[31] Moltmann, 'Hope and Reality', 82.
[32] Bauckham, 'Eschatology in *The Coming of God*', 2.
[33] Bauckham, 'Eschatology in *The Coming of God*', 2.
[34] O. Sacks, *Seeing Voices* (London: Pan Books, 1990) 19.

proceeds to emphasise the importance of the development of 'inner speech'. 'Inner speech', says Vygotsky,

> is not the interior aspect of external speech, it is a function in itself . But while in external speech thought is embodied in words, in inner speech words die as they bring forth thought. Inner speech is to a large extent thinking in pure meanings.[35]

Sacks proceeds, '...our real identity lies in inner speech ... and the inner speech (or inner Sign) of the deaf may be very distinctive'.[36]

It is useful to consider how much propositions are involved when we have a revelation of God. Helm in his discussion of the arguments surrounding propositional special revelation makes the point that 'The personal directness of the propositional view of special revelation is saved if it is borne in mind that the propositions may be "response invoking", not just reporting facts but calling for a response'.[37]

Moltmann's eschatological ontological view of reality is 'response invoking' as it makes use of his concept of time and history. The eschaton, being pre-existent, influences the present. It forms our experience of the present through the attitudes and expectations we have. Its power comes from our assured hope that a certain future state will come to pass. This gives us the assurance in the present that we are on the way to that future state. Its adaptability means that both hearing and Deaf people can make use of it despite some differences that may exist in the way they conceptualise reality.

d. Dialectical Encounter, Immediacy and Conceptualising Reality

Moltmann's dialectical view of the identity of the crucified and resurrected Jesus, who is coming again, as the origin and centre of the church also provides us with a basis for our knowledge of all reality. This is not a subjective view mediated by experience. It is a dialectical encounter interpreted through a biblical understanding of promise and fulfilment as the practical basis for our concepts of reality. In our understanding of how revelation occurs, eschatology will take either a central or a peripheral place. Moltmann not only places eschatology centrally, but also makes it the lens through which we are to interpret everything else. He does this by redefining how we understand the process of history. Dialectically taking the future of Christ's return as a

---

[35] L.S. Vygotsky, *Thought and Language* (Cambridge, Massachusetts and New York: MIT Press and John Wiley & Sons, 1962) 149.
[36] Sacks, *Voices*, 72-73.
[37] P. Helm, *The Divine Revelation* (London: Marshall Morgan & Scott, 1982) 27.

promise that changes the present, he allows the future to be the determining factor in time.

For Moltmann, we interpret our experience of reality through dialectically encountering this Jesus Christ, whose identity we understand not just in terms of who he was and what he did but also in terms of his relationship to God the Father and what he will accomplish at the eschaton. This way of understanding reality has a sense of *immediacy* inherent in it, which we will now link with a distinctive characteristic of the way that Deaf people experience and understand reality. Deaf people's process of conceptualising reality involves an experience of a greater sense of *immediacy* in their encounters with others.

As we involve ourselves in the process of understanding reality and acquiring knowledge, we do this either analogically or dialectically. When we first encounter something new we can say it is analogous to something we have encountered previously. Alternatively we can proceed dialectically and note how it is unlike anything we have encountered earlier and develop an identity for it in this way. Deaf people use both methods but they can appear to be more polarised in this than hearing people. Deaf people propositionize using inner speech but perhaps because their inner speech is a visual process the clarity and definition of the concepts sometimes appear to be heightened.

Moltmann's theology has an integral response invoking style and has echoes of Kierkegaard's existential dialectic.[38] Commenting on Kierkegaard, McGrath says 'he stressed the importance of the personal experience of faith, and argued for commitment and obedience over against mere proposition as the condition of knowing God'.[39] The experience of reality and self for Deaf people involves a similar emphasis on involvement compared with the more propositional or abstract understandings that hearing people primarily use.

e. Narrative and Storytelling

We will now look at some characteristics of narrative and storytelling and the way in which these influence our conceptualising of reality. There would appear to be an important point of contact between Moltmann's approach, and the approach of Deaf people, to understanding reality. In his scheme, the narratives and stories of Scripture provide access to the reality of God. This comes through a process of engaging with the stories that tell us of God's promises and their ful-

---

[38] With which he opposed Hegel's dialectic, and which Moltmann developed through the dialectical theology of the early Barth.

[39] A. E. McGrath (ed.), *The Blackwell Encyclopedia of Modern Christian Thought* (Oxford: Blackwell Publishers, 1993) 301.

filment. In the process of this engagement, we necessarily adopt a *perspective* on that with which we are engaging. The storytelling process used by Deaf people in everyday life has a similar function and also involves the signer utilising and showing the perspectives and relationships that are believed to exist between the people or things in the story. It provides access in a narrative form to the reality of life and invites us to be involved in it. This similarity could be one element among many that makes Moltmann's theology peculiarly accessible to Deaf people.

For Moltmann, the narratives of Scripture always provide us with a perspective from which we are then led to view all reality, including the nature of our relationships to God and each other. Although this providing of a perspective can sometimes be viewed almost as a by-product of the storytelling process it is seen by Moltmann as a fundamental factor in the process of conceptualising reality.

Storytelling is intrinsic to Deaf culture. Deaf people use it to pass on information and to help them cope with life. In their stories, they include self-mocking elements and make fun of interactions with hearing people. Storytelling also influences how they conceptualise reality and create their worldview. In Deaf culture the storytelling mode, the dialectical nature of encounter and the greater experience of immediacy create differences in the backdrop against which reality is interpreted.

Within the narrative form the composer of the narrative is the authority not the person reading or signing it. The recipient of the message relates to that authority and not to the authority of the person communicating the message. In Scripture, the promises of God often carry with them moral warnings. We may receive these not as directives from a person with power dependent on a hierarchy, such as a priest or teacher, but as moral consequences that will inevitably follow certain actions. The authority exists in the Scripture itself. This can enable the recipient of the message to view the teacher in a non-hierarchical way.

Scriptural stories that tell of past liberation like the Exodus narrative hold the implicit or explicit promise of liberation from oppression in the future. These stories have often found a welcome amongst oppressed and marginalized peoples. In the storytelling mode of communication there is a natural and yet under-used resource.

This is the way in which storytelling provides a perspective. Deaf people convey this in sign language by their use of body language and facial expression and by using a physical signing space for the 'placing' of the characters in a story. We should also note that verbs in BSL provide information on the perspective in the story. Sutton-Spence and Woll have said:

> BSL verbs contain a considerable amount of morphological information, and very much more than English verbs do. The three types of information ... (aspect, manner and mood) are usually provided in English through the use of separate adverbs; in BSL the information is often incorporated into the verb itself.[40]

A term used by Lessing, which has links with the nature of communication that we are describing, is that of 'gestus'. This has been described as meaning '... something distinct from "gesture" and adopted in Brechtian parlance around 1930 to convey much the same as the old English "gest", meaning bearing, carriage, mien, i.e. a mixture of gesture and gist, attitude and point'. In Brecht's view, an expression was 'gestic' when it communicated 'not merely the meaning but also the speaker's attitude to his listeners and to what he is saying'.[41] In storytelling, both in Scripture and in Deaf people's use of narrative, the 'attitude towards' others, of the characters and the storyteller, form an important part of the story. This emphasis on the perspective of the storyteller and the characters in the story is used in a more prominent way in sign language, than in spoken and written English. McDonnough has noted that

> the styles of narrating that Deaf people use are different to hearing people, not simply because the signs are in the religious context, but because of the semantic and syntactic nature of our language. It is also because of our culture which is encoded in our idiomatic language and is externalised to a far greater degree.[42]

It is a factor that helps Deaf people access these aspects of the stories in Scripture. It is also something that could be of benefit to hearing people if they gave more prominence to the perspectives inherent in the narratives of Scripture.

f. Scripted Reality and Rituals

In this section, we will consider the way in which rituals, including the small rituals of our everyday lives and the rituals of the church, provide a ready-made way of understanding our relationship to others. Another way of describing these rituals is to call them 'scripted reality'. Moltmann sees scriptural stories not only as providing us with information concerning the promises of God and their fulfilment but also a framework and relational categories that we can use to interpret

---

[40] Sutton-Spence and Woll, *Linguistics*, 115.
[41] J. Willett, 'Gestus' in A. Bullock and O. Stallybrass (eds.), *The Fontana Dictionary of Modern Thought* (London: Collins, 1977) 265.
[42] McDonnough, 'Deaf and Made', 9.

and live our lives. In the same way that stories can provide us with an understanding of our place in the larger scheme of things rituals, which present reality to us in a 'scripted' way, can also help us. Rituals can be viewed as being written, spoken or acted narratives that have the potential to provide us with a 'script' which can help us live our lives. For Moltmann, a key category is that of *anticipation*, and we can note that the scripted reality of rituals can help us with the anticipation that is necessary for us to live our lives effectively.

Rather than life consisting of a process of original actions, each decided upon by us just prior to their occurrence, life often consists of us taking actions that are simply *learned responses* to situations. These rituals may be specific to the context of particular cultures. More importantly, they provide us with a perspective with which to view things. We have noted already the importance of *perspectives* both for Deaf people and Moltmann. Perspectives are important because they reveal to us the place we are to adopt as we conceptualise our relationship to God and all reality.

In church life, we can view the church liturgy as the vessel that holds within it 'the script' that appears to determine reality. The church liturgy contains words, actions and other information that is believed to be necessary in a particular tradition. In different traditions there may be an emphasis on differing elements such as incense, robes, statues, banners, different styles of music, layout of the building and seating.[43] Some traditions will see the eternal truths contained in the liturgy itself, and preserved as it is passed from generation to generation. The various 'actors' in the liturgy are the priests and the general congregation. Priests will normally maintain the status quo and among the congregation, the acceptance of the 'script' of the liturgy will challenge any 'acts of deviance' by the actors and the 'gestus' that exists within the setting. For a person to participate in a church they will normally need to anticipate what is expected of them and they will gain this as they experience the significance and function of the key elements in the liturgical 'script'.

In early life, parents, teachers and peers teach us how to react in specific situations in our social interactions. We later internalise these reactions and reality for us exists within these internalised scripts that

---

[43] Churches that do not follow written liturgies, emphasising informality of worship and forms of service, almost inevitably develop repeated elements that by consensus, or by the decision of the leaders, the group consider necessary for the functioning of the church.

form the basis of the roles we adopt in our daily rituals.[44] They provide an understanding of the relationship between people and things that save us the intense process of continually trying to establish these on a moment-by-moment basis.

Rituals are culturally specific. Within Deaf culture the rituals and expectations of the roles people should adopt may be different to those with which hearing people are familiar. Our understanding of role expectations in different situations contributes to how we act. For example, teachers may act as if they are actors going 'on-stage' when they leave the staff room.

Some ritual may be discouraged by the dominant culture if it is viewed as subversive. With an oppressed group such as Deaf people, there will be attempts by the dominant culture to prevent certain rituals because they could be seen as subversive. The oppressed group may actually reinforce the oppression by conforming to the wishes of the dominant group because the sanctions against non-conformity are too severe to bear.

Sometimes Deaf people cover up their deafness when mixing with hearing people.[45] When they do not understand they give the impression that they have understood. They may 'nod and smile'.[46] We can view this sort of action as a denial of the effects of deafness and a repression of appropriate reactions or as an attempt to keep 'the flow' of conversation going. On the other hand it may be a highly stylised ritual which itself forms part of the coping repertoire of Deaf people.

An example of difference in ritual exchanges is the way that people greet each other. Deaf people meeting other Deaf people in a church setting would ensure that they greet everyone in the group in a way that would seem excessive to hearing people. Similarly, on leaving a group of Deaf people, they would give attention to ensure that no-one

---

[44] We are following the approach of Goffmann to ritual here, see particularly E. Goffmann, *The Presentation of the Self in Everyday Life* (Harmondsworth: Penguin, 1969).

[45] See E. Goffmann, *Stigma* (Harmondsworth: Penguin, 1968) 95, on 'passing', and the section on this subject in S. Gregory and J. Bishop 'The Mainstreaming of Primary Age Deaf Children' in Gregory and Hartley (eds.), *Constructing*, 170. Alternatively, some Deaf people may choose to emphasise their deafness, perhaps to show the need for hearing people to make more effort in communicating with Deaf people.

[46] This practice is not unique to Deaf people. Many hearing people might acknowledge that they at some time gave the impression of having understood, when in fact that was not the case. They hoped that they would understand later.

was left out. For English hearing people this practice is unusual but in other countries, for example, France it may be normal polite practice.

Rituals in a church setting sometimes involve considerable attention to detail. Words and actions can be used in achieving what otherwise would take much time and effort because of the symbolism inherent in them. The effect of symbolism in a simple ritual can be satisfying to both parties and very effective. We can take as an example a church leader's position at the door after a church service. Very simple but highly symbolic words and actions are used. The leader smiles, shakes hands and warmly and says, 'How lovely to see you. How are you? Thank you for coming'. The physical touch, the expressed concern for the other, the affirmation of their existence by these things, the representational nature of the action on behalf of the local church, can be summarised, abbreviated and carried out efficiently in these simple actions and the few well chosen and effective words.

We have seen how we use rituals in our conceptualising process and that to live authentically we do not always have to interact with people and our surroundings in a vigorous and over-conscious way because our conceptualising of reality can occur in the context of our involvement in rituals. We have seen that there is also a large element of non-verbal creation of reality within most settings where 'scripted reality' or rituals are used. Deaf people may value situations where rituals are used, particularly when interacting with hearing people because rituals can give a greater sense of assurance concerning the perspective Deaf people should have, and the place they should adopt, in relation to that which is occurring.

g. Conceptualising Reality Using our Worldview and Model of the World

In this section, we will look at how Moltmann's theology affects our worldview and model of the world. Whilst looking at the process of conceptualising reality we need to remember that a mental image of God is not God. As Johnson has said, 'For God is not our mental construct, but the One who is "Wholly Other" than we. To speak of God in concepts appropriate to a mere construct of Reason is to make God into an idol'.[47]

Moltmann's use of Aristotelian categories that emphasise the concrete reality of all sense perceptions also draws on Hegel's similar emphasis on concreteness and the fullness of all created and perceived reality. This contrasts with Plato's understanding of the eternal truths

---

[47] R. A. Johnson, *Rudolf Bultmann. Interpreting Faith for the Modern Era* (London: Collins, 1987) 25.

of reality existing over and beyond us yet represented within the forms of our mental concepts. Moltmann seems to pick up and develop Hegel's view of the dynamic motion of conceptualising reality. Friedrich describes this as being for Hegel,

> ... not the process by which a general or abstract concept or thought is manifested in a particular thing or event (*Dingheit*) but the process by which thought takes hold of any real something, no matter how spiritual or general. It is motion, a continuous weaving back and forth.[48]

Moltmann also stresses Hegel's emphasis on the dialectical encounter of the other as being fundamental to establishing identity of reality and self. He then follows with Hegel the process of concretization and avoidance of the abstract. Through this he reinforces his similar avoidance of the dangers of objectifying from which Bultmann also sought stridently to distance himself.[49]

Moltmann speaks of '... the concept of God and the understanding of the Word in which God proclaims his presence'.[50] He describes an opening up of 'history and existence within a new horizon, [that] becomes even clearer in the fact that revelation is always concerned with calling, commission and sending into historical service in the promised future'. He says 'Revelation in promise and sending does not, then, effect a new self-understanding and a new world-view, but rather an openness to that future of God which is conditioned by hope'.[51] Of our experience of the presence of God, Moltmann says 'God is not yet present in such a way that everything is silenced in us. He is, however, present in Word and Spirit in such a way that everything in us and with us questions, searches, hopes and also begins to suffer from the misery in the world'.[52]

The key element in Moltmann's scheme of the understanding of the revelation of God is the possibility of the new thing that the future can bring. We face two psychological aspects as we encounter this new thing. These are our 'model of the world' and our 'worldview'. We use our worldview to understand our model of the world and thus understand reality. We can liken the mechanism by which we manage reality to the governing body for a sport that has the power to change the rules of the game. They do this 'behind the scenes'. The game has historical

---

[48] Friedrich notes that this is the central theme of Marcuse's work. C.J. Friedrich (ed.), *The Philosophy of Hegel* (New York: Random House 1954) xix.
[49] Johnson, *Bultmann*, 25.
[50] Moltmann, *Hope and Planning* (London: SCM Press, 1971) viii.
[51] Moltmann, *Hope and Planning*, 18.
[52] Moltmann, *Hope and Planning*, 26.

roots and the governing body is constrained from making changes that would alter the 'ontological status' of the game. Its status means that it must contain certain elements. When we make major changes these may change the very nature of the game. This at least is our perception of the paradigm shift that has occurred. When this happens, as we cannot change reality itself, we have to change our internal memory of it because this tells us about its ontological status. The power behind the scenes can decide. The mechanism exists either for the current model to continue to or for it to be changed.

We can only speak of these processes by analogy but the models of a worldview and the model of the world that we have described, adequately enable us to envisage the processes that we go through when we conceptualise reality.

h. The Social, Suffering Trinity and Non-Hierarchical Relationships

In Deaf culture, there is evidence that Deaf people view their identity as existing in the interdependent relationships they have with one another rather than on their own deliberations and reflections of who they are.[53]

It will help us at this stage to consider some of the characteristics of Moltmann's doctrine of God. His different perspective of God and consequently of creation challenges some established views. Because of their own distinctive characteristics, Deaf people may be more able to view God from Moltmann's perspective.

God is involved at an experiential level with the temporal history of the world.[54] God experiences the pain of separation between Father and Son as he takes up the suffering of the crucifixion into himself. Moltmann's panentheistic understanding of God and his pneumatology provide a view of God and the world as being one of mutual involvement.

The social doctrine of the Trinity is important for Moltmann as a way of determining the nature of our own personhood. He says, '[t]he Christian doctrine of the Trinity provides the intellectual means

---

[53] See the next section for a fuller look at this.

[54] Bauckham has helpfully noted how '... the potential for speaking of the experience of the presence of God in both the contradictions of life in hope and the anticipations of the kingdom in the present is implicit in Moltmann's early theology. What made it increasingly explicit, however, was Moltmann's developing understanding of God's involvement in the history of the world, in *The Crucified God* and *The Church in the Power of the Spirit*'. Bauckham, *Theology*, 218.

whereby to harmonize personality and sociality in the community of men and women, without sacrificing the one to the other'.[55] Moltmann emphasises that we should not view the unity of the Trinity by considering God as a single subject. He says '[t]he reduction of the Trinity to a single identical subject (even if the subject is a threefold one) does not do justice to the trinitarian history of God. The reduction of the three persons to three modes of subsistence of the one God cannot illuminate salvation history in the fullness of God's open trinitarian relationships of fellowship'.[56]

Bauckham notes that for Moltmann '[t]he trinitarian perichoresis, in which the divine Persons are themselves in their distinction from and (equally) at-oneness with each other, provides a pattern of personhood as that of individuals in relationship'. Later he notes that for Moltmann ' ... the perichoretic unity of the three divine Persons is a non-hierarchical fellowship of open love'.[57] This is also a model for our own relationships.

> So, in place of the concept of God as divine monarch providing the prototype for human domination, at the expense of freedom, the social Trinity provides a model for human community in which people are free for each other and find freedom in relationship with each other.[58]

These suffering, relational trinitarian understandings of the being of God and the being of man underpin Moltmann's ecclesiology. Bauckham rightly notes concerning Moltmann's "messianic ecclesiology" or "relational ecclesiology" that '[b]oth terms serve to situate the church within God's trinitarian history with the world, more specifically within the missions of the Son and the Spirit on their way to the eschatological kingdom'.[59] The dynamic, constitutive relationships, which Father, Son and Holy Spirit experience, are mediated to the world in the present time through the action of the Holy Spirit who brings the reality of the eschatological future. The world as we know it exists between the historical past including, most significantly, Christ's crucifixion and resurrection and the anticipated future kingdom.

This is how the church currently manifests itself as an anticipation of that future kingdom. Its members embody this in their relationships between themselves and with the trinitarian God, who has given them their very being by entering into relationship with them.

---

[55] Moltmann, *Trinity*, 199.
[56] Moltmann, *Trinity*, 157.
[57] Bauckham, *Theology*, 176.
[58] Bauckham, *Theology*, 176-177.
[59] Bauckham, *Theology*, 13.

Moltmann's ideal view of the church is where people relate to one another as a fellowship of friends in free open friendship with each other. He provides a theological critique of the church[60] and argues for a theological understanding of the church that is trinitarian based. He views his form of the congregational model as being ideal. He acknowledges that '[o]f course most churches will in actual fact have mixed forms, with episcopal and synodal elements'.[61]

Concerning the ideal nature of the church, as seen by Moltmann, Bauckham notes that:

> The ideal is a church *of* the people, a fellowship of committed disciples called to responsible participation in messianic mission. Membership of the church must therefore be voluntary (from this follows Moltmann's critique of infant baptism) and characterised not only by faith but by discipleship and a distinctive lifestyle.[62]

We should note that not everyone has viewed Moltmann's radical approach sympathetically. Otto, concluded his 1991 study with the ungenerous observation that 'Moltmann has through his sinful reason and idolatrous imagination formulated a theology that appeals to the rebellious desires of man to be as God, to create a world of his own, a world better than God himself did create'.[63] Bauckham describes the argument of Otto's book, correctly in our view, as an 'extraordinary argument ... that "Moltmann's God is the idea of human community" ([Otto] p.11)' and concludes that 'The book is a remarkable example of understanding grossly distorted by polemical determination'.[64]

We believe that the 'ideal' nature of the church that Moltmann presents can be rightly criticised. It seems to imply that what is expected of the members of this ideal church in the words 'discipleship and a distinctive lifestyle' is a rather more demanding expectation on believers than other parts of Moltmann's theology would seem to require. It is possible to read into this expectation a responsibility that may be beyond the ability of some people, who because of personal circumstances, illness, disability or other reasons are unable to commit themselves to the level of participation Moltmann seems to require. We have suggested previously that one solution to this problem that we

---

[60] 'Moltmann is engaged in a trinitarian critique of ecclesial structures as well as political systems' W.W. Willis, Jr., *Theism, Atheism and the Doctrine of the Trinity. The Trinitarian Theologies of Karl Barth and Jürgen Moltmann in Response to Protest Atheism* (Atlanta: Scholars Press, 1987) 191.
[61] Moltmann, *Trinity*, 202.
[62] Bauckham, *Theology*, 14.
[63] R.E. Otto, *The God of Hope: The Trinitarian Vision of Jürgen Moltmann* (Lanham/London: University Press of America, 1991) 232.
[64] Bauckham, *Theology*, 24.

see in Moltmann's ecclesiology is to 'use a sacramental interpretation of aspects of the church as community, which would make the 'open' church he seeks after, more of a reality'.[65]

Conyers' approach represents a more measured and sympathetic critique of Moltmann's theology. He challenges his outright rejection of hierarchy and calls instead for a need to see '*[h]umility as the resolution of hierarchy*'.[66] Conyers' main critique is of Moltmann's total rejection of hierarchy and its relationship to 'monarchical monotheism'. Conyers says: '[f]ew will deny that hierarchies can, will, and even must be changed. The apparent must be judged by the real, the temporal by the eternal. But it is entirely another question whether we can do so without a *sense* of hierarchy'.[67] When Conyers speaks of a *sense* of hierarchy he refers to a social articulating of values. He views this as a 'natural' process and as common practice in many societies that use hierarchies to demonstrate what is most valued and revered in them. He says (agreeing with Weaver) that 'every advanced society articulates its values in terms of its social and political hierarchy'[68] and that this ' ... irreducible fact is simply the natural tendency to give incarnate expression to, and to communicate within society, what is most to be desired and most to be esteemed'.[69]

In society we often seem to need to express the values that are important to us. We commonly do this by giving *roles* and a corresponding *status* to people in the organisations within society. Conyers views the church as an organisation that exercises power that can be restrained by the virtue of humility.

Moltmann's view is that the concept of hierarchy cannot be appropriate in the church for its actions are only those of love. Moltmann says of the church '... as the community of the cross it consists of the fellowship of the kingdom – and not of church members; and as the community of the exodus – and not as a religious institution'.[70]

Conyers is right when he says that hierarchical institutions that exercise power can contain elements which protect the vulnerable and restrain the powerful. He says, '[h]eirarchy, therefore, like ethics and religion in general, involves a dialectic that certainly refers to force and domination but also to freedom, and love, which entail choice'.[71]

---

[65] Hitching, *Moltmann's Radical Church*, 79.
[66] A.J. Conyers, *God, Hope and History* (Macon, Georgia: Mercer University Press, 1988) 199.
[67] Conyers, *God*, 16.
[68] Conyers, *God*, 14.
[69] Conyers, *God*, 14.
[70] Moltmann, *Church in the Power of the Spirit*, 75.
[71] Conyers, *God*, 198.

He argues for a joining of piety and hierarchy that follows from a strongly messianic theology and sees that we will then have access to the power to restrain that which threatens.

> From the standpoint of a world open to God in humility, hierarchy can mean precisely the opposite of the presumptuous and calculating use of power—in fact it is the restraint of power and becomes so by resisting the temptation of power.[72]

We need to concentrate on Conyers' main difference with Moltmann which is that, for Conyers, it is appropriate for the structure of 'the church' to mirror the structure of organisations in society. The exercise of power by the church is then seen primarily as a demonstration of the value considered most important by the organisation. Conyers seems to view this as being possible even within a federalist approach to theology. It could be seen as a model of the church founded on the gifts of its members. The value of these gifts is recognised by giving status to individuals. This results in a collection of varied and interrelating hierarchies, which may be temporary in their existence. For example, church members may defer to a person, viewed by the church community as having a gift of teaching, when he is teaching. He in turn may defer to others in a different context where they have a status that requires such deference. This may occur within covenant relationships and we can see how Conyers can hope that our freedom may be protected in such a model of the church by the exercise of power in the way he suggests. We agree that we must acknowledge our humility before others, as Conyers argues, if we are faithfully to respond to Scriptures such as Phil. 2:3 and 2:7 and 1 Peter 5:6.

We agree, however, with Moltmann's view of hierarchy that it is the form of organisational structure most prone to produce situations of oppression and subjection, because of the temptations accompanying the concentration of power.

Moltmann reveals that he sees three ways in which power may be dealt with theologically, the justifying and sanctifying of power resulting in *hierarchy*, the opposite being *anarchy,* and the third way which is the *federalist* way. This latter emphasises covenant relationships. He says

> [f]ederalist theology presupposed that, according to the Bible, the relationship between God and humans is not one of domination and submission, but rather one of covenant. The covenant is given by God and it entails mutual loyalty and commitment.[73]

---

[72] Conyers, *God,* 199.
[73] Moltmann writing in the foreword to Conyers, *God,* viii.

We also agree with Moltmann when he says,

> [t]he hierarchy which preserves and enforces unity is replaced by the brotherhood and sisterhood of the community of Christ. The presbyterial and synodal church order and the leadership based on brotherly advice are the forms of organisation that best correspond to the doctrine of the social Trinity.[74]

For Moltmann, God's 'kingly' rule is an eschatological reality and is to impact on us only in a dialectical way. We will then reject temptations to exercise power over others but instead serve them in love. Even then we are to avoid the temptation to subtly dominate them through creating a dependence on our service to them.

Many churches use hierarchical structures well and for the good of others but we must question whether this acceptance of the need for domination in some circumstances really fits in with Christ's ideal for us. Moltmann would see us embracing that which is 'other' rather than seeking to dominate it even when we may have good reasons for doing so.

The individualism in modern Western society has often resulted in a tendency towards the individualisation of perceptions of experience. Moltmann's doctrines of God and man are a constructive and creative challenge to this. Relationships that we form will involve acknowledging differences and states. At a functional level, within the wider society, we are used to operating with hierarchies in specific contexts, deferring to others who can perform the functions that we need. If we are to follow Moltmann and be open to others and their ideas (as he is to Conyers concerning this matter)[75] then we must be open to the *possibility* that hierarchical structures in the church might sometimes be used positively.

i. Deaf People's Understanding of Self and their Interdependence

There are links between Moltmann's ecclesiology and his views on the type of relationship that can exist within the church and the existing types of relationships amongst members of the Deaf community. The most significant of these is the 'closeness and acknowledged interdependence' already typifying existing relationships between members of the Deaf community. Most Deaf people are scattered geographically among the general population and when they do choose to meet together, in some parts of the UK, this may be only once or twice a week. 'This produces a community pattern which is rather fragmented

---

[74] Moltmann, *Trinity*, 202.
[75] Conyers, *God*, ix.

in the time spent together but extremely closely bonded in the friendship of the members'.[76] For Moltmann, ideal relationships within the church are similar. He refers to them as 'friendship type relationships' and interdependence is central to these.

Another link that makes Moltmann's ecclesiology particularly appropriate to Deaf people is the emphasis he places on freedom of 'choice'. Throughout his ecclesiology he is concerned to avoid the creation of relationships in which one person can dominate another. The right of the individual to choose is coupled with a responsibility to other people in the community. Deaf people will be attracted to this aspect of Moltmann's thinking because many of them have suffered in the past from a lack of freedom of choice.

The way in which Deaf people view their relationships with other Deaf people is different from the way in which hearing people view relationships and we will consider this in more detail later. We should note that one characteristic of Deaf people is that within their relationships they often need more information sharing. This is because they can find themselves separated from some media sources of information such as sound on radio and television. They are also cut off from the informal 'overheard in the background' sources of information to which hearing people have access, and often take for granted. Consequently, Deaf people have a greater need for social interaction with people who use their language because isolation is often a part of their normal experience. We should note, however, that there are Deaf people actively involved in the hearing world, some working alongside hearing people, who consider that their access to information is, in many respects, satisfactory.

New technology such as mobile telephone text messaging now enables Deaf people to access and share information more easily and they now often meet in 'hearing' environments such as public houses rather than Deaf clubs.

When Deaf people are relating to hearing people where spoken language is used, they are also deprived of the process of 'rehearsing' words, by which we mean the hearing of them repeatedly in diverse contexts. In hearing people, this helps them develop their lexicon, which is the store of usable words in their memory for use in spoken or written language. When Deaf people are relating to others through sign language, however, the 'rehearsing' of words in sign is enriched by the unique conceptual imagery, identified as existing in sign language. Later in the work we will be linking this with the way in which theological conceptualization occurs, and especially with Moltmann's

---

[76] Kyle and Woll, *Sign Language*, 10.

'open' categories that use our imaginative capacities and which form so much a part of his theological approach.

j. Moltmann's Cosmological and Ecological Understanding of Redemption and its Benefit for Deaf People

The particular significance for Deaf people of Moltmann's cosmological and ecological understanding of redemption is that it can provide a liberating perspective. Deaf people may have an understanding of who they are and how they relate to the world that is restrictive and oppressing. Through the dominant ideology in society they may often have a sense of identity arising from an assumption that people 'become' Deaf at a certain point in time and that there is only one way of being Deaf. Moltmann emphasises the fact that we are all involved in a *process* in life and that we should view our identity against the all-encompassing backdrop of a God who will redeem all things. This is important as it extends our understanding of what it is to be, and to be in relationship with others and with God.

In Moltmann's cosmological and ecological approach to redemption, the atoning and reconciling work of Christ extends beyond the salvation of individuals to all of creation. He notes the relationship between human beings and nature.

> Just as soul and body interpenetrate one another, so human beings and nature find one another in mutual perichoresis. Civilization can be brought into a relationship which promotes the life of both by way of a *covenant*.... Human beings cannot redeem nature, and nature cannot redeem human beings. The divine redemption must reach them both.[77]

His purpose would seem to be to allow for the provision of a 'horizon of expectation' that belongs to the hope of the resurrection.[78] This develops a relationship in which nature is not subjected to the domination of human beings. 'Instead a brotherly and sisterly relationship to fellow-creatures will spring up.... All creatures on this earth find their way to one another in the community of a common way, a common suffering and a common hope'.[79]

After developing his cosmic Christology, he speaks of the completion of creation.

---

[77] J. Moltmann, *The Way of Jesus Christ. Christology in Messianic Dimensions* (London: SCM Press, 1990) 272.
[78] Moltmann, *Way,* 272.
[79] Moltmann, *Way,* 273.

> [I]t is only the reconciliation of all things, whether on earth or in heaven (Col. 1.20), and their redemption from the fetters of the transience of the times which leads to the gathering together of all things in the messiah, and therefore to the completion of creation.[80]

This strongly perichoretic understanding of Christ's being, which is linked with all of creation, forms a model for relationships now and provides a hope for the future reconciliation of all things. This is also a constituent in the current process of our relationship forming activity.

We can see how we can connect some of Moltmann's thoughts here on how we are to view ourselves by looking at an article by David Moorhead. In his recent research into the aspects of social work service provision to Deaf people, he draws attention to the place of *autobiography* in understanding the concept of the self and the importance of the category of *process*.

Moorhead draws on the work of sociologist Giddens who suggests that autobiography provides the anchors, framework and certainties that individuals need to place themselves in the world.

> In some ways, it may, in a modern world, replace the anchors and certainties that Giddens suggests were relatively fixed in pre-modern societies in Europe – lineage, gender roles, social status.... [these] may still be strongly institutionalised in the structure of our lives. For deaf people, these fixed relationships can be more imbedded in their lives than in those of others, through the meanings of their experience which are imposed on them by others, or by the mediating relationship which governs their contact and connection with others.[81]

Moorhead suggests '... that we use a combination of individual and institutionalised anchors to create our sense of who we are' but that 'a single defining experience, especially if it is defined or imposed on us by others', may prevent us using our institutionalised anchors 'because they do not fit in with the defined experience'.[82]

His research identifies processes in which Deaf and deafened people report themselves to be involved.

> There are different ways of being deaf and becoming deaf ... It is clear that these are both processes which are continuous, processes

---

[80] Moltmann, *Way*, 304.
[81] D. Moorhead, 'Meanings of Deafness' in *Deaf Worlds* 13 Number 1 (March 1997) 4.
[82] Moorhead, 'Meanings', 5.

through which Deaf and deafened people understand and develop their sense of identity and their relationship with others.[83]

He sees the mediating relationship as 'central to the understanding of deaf people'. He says that sign language users '... seem to have larger areas of their experience mediated to them through third parties, both as a result of their deafness and their use of a different language, than might be the case for other groups of deaf people. This means their opportunities for direct experience ... are limited'.[84]

In family relationships where a Deaf person has a relative who acts as an interpreter and mediator for them, he makes the point that there is a third party in the relationship. This is the 'the expectations and demands of the dominant political and social ideology'[85] and it is this that defines the meaning of disability and other differences within relationships.

Aspects of disability and other factors normally define for Deaf people, identity and the nature of relationships. Moltmann's approach, sees our personal autobiography as existing within the overarching and all encompassing autobiography of God's dealings with his creation as revealed in Scripture. This includes the redemption of all things, which God has promised in the eschaton, and can provides an accessible, safe and valuable way for Deaf people to understand who they are and how they actually relate to others.

k. The Use of Biblical Categories in Viewing Reality

In exploring the ways in which the Christian truth claims may be presented, it is useful to attempt to correlate some of the approaches of Colin Gunton with Moltmann's invitation to engage in being open to the future through an eschatological ontological understanding of reality. Gunton has re-emphasised the place of the Trinity in doctrinal formulations. He also emphasises the pre-eminence of biblical thought forms and categories.

We establish the *a priori* categorisation and the nature of relationships in philosophical and theological constructions as we use thought forms and language, whether these are biblical or otherwise. In order to overcome the inadequate, restricting, and oppressing results of modern and Postmodern constructions and deconstructions both Moltmann and Gunton are advocating the adoption of biblical forms.

---

[83] Moorhead, 'Meanings', 6.
[84] Moorhead, 'Meanings', 7.
[85] Moorhead, 'Meanings', 8.

Gunton's arguments put the category of relationality based on a trinitarian theology back in a central place in theology. Thompson draws attention to Gunton's use of what Barth has called the 'biblical thought form'.[86] In addition, Thompson notes that Gunton opts for a Christological focus for interpreting the biblical record and critiquing Enlightenment approaches which have overemphasised the human individual's place in philosophical and theological reasoning.

Moltmann, throughout his career, has emphasised the relational aspects of the Christian faith, based on a relational understanding of the nature of God, the Trinity.

The structures of reality we choose can determine the nature of the outcome of our deliberations, the very language of our proposals determining normative and prescriptive categories within our theologies. It is important to be aware of the main categories, the relationships between categories and people, and thought forms that we use in any theological system, or proposals for dialogue within a theological context.

We need to be aware how it is possible for anyone to manipulate his or her perception, or mental image, of reality. C. S. Lewis comparing the mental image with reality rightly noted that [the image] 'is a puppet of which you hold the strings'.[87] He makes the challenging statement that all reality requires a shattering of images '[a]ll reality is iconoclastic'.[88]

Hearing people discriminate against Deaf people not only as individuals, but also through the systems of society and the dominant belief systems. These have often over-emphasised an ideal concept of the normal, fully functional and integrated human being. The biblical emphasis is on our responsibility to take care of those who are consid-

---

[86] J. Thompson, *Modern Trinitarian Perspectives* (New York: Oxford University Press, 1994) 9. Thompson notes that Gunton is following the view of B. Childs and R.E. Clements, which emphasises the unity within diversity within the biblical record, and which is indicative of a similar unity within diversity within the trinitarian Godhead. It is this biblical, theological thought form which is prior to any dogmatic categorising and formulating which may follow.

[87] C.S. Lewis, *A Grief Observed* (London: Faber & Faber, 1961) 20. His fear, in wanting to retain an accurate memory and impression of his wife, who had recently died, was that he would mentally manipulate the image of her within his consciousness, perhaps gradually leaving aside any negative or challenging aspects of her being, so leaving him with a corrupted mental model of what she was really like. He recounts meeting a friend he had not seen for some years, and his surprise that he had forgotten particular distinctive characteristics and mannerisms. His fears turn out to be valid but he has no option but to eventually accept his own memory and interpretation of what his wife was really like.

[88] Lewis, *Grief*, 52.

ered the outsider, the foreigner, the sick and the lame, the broken reeds of humanity—those who are different. This we are to do in such a way that their difference is not emphasised in the process, as to emphasise difference could cause suffering. In the thought forms we use, such as our concept of an ideal healthy person, there is a shift from the biblical view, which emphasises caring, to an attitude which refuses to acknowledge incompleteness in people.

Volf, in an essay, which seeks constructively to criticise some aspects of Lindbeck's post-liberal theological methodological revisions, acknowledges that '... Lindbeck tells us that Christians should redescribe this world with the help of biblical categories'.[89] He makes various points such as the need to note the public nature of the Christian truth claims but, of most importance for us, Volf rightly concludes that '... theology in a post-Christian and post-industrial context should celebrate the social space it was forced to inhabit — the margins — and shed all traces of nostalgia for the life in the centre'.[90]

The constant danger that accompanies Christianity is the possibility of people being deceived into believing that the acquisition of worldly power will enable them more successfully to communicate the gospel. Volf notes that the Christian responsibility is to operate in the margins and to insert a different set of relations of power. Within this proposal the text of the Bible provides a language, categories and relationships. These can then dialogue with the cultures within which Christians exist in a public way and use propositional truth claims, which summarise existential experiences of the Christian faith.

Of primary concern to many modern theologians is the functionality of systems or approaches. Moltmann's adoption of eschatology, history, promise and hope as primary biblical categories, which are intended to shape the form and content of theological dialogue, provide both a dynamic and effective starting point. This is particularly functional 'in the margins' that may include the social margins of deprived, oppressed and suffering social people groups. It may also include marginalized people groups such as Deaf people and disabled people who move in and out of the mainstream of culture as they engage in work or social activities.

An emphasis on biblical thought forms will include the liberation stories of Scripture, both personal and group, as these can provide the basis for a theology that is attractive and functional for Deaf people. Such a theology may provide the intellectual platform from which

---

[89] M. Volf, 'Theology, Meaning and Power' in M. Volf, C. Krieg and T. Kucharz (eds.), *The Future of Theology* (Grand Rapids and Cambridge: Eerdmans, 1996) 99.

[90] Volf, 'Theology' in Volf *et al.* (eds.), *Future*, 113.

social change may occur. Groups and individuals can experience a transformation of their perceptions of reality as they view themselves through the lens of biblical norms.

1. Openness to Others and the Function of Myths in Perceiving Reality

In this section, we will look at openness to others and view personal and social interactions using the category of 'myth'. This will help us understand the processes involved in perceiving reality. The way in which we perceive and describe reality depends on the perspective we have. The future is part of Moltmann's perspective. The dominant ideology within which we live will also have its own *a priori* assumptions about the nature of God, society and mankind, and we believe these may usefully be described as existing at the level of myth. Theological discourse uses language to describe basic assumptions and interpret reality. When we use language, including metaphors, to understand reality in the way that we are describing the process in this section, we are using mythical categories that function as tools.

At the outset we will define the term 'myth' as we are using it here. We are not using it in the sense of 'a sacred narrative from which legends and fairy tales are not always distinguishable' but in an anthropological sense of 'that which describes a whole value bestowing area of belief'.

This follows from

> Levi-Strauss's thesis that the meaning of a myth lies below the narrative surface, being detectable by a close analysis of the individual incidents and items in the narrative, by their regrouping, and by their study in the context of the transformations they undergo in all versions of the myth. They then reveal an endless struggle to overcome 'contradictions'.[91]

The meaning of myth we are using here is that described by Douglas who says 'the function of myth is to portray the contradictions in the basic premise of the culture'.[92] We see that the special value of using this term is in its ability to *combine*. We are able to successfully combine in the one concept of 'myth' ideas, which could not otherwise be combined, because they would contradict each other and mean nothing. There is a dialectical relationship between the components that are combined in the 'myth'.

---

[91] M. Freedman, 'Myth' in Bullock and Stallybrass (eds.), *Fontana*, 556.
[92] M. Douglas, *Implicit Meanings* (London, Boston and Henley: Routledge and Kegan Paul, 1975) 156.

For example, when we encounter a Deaf person, we probably have in our mind a concept that represents 'Deaf person-ness'. This concept may be made up of a 'whole value bestowing area of belief' that consists of knowledge about Deaf people, personal experience of interactions with Deaf people, and attitudes, beliefs and prejudices concerning them. The concept may have within it both accurate and fully formed ideas and inaccurate and partly formed ideas. These may, individually, actually contradict each other, but combined together they form the concept that we use when we try and define 'Deaf person-ness'.

'Myth' is thus able to combine the contradictions and indefinite, and sometimes incomplete, components of what we perceive to be our 'knowledge' of reality. As Moltmann, in his theology, uses dialectical processes for understanding reality and emphasises the tentativeness with which we should approach 'the other', it seems to us that this use of the term myth is a convenient and helpful way of understanding how perceiving reality occurs.

The myth provides a model for group and individual identity. It operates dialectically within itself, reforming its content with experience of the reality of the social world. The external identities of a Deaf person and Deaf people as a group can be seen in the 'myth of Deaf identity' and this 'myth' will change as they interact with it.

As Horne has rightly said, '[w]ithout the ordering of reality into mythical structures the self disintegrates'.[93]

We can view the 'openness' aspect of Moltmann's theology as a myth for the purposes of this discussion. As we have already indicated this does not mean that it lacks truth, but that it functions as something that can take us closer to the meaning of that to which we are referring. It enables us to accept that apparent contradictions may co-exist and yet be constructive. One of the strengths of Moltmann's approach, especially for the purposes of promoting dialogue, is that he does not offer a closed systematic theology. He makes suggestions and proposals, and offers an invitation for dialogue. His openness to others, and to their beliefs and practices, is a tool that we can use to counter prejudice. Suggesting that dialogue with the 'other' is even possible opens possibilities of understanding and acceptance without the need for assimilation. The very existence of dialogue reduces the likelihood of prejudice. From this flows the possibility of political implications. These may result in the formulation of laws and policies that reflect a

---

[93] B. Horne, 'Theology in the Narrative Mode' in P. Byrne and L. Houlden (eds.) *Companion Encyclopedia of Theology* (London and New York: Routledge, 1995) 958.

more accepting understanding of the needs of all the members of society.

Pinker has made the point that language is 'combinatorial'.[94] Consequently, it provides a large number of possibilities, as does music, which is also a combinatorial system. Language is just one of the channels through which perception occurs.

Mary Douglas uses this combinatorial approach when she says '[i]n both language and myth the separate units have no meaning by themselves, they acquire it only because of the way in which they are combined'.[95] In her discussion of the limitations of Levi-Strauss and his work on myths, she identifies some positive aspects that we wish to draw upon. She says that his structuralist approach, identifies the dialectical method by which myths function. According to Levi-Strauss,

> the structure of myth is a dialectic structure in which opposed logical positions are stated, the oppositions mediated by a restatement, which again, when its internal structure becomes clear, gives rise to another kind of opposition, which in its turn is mediated or resolved, and so on.[96]

Douglas later shows how Levi-Strauss, speaking of his unusual use of the term *myth* says that 'Not only is the nature of reality dialectical, and the structure of my myth dialectical, but the relation of the first to the second is dialectical too'.[97]

Douglas makes the valid point that Levi-Strauss ends up with an analysis of myth which can only 'reveal myths as timeless, as synchronic structures outside time'.[98]

When we refer to any community, including the Deaf community, we are dealing with an entity that in sociological terms functions and exists by way of a myth. Using the term as we have done here, it also enables us to grasp seemingly contradictory aspects of Moltmann's theology that would otherwise be beyond our reach.

Summary and Conclusion

In this chapter, we explored the nature of Moltmann's ecclesiology noting his stated intention to use new thought forms and modes of action. We saw how his methodology liberates the future from the

---

[94] Pinker, *Language*, 17.
[95] Douglas, *Meanings*, 154.
[96] Douglas, *Meanings*, 156.
[97] Douglas, *Meanings*, 161.
[98] Douglas, *Meanings*, 171.

power of the past through the messianic understanding of a suffering God's dealings with the world. We saw how Moltmann's view incorporates openness to the future and thus to the power of God. This comes through his promises about the future and remembrance of his fulfilled promises about the past and provides us with a means of entering into an experience of the transcendental. God is experienced in his coming towards us as we adopt these thought forms and associated actions. Our dialectical encounter of the coming God and his promises exerts a strong power on us, pulling us towards the future.

We noted how Moltmann's eschatological ontology could have a special application for Deaf people as, compared with hearing people, their self-awareness is at a less abstract level. Their inner-speech is also less likely to include propositionizing than that of hearing people and their categorization of experience appears to involve fewer linguistic based propositions, possibly due to the visual nature of sign and the iconic nature of some signs. Research indicates that there may be a heightened clarity and definition of concepts in Deaf people which results in a greater sense of immediacy.

We saw how Deaf people use narrative and storytelling as a part of their everyday communication and as a way of coping with the results of oppression by hearing people. Sign language provides valuable information on the *attitude* of the signer. This is communicated not just through linguistic signs but through the visual facial expressions, stance, etc. that are sometimes present in communication by hearing people but are there to a greater degree in sign language.

We considered the place of ritual in Deaf experience and within the liturgy of the church. There was evidence that some Deaf people might find a scripted version of reality helpful for understanding their church experience.

We saw how Moltmann uses Hegel's view of the dynamic motion of conceptualising reality that is 'a continuous weaving back and forth'. This provides an understanding of God and reality that is formed through a dialectical encountering of that which is 'not yet' or 'totally other'. We also saw how Moltmann has a strongly social understanding of the Trinity that incorporates suffering which he views as a perichoretic unity of the three divine persons in a non-hierarchical fellowship of open love. It is a pattern and model for human community in which we may discover freedom within relationships. We saw how Moltmann viewed the experience of church in an idealistic way. We see the action of the Holy Spirit in the church in the actions of those who follow Christ as he draws attention to the past death and resurrection of Christ and the future through his messianic promises. We noted the contrast between the interdependent relationships modelled in the Trinity that produce a community-based model of the self and the individualistic emphasis of modern Western society. In Deaf culture, such interdependent relationships may be easier to achieve because of the greater sense of community that already exists among Deaf people.

We showed that Moltmann's use of a cosmological and ecological view of theology stresses a redemption, liberation and salvation of all creation. This provides an all-encompassing theology that may have particular attractions for Deaf people because it provides reassurance that all things are 'under control'. Some research has indicated that the notion of 'autobiography', as used by Giddens, is more prominent in the lives of Deaf people. This 'autobiography' catalogues and defines fixed relationships within our experience of the world and provides the anchors, framework and certainties that we need for our survival and for an adequate understanding of reality. Hearing people may use a variety of such anchors but Deaf people are more likely to consider themselves institutionally classified by the single defining experience of 'being Deaf'. This occurs partly because they often experience the mediation of reality through third parties.

We showed correlation between some of Gunton's concepts and those of Moltmann noting particularly the centrality of a trinitarian understanding of God, the pre-eminence of biblical thought forms and categories, and the relational nature of reality constructed with these. We noted the importance of the language used in describing and understanding reality and the way in which language can distort our perceptions of reality. We saw that biblical norms are essential if we are to avoid modern, inadequate worldviews. Moltmann sees political awareness, action and involvement as a natural out-working of a faith based on biblical stories and promises of liberation.

We showed that Moltmann has an approach which, rather than providing a closed system of ontology or epistemology, gives an *invitation* to dialogue. This has a positive value when considering how we can form evangelical and ecumenical bridges to reach others who think differently, whether they are hearing or Deaf people.

We examined the way in which mythical categories function dialectically within societies to define seemingly opposing realities. We drew a parallel with the way in which the 'myth' of the identity of Deaf people dialectically encounters the 'myth' of particular theological paradigms.

To briefly summarise, in this chapter we have examined some of the distinctive characteristics of Deaf people that originate in their cultural and social situation and in the nature of sign language. Our initial exploration of Moltmann's ecclesiology seems to indicate it can have particular relevance to Deaf people. Deaf people rely on the Deaf community for a sense of personal identity because society has marginalized and oppressed Deaf people. Anxieties can more easily arise because of limited access to peripheral contextual social information and this means that they may welcome assurances that come from a strong community experience of church. There is a significant reliance by Deaf people, within their culture, on storytelling and therefore Moltmann's theology may be useful to them because of its emphases on the dialectical process of understanding reality and its use of narrative in that process.

Chapter 3

A Discussion with Moltmann Concerning his Theology and Deaf People

Introduction

In this chapter, we will look more closely at perceptions of reality, meaning, truth, identity and relationships through a discussion with Moltmann.

Our view on the relationship between knowledge and meaning, language and truth affects the way we express eternal truths and how we communicate them. If we are to understand reality by using dynamic conceptualities, we need to consider the use of metaphor.

a. The Tentativeness of Communication Using Metaphors and Signs and its Basis in Community

In this section, we want to note the evidence for the way in which communication is often more tentative than we normally understand it to be. We also want to note the valuable way that metaphors can help in communication because of their ability to 'stretch' meaning and communicate at a revelatory level.[1]

Cherry states that '[a]ll communication proceeds by means of *signs*, with which one organism affects the behaviour of another'.[2] In talking about signs, he differentiates between events and types. 'The distinction between an event and a type is important'. A type may remain static but in events we interpret signs on a probability basis. The meaning will vary according to time, place, mood and other contextual factors.[3]

Cherry says '[p]utting yourself in the position of observer-communicant ... you might speak in terms of the probabilities of sign

---

[1] See Chapter 5, section b, for a more detailed look at 'the effect of symbols and signs on the formation of theological concepts, and how they differ from icons'.

[2] C. Cherry, *On Human Communication* (Cambridge, Massachusetts and London: MIT Press, 1980) 221. We shall argue later, that it also affects the *state* of another.

[3] Cherry, *Communication*, 227.

events *to* you'.⁴ This naturally involves a degree of subjectivity but we moderate this by the objective knowledge we hold and receive from the community in which we exist. The important matter for our purposes is the dynamic, dialectical and communal nature of the process, reflecting Moltmann's approach to theological concept-ualities.⁵

Cherry says, when we first start to talk about something, we can only define it in approximate terms. A kind of 'bargaining' takes place in our minds and that of the person receiving the communication. This is a constant process of trying to match expected reality with the reality described. There is therefore tentativeness in the process.

This tentativeness is similar to the flexibility that Moltmann says is one function of metaphors as symbols of transcendence.

> The purpose of the Israelite prohibition of images is to preserve the mystery of God and at the same time to keep open the future of his glory. Religious symbols and metaphors are built up out of religious experiences. If they are dogmatized, these experiences become fixed, and their fixation makes them 'fixed ideas' – and that puts an end to the journey. The metaphors for experiences of God in history have to be flexible, so that they invite us to voyage into the future and encourage us to seek the kingdom of God. The true symbols of transcendence impel us to transcend. ... They become signposts, and search images for God's future.⁶

Forms of expression of the truth derive from the interaction of people communicating with each other and as they receive revelation from God. Speaking of the variety of method in sign language, which includes the use of metaphor, Kyle and Woll say 'British Sign Language is a language of movement and space, of the hands and of the eyes, of abstract communication as well as iconic story-telling ...'.⁷ We create the forms of metaphor in community. Language, although used by individuals, has its being in community. We own it and create it communally. We often use metaphors to describe things, but when we use them, it is to describe things in a tentative way.⁸ Even so, they have

---

[4] Cherry, *Communication*, 247.

[5] Moltmann says, 'The forms of theological thinking, theological language and theological metaphors are contextual, always and everywhere. They are determined by their situation and are guided by particular interests'. Moltmann, *Experiences in Theology*, 59.

[6] J. Moltmann, *The Spirit of Life. A Universal Affirmation* (London: SCM Press, 1992) 300-301.

[7] Kyle and Woll, *Sign Language*, 5.

[8] Moltmann notes how this necessary *tentativeness* is helped through the use of metaphor, he says 'Conceptual definitions limit and demarcate – they are, in

considerable value in leading us from that which we can only describe in an approximate way to a point where our description accurately reflects reality.

Gunton says that '[t]he great atonement metaphors, because they have articulated and made real certain ways of inhabiting the world, continue to have currency even where they have become debased or dead metaphors …'.[9] Gunton has argued strongly that metaphor is the main way in which we speak of the world and God.

He says,

> [w]e have seen that the metaphorical use of language is the heart of the way in which we come to speak of our world, approaching it as we do indirectly in the hope that by forcing changes in our language it will enable us to come to a measure of understanding of its structures.[10]

He goes on to use Berggren's suggestion that '… because metaphors operate, at least in part, by creating a tension between two ideas or subjects, the meaning of both terms may be transformed and yet preserved'.[11] There are two points here. Firstly, Gunton is pointing to the tentative nature of all language statements about the nature of reality, and the value of metaphor in allowing us to come more closely to expressing accurately that which we perceive. Secondly, he allows for the 'catalyst' nature of metaphor, which transforms words and produces something new, whilst remaining separate from that which it affects. Thus, '… metaphor can have a revelatory function'.[12]

Gunton says the '"deadness" of our language is a symptom of our historical disorientation'.[13] Throughout his book, he argues in favour of recognising the value of the metaphor 'as a vehicle of knowledge'.[14] In his final chapter on 'The Community of the Reconciliation', he speaks of how words create space.

> Like the preached word, the visible words have as their end the creation of space: or rather they are concerned with the realisation in the present of the achieved space of the atonement and the promised space of the new heaven and new earth.[15]

---

fact, distinctions. But metaphors can also *de*-restrict and can throw open the realm of possibilities'. Moltmann, *Experiences in Theology*, 162.

[9] C. Gunton, *The Actuality of the Atonement* (Edinburgh: T & T Clark, 1988) 50.
[10] Gunton, *Actuality*, 47.
[11] Gunton, *Actuality*, 51.
[12] Gunton, *Actuality*, 51.
[13] Gunton, *Actuality*, 176.
[14] Gunton, *Actuality*, 173.
[15] Gunton, *Actuality*, 184.

Although Gunton understands the being of God in a different way to Moltmann both writers offer a concept of the church as ideal, but Gunton's model emphasises the possibility that the concept should be descriptive. Moltmann, however, provides a more dynamic and open model which reflects his overall theological approach and which is perhaps more adaptable.

b. The Impact of Social Forces on Views of Self and Relationships

In this section, we will look at some of the ways in which we can develop a view of our 'self' and the impact of social forces on this and our relationships.

We will do this by looking at the work of Corker who can help us relate the importance of Moltmann's dynamic, relational, trinitarian theology to Deaf people. She does this by her observations on the diversity of states of being and ways of acting among Deaf people. She sees a need to break away from fixed and predetermined conceptions of Deaf people when considering their social and private selves. Her experience of counselling Deaf people is illuminating.

> The evidence of my own counselling experiences is that the insidious focus on Deaf people's difference *in a negative way,* not only by hearing people in general but also by significant others and those in their immediate socio-cultural group, is the single most common factor that leads my clients to seek counselling.[16]

She is keenly aware of the impact on Deaf people of community and significant others who relate to the individual at a personal developmental level. She agrees with Allport who noted that prejudice and conflict are reduced by relating.[17] She notes that '[d]eafness and disability are, *for many of those who are deaf and disabled and for those who live and work with them,* defining characteristics'. As a humanistic counsellor she seeks to find answers to the problems of her Deaf clients by helping her clients to learn to '... *negotiate shared meanings* and *translate societal definitions* for themselves'.[18] She sees narrative as a primary means by which Deaf people can convey values and beliefs as well as facts and details of relationships.

In her excellently argued book, Corker adopts in her discussion of Deaf identity what she refers to as '... that group of theories which

---

[16] M. Corker, *Deaf Transitions* (London and Bristol, Pennsylvania: Jessica Kingsley Publishers, 1996) 9.
[17] Corker, *Transitions,* 9.
[18] Corker, *Transitions,* 9.

suggest that identity is constructed'.[19] She takes Erikson's model as typical[20] and shows how a person's internal centre develops from identification with significant others in childhood, role diffusion experiences in early adolescence, role experimentation experiences in adolescence and achievement of identity in adulthood. These four stages of personality integration, or identity formation, draw on the apparent effects that our experiences of our surroundings influence, and create, the reality that we call our selves, our identity.

Corker rightly draws attention[21] to the similarity with the process of self-actualisation that Maslow in his 'hierarchy of human needs' indicates is the way of growth, accomplishment and personal development.[22] Corker makes the point that '[t]he core of the Deaf community is formed by Deaf people who come from Deaf families which sometimes go back generations'.[23] Deaf cultural centres are predominately the Deaf club and the Deaf school, where socialisation takes place and Deaf people form and maintain networks of relationships. Deaf people whose first language is BSL find within them their cultural and personal identities. Other partially or fully hearing people, such as the parents of a Deaf child, are able to become members of the Deaf community through involvement in this sub-culture. Corker rightly makes the point that '... the cultural model is a valid representation of *one* Deaf reality, though not the only reality'.[24]

She goes on to show that the 'disabled identity', which derives from the hearing medical specialist's need to define adequately, with a blanket term, all people with a 'hearing impairment', is often strongly rejected by those at the core of Deaf culture. For these Deaf people any sense of loss is lacking and they often view hearing people as lacking because hearing people lack the ability to converse in BSL and do not understand the elements of difference within Deaf culture.

These discussions by Corker, whilst illuminating in the field of counselling, tend to point towards a mode of being which is achievable and with which we can identify. We experience this modalism as we adopt different roles within modern Western society.

Both Maslow and Erikson can be criticised for oversimplifying what is a very complex process and for viewing the identity formation proc-

---

[19] M. Corker, *Counselling – The Deaf Challenge* (London and Bristol, Pennsylvania: Jessica Kingsley Publishers, 1994) 20.
[20] E. Erikson, *Identity: Youth and Crisis* (London: Faber, 1968) Chapter III, see Corker, *Counselling*, 20-22.
[21] Corker, *Counselling*, 22.
[22] Corker, *Counselling*, 13.
[23] Corker, *Counselling*, 24.
[24] Corker, *Counselling*, 24.

ess too idealistically. Running counter to the socialisation arguments are the experiences of individuals whose strongly held values, beliefs and attitudes enable them to avoid any change of identity in the direction of socialising forces.

There have been strong and convincing arguments made by Berger for the 'Social Construction of Reality'[25] and sociologists have used a number of experiments to demonstrate that people are at least temporarily vulnerable to the influences of others, particularly peers, in causing them to act in an unexpected way. It is evidently easy to take advantage of people's suggestibility. This is not to say that we can easily change the identity of people, although repeated re-enforcement of behaviour or attitudes often seems to effect permanent change.

The contemporary possibilities of religious affirmation that Berger is later concerned with, can provide a way of understanding how positive recognition of other approaches to affirming faith may be accepted. The liberal approach can also be a means of ensuring that the identities of the more vulnerable are not unduly threatened by our assertions concerning belief. Arguing for a liberal approach in religious matters, which would be especially sensitive to the beliefs of others, Berger says,

> ... there is a kind of mellowness that comes out of great inner strength. And apodictic certainties have a way of collapsing overnight. One could even suggest that those who have truly encountered the 'reality of the unseen' can *afford* the mellowness of liberality, both in their lives and in their thinking.[26]

Berger represents a direct contrast to the seemingly non-dogmatic dialectical approach of Moltmann, yet both are keen to explore common ground with those of other faiths by pointing to the commonality of mystical experiences. Moltmann also wants openness to others but bases his approach on what he sees as the objective facts of history and divine revelation. He sees these as vital components in determining what constitutes identity.

Corker views identity almost in terms of self's role, or mode of being, differentiating between self and identity. She then views the self as consisting of a private self and a public self. In contrast Kierkegaard views self and self's perception, awareness or consciousness of itself as being the two constituents of a trinitarian model of self, the third being the dynamic process of self observing and processing information about the self. This would seem to be the model of self which

---

[25] P.L. Berger and T. Luckmann, *The Social Construction of Reality: A Treatise in the Sociology of Knowledge* (New York: Doubleday, 1966).

[26] P.L. Berger, *The Heretical Imperative* (London: Collins, 1980) 156.

Moltmann holds and one which emphasises the perichoretic, mutual indwelling of the constituents of self and which model he extends to include the place and relationship of self dwelling within the world and within God.

There is significance in this for the way in which individual and group identities are viewed, both by hearing and Deaf people. Ultimate identities, as the source of power and movement, are able to draw current identities out of themselves by dialectically challenging the status quo.

Moltmann's model clearly shows a Barthian influence with this view of God, who axiologically enters into the world. Moltmann emphasises the transcendence of God yet he combines it with a strong emphasis on God being immanent in the more obviously material realm of the created world. He uses a strong perichoretic understanding. The created self and the created order mutually indwell each other and exist within God who is within them. The power, of the future hope of the Christian eschaton, dwells within the present and we all live within this power.

c. Identity of the Self through the Identity of God as Trinity

A valid theological approach to the subject of identity would allow for the identity of God to be in some way constitutive of the identity of the human self. We can achieve this by showing through the 'otherness' of God, how human identity differs from the identity of God. We also see through a doctrine of the *imago dei* the similarities in our identity.

We can note the considerable academic work carried out on the subject of 'the self' in a variety of disciplines. Psychology, sociology and anthropology have drawn upon and provided inspiration for the quest carried on by philosophy and theology for millenia. It is not possible to conduct here a complete survey of thought on this subject, as we consider it more productive to look at recent attempts at defining identity.

For the purposes of this section, we are concerned with the matter of identity as it relates to our idea of self. That is, how we describe and understand who we are and how we relate to God and others. Our description and understanding of ourselves may differ from the view other people have of us, but it is easier for us to say how we identify ourselves than to seek an understanding of what it is for us 'to be'. By concentrating on the phenomenological aspect of self, that is identity, it will be possible to make some comparisons between Deaf and hearing understandings and note their differences. Current theological explanations of how we should understand self will help us in our task of seeking to show the relevance of Moltmann's theology to Deaf people.[27]

Thiselton provides an excellent survey of theology's attempts to define and explain God and the self in a Postmodern context. To view being as consisting merely of modes of being, which some Postmodernist approaches do, is to provide a successful hermeneutic, in the sense of being efficient, for understanding reality, though it may not endure. Thiselton, is positive about Moltmann's significant contribution in promoting the search for a valid 'promissory perspective'. He says

> ... 'the image of Christ' assumes a fundamental role in relation to *future* promise. To be transformed into 'the image of Christ' and to become 'like him' constitutes the heart of the divine promise which lifts the self out of its pre-defined situatedness and beckons from 'beyond' to a new future ... [which] is by no means itself pre-packaged by fixed horizons fully determined in advance.[28]

Noting the importance of viewing the nature of the 'new existence' we have in Christ as being *dynamic*, he says, '[f]or the Hebrew people and the biblical writers, to be "living" was to be "on the move". ... [E]ven the post-resurrection mode of existence ... cannot be conceived of as a static existence'.[29]

Thiselton draws together the ideas of promise, future and the dynamic nature of self, both human and divine. He notes Moltmann's contribution, and those of Pannenberg, W. Kasper, Boff and Gunton, towards '... interpreting God as Trinity for inter-personal understandings of love, respect, mutuality and more broadly human society ... '.[30] Thiselton then clearly describes an understanding of God's identity that can flow from this approach. He says,

> [i]f God's identity (to follow Barth) consists in his self imparting love as Trinity, divine personhood, independently of his creation, embodies the capacity for interactive reciprocity. At the same time, God's 'oneness' represents neither solitariness nor self-love of the like-minded, but that which *could be no other* if love is pure, non-

---

[27] For Deaf people who have suffered oppression, any identity will have political consequences. This will be yet another force affecting the development of identity.

[28] A.C. Thiselton, *Interpreting God and the Postmodern Self* (Edinburgh: T & T Clark, 1995) 153.

[29] Thiselton, *Interpreting*, 153-54.

[30] Thiselton, *Interpreting*, 156.

manipulative love 'serving the interests of the Other as one's own' (to paraphrase Brümmer).[31]

Thiselton points out that '... Pannenberg works out a trinitarian theology in which love constitutes the ground of selfhood'.[32] Pannenberg rightly says 'Persons do not have power over love. It rises above them and thereby gives them their selfhood. It manifests itself through the reciprocal relation of those who are bound together in love'.[33]

We are urged by Thiselton not to dismiss approaches such as these simply because they suggest a social model of the Trinity. He feels, and we agree, that we should exercise caution because there may be hidden agendas, conscious or sub-conscious, in any theological approach. We should constantly be aware those who recommend either adopting, or rejecting, a social model of the Trinity may have ulterior motives. He says '[i]f ... we are tempted to opt for a "social" Trinity in order to legitimate an egalitarian view of society, this becomes manipulation in the service of power-interests and ceases to be a quest for theological truth'.[34] Moltmann has sought to introduce a new paradigm where we are to assume from the outset that any hierarchy is contrary to God, either in himself, in his dealings with his creation or in the human self and the interaction between people. At first glance, it might appear that Moltmann's theology is less concerned with the pursuit of theological truth and more with achieving an egalitarian society. However, it seems to us that Moltmann's primary motive has never been 'manipulation in the service of power interests' for there is no evidence of this. His efforts have consistently been targeted at understanding faith and providing ammunition for use against those evil powers that oppress and cause suffering in the world. His stated purpose has been to provide new perspectives from which to view theology and he has provided these.

d. Moltmann's Use of Trinitarian, Relational and Dialectical Processes to Define Being

Commenting on Moltmann's stress on perichoresis, within the Godhead, and of people within creation, Thiselton says '[a]t the beginning of *The Spirit of Life* Moltmann observes: "[p]ersonhood is always being-in-relationship". ... The personhood of the Holy Spirit is per-

---

[31] Thiselton, *Interpreting*, 156.
[32] Thiselton, *Interpreting*, 156.
[33] W. Pannenberg, *Systematic Theology, Volume 1* (Grand Rapids: Eerdmans, 1991) 426.
[34] Thiselton, *Interpreting*, 157.

ceived *as personhood* within the context of the mutuality of the Trinity'.[35]

The particular passage that Thiselton refers to is a splendid systematic exposition by Moltmann of his understanding of the trinitarian personhood of the Holy Spirit, where he moves through four conceptions of the Trinity.

> In the monarchical Trinity the unity of the three Persons comes into being through the unified movement of *God's sovereign rule*. In the historical Trinity the unity comes into being through the direction of time, which thrusts towards *the future*. In the eucharistic Trinity the unity of the divine Persons comes into being through the unified movement of *thanksgiving*. It is through the trinitarian doxology that we first perceive the immanent Trinity as it rests and revolves in itself, and whose unity lies in the eternal *community* of the divine Persons. The essential nature of the triune God *is* this community.[36]

Moltmann, in speaking of trinitarian doxology says it is 'the *Sitz im Leben* for *the concept of the immanent Trinity*'.[37]

> [T]he trinitarian doxology is the beginning of the seeing itself, for the seeing of God's glory is the goal of salvation history, and the trinitarian doxology anticipates this goal in the very midst of salvation history. What corresponds in life to the trinitarian doxology in the divine liturgy is the perception of *the eternal moment*. I mean by that an awareness of the present which is so intense that it interrupts the flux of time and does away with transience. ... We perceive these exceptional ecstasies of life with all our senses, and yet they reach beyond our sensory perceptions – not as if they were 'supersensory', but because they are so intensive that the distance we need if we are to perceive them is taken from us, and we ourselves become wholly present and wholly living in the ecstasy of life.[38]

Moltmann moves from the monarchical concept of the Trinity, where experience of God is at a distance and mediated, to this ecstatic understanding of certain moments experienced in doxology. Is Moltmann, in referring to *the eternal moment*, departing from his argument for an eschatological underpinning of all theology? He certainly comes close to seeming to mean this, however he is careful to say that there is a *correspondence* between the *trinitarian doxology* and *the eternal moment*. His point is that by involving ourselves in the earthly liturgy

---

[35] Thiselton, *Interpreting*, 157.
[36] Moltmann, *Spirit of Life*, 309.
[37] Moltmann, *Spirit of Life*, 302.
[38] Moltmann, *Spirit of Life*, 303.

we experience 'unutterable points of rest'.[39] These are statements referring to *correspondences* and are not intended to be *descriptive* in themselves.[40] As our eucharistic liturgical practices and experiences correspond to 'heavenly' realities so our momentary ecstatic experiences (that impress by with their vividness and immediacy) correspond to, and speak to us of, the 'heavenly' rest that will be ours in the eschatological fulfilment of God's promises.

Moltmann's proposal for defining the being of God is effective in that it incorporates narrative at a number of levels. He utilises the power of the naming of God through our human experience of him. As we adopt the power of a hope in the eschatological future, we have a power that is effective against existential angst.

Moltmann emphasises the incorporation of the dialectic of the cross and resurrection that inverts earthly values and power. By making the cross and resurrection central, Moltmann is able to provide a firmer concept of identity than a static, non-relational model can provide. He provides a way of negating all that might threaten to destroy our being and stresses the interim nature of all being in the light of the eschaton. This theology is particularly useful in an environment where change is the norm rather than the exception.

Moltmann reaches his view of reality by juxtaposing the complete with the incomplete, the whole with the partial, the permanent with the transitory and the static with the dynamic. For a basis of the identity of disabled people, including Deaf people, this is a helpful process.

He poses the question 'What is a human being?' and in his answer says

> [w]e only have to set the Gospel picture over against the Greek ideal of a human being, bursting with health, strength and goodness, in order to sense the difference. In the Gospels sickness is part of the definition of the true person. For wherever the Saviour appears, the sick appear too.[41]

The picture that we have in the modern world of what it is to be fully human is so affected by the Greek ideal that we find it difficult to think of wholeness in other ways, and we often judge others accordingly.

---

[39] Moltmann, *Spirit of Life*, 303.

[40] Note, for example, Moltmann's use of the term *correspondences* in his understanding of *messianic* situations that are 'correspondences to God's kingdom and his righteousness and justice'. Moltmann, *Experiences in Theology*, 101. Similarly, see his use of the term when referring to political theology, '[a] political theology ... will ask what is in accord with God – what his correspondences on earth are – which means among other things: in the political constitution of a community'. Moltmann, *Trinity*, 198.

[41] Moltmann, *Power*, 145.

> We who judge according to the standards of our own ideals may think that a blind or deaf or lame or mentally sick person has a 'diminished' life — life which is less than the life of other people. But God loves every human life. ... Every life is in its own way divine, and must as such be experienced and respected.[42]

We can gain some insight into Moltmann's theology by being aware of his view of his past. In his post-war theological studies, he wanted to go beyond Barth's theology 'toward the eschatological, toward the theology of the cross, and toward a politically critical theology'.[43] In the foreword to Meeks' book Moltmann writes about the personal context of the origins of his theology of hope. He describes the horizon seen from the window of his parent's home in northern Germany. He gazed on this as a boy and describes it as a 'boundary which does not confine but rather invites one to go beyond'.[44] Moltmann speaks of his experience as a young prisoner of war, where the 'horizon ... is the barbed wire' and where '[h]ope made him free to accept, even laugh at the barbed wire, and to discover in his fellow prisoners human beings whose company he enjoyed, with whom he could be happy even in suffering'.[45]

Meeks maintains that behind Moltmann's theology is one methodology. 'The dialectic of reconciliation ... is a theological methodology which aims at demonstrating the thorough interdependence of the relevance and the identity of Christian theology'.[46] Concerning Moltmann's view of existence itself he says, 'the dialectical mode of Christian existence is the dialectic between hope and our suffering from real contradictions of our humanity'.[47]

We have seen in this section the various ways in which Moltmann cleverly incorporates a dynamic dialectical process in order to define the trinitarian 'being' of God and derives from this an understanding of our own 'being'.

e. Openness in Moltmann's Ecclesiology

A further result of Moltmann's emphasis on openness is its impact on ecumenical dialogue. From this we could expect that it would be conducive to encouraging dialogue between hearing and Deaf people

---

[42] Moltmann, *Power*, 148.
[43] M.D. Meeks, *Origins of the Theology of Hope* (Philadelphia: Fortress Press, 1974) xii.
[44] Meeks, *Origins*, x.
[45] Meeks, *Origins*, xi.
[46] Meeks, *Origins*, 3.
[47] Meeks, *Origins*, 7.

concerning the place of Deaf people within society and the church. In viewing theology itself, Moltmann prefers an open rather than a closed approach to conceptuality. This means that rather than providing a closed system of theological thought he prefers a scheme that offers an invitation to explore possibilities that may, or may not, provide fixed or closed interpretations of theological truth. He is using Bloch's category of 'not yet' in adopting this approach. He also extends the method to include attitudes towards others who have different understandings of truth claims. Openness towards those who are different, in Moltmann's thinking, stems from his adaptation of the Old Testament command always to consider favourably, and with a sympathetic approach, the 'foreigner in your midst'. Thus, within Moltmann's theology is a built-in expectation that dialogue will occur with those who hold different beliefs. In his own career, he has had dialogues with representatives of Orthodox and Pentecostal churches as well as those from the Jewish faith.

This distinctive within Moltmann's theology affects those who choose to adopt his methodology. It encourages a way of thinking which is less dogmatic than other approaches, and which is more willing to consider the point of view of the other. In place of a competitive approach to the question of beliefs, which may result in the success of one over another, Moltmann adopts a co-operative approach that can be more constructive. This can be the case particularly in times of change when existing belief systems are proving themselves inadequate. In the Western world, there is an inbuilt attitude of scepticism towards traditional beliefs and practices in society generally, as well as within religions in particular. Moltmann's openness, offers a positive and constructive way of allowing for the possibility of change.[48] This can occur without the need for the immediate rejecting of traditionally held beliefs. Moltmann is far from weak in the areas of what can and cannot constitute non-negotiable elements in the Christian faith. His radical and innovative approach to openness allows people, who otherwise would be unable to talk or listen constructively to others with different views, to enter into dialogue. His church is an open church that exists for all its members and in which members of the congregation care for one another, even if they are on the margins of society and of the church.[49]

One outcome of using this open approach is the countering of prejudice. Geertz has said '[i]deology bridges the emotional gap between

---

[48] The adoption of the tentative point of view that 'I may have got it wrong' can be used as a tool to adapt belief systems to changing circumstances.

[49] Concerning this, see his small but important book, J. Moltmann, *The Open Church. Invitation to a Messianic Lifestyle* (London: SCM Press, 1978).

things as they are and as one would have them be ...'.[50] This openness can also provide an experience of solidarity for those of similar beliefs that results in us needing to be separate from others, in our view of ourselves as well as in practical day-to-day living. Prejudice causes a scapegoating of those who do not conform within our society. The prejudices of society are against those whom we perceive to be 'not normal'. This may be because of how they appear or act, because of their beliefs, or the spiritual powers we believe them to have.

Where there is a strong and dominant ideology, the powers of those who hold the dominant ideology are more likely to be extreme in the scapegoating of others. Deaf people have experienced social and personal ostracising through practices such as mockery and ridicule. The closed approach to belief and value systems causes people to deal with non-conformity in this way. A system using an open approach counters prejudice and discrimination and allows people to challenge established notions of normality.

Speaking of *cultural* systems, Geertz has rightly said 'coherence cannot be the major test of validity'.[51] We sometimes use cohesiveness and coherence as initial categories for evaluating *theological* systems or methods. We assume that the more obviously cohesive and coherent a system appears to be the more valid it is. Cohesiveness and coherence are necessary but are not always obviously apparent. Moltmann's open approach allows for the fact that our initial judgement concerning validity may be deficient and that we may only subsequently become aware of coherence and cohesiveness.

Moltmann's approach sometimes provokes resistance to the suggestion that any worthwhile progress is possible outside a closed systematic theological system. The necessary tentativeness such openness requires at certain stages, and which is evident in much of Moltmann's writing, has a fear inducing quality. Farrow has rightly noted that '[w]hilst it is commonly held that Moltmann's conceptual looseness and spotty engagement with the tradition exacerbate his readers difficulties ... it is also widely agreed that the seminality of his thought goes a long way to compensate for that'.[52] Jesus was anti-systemic in many of his pronouncements emphasising instead the need for his listeners to change their attitudes especially as they related to the outsider.

At an anthropological level Geertz has rightly acknowledged the public as well as the personal dialogue that an individual enters into when making sense of the world. He says '... the existence of cultural

---

[50] C. Geertz, *The Interpretation of Cultures* (London: Fontana, 1993) 205.
[51] Geertz, *Interpretation*, 17.
[52] Farrow, 'review', 427.

resources, of an adequate system of public symbols, is just as essential to this sort of process [of clarifying feelings] as it is to that of directive reasoning'.[53] He argues effectively for an acknowledgement that our thinking is not as purely a personal, internal process as some would hold, but is really a dialogue between the inner self and its set of symbolic understandings, or models, of the outside world, and incoming symbolic perceptions of that world which do not fully comply with it.

There are two important points in his discussion for our purposes. The first is that selectivity over our incoming perceptions occurs through our 'determining of the affective significance, the emotional import of that pattern of events'. The second is that 'not only ideas, but emotions too, are cultural artefacts in man'.[54] For Geertz, the public nature of symbols that interpret reality is important. By this, he means that we establish symbolic meaning within community rather than internally in the person. Our culture produces commonly held symbols that we internalise. A dominant ideology will have its own set of agreed and accepted symbols which will need to be conformed to, and accepted by, its members in order to achieve cohesiveness.

At first glance, openness appears to suggest a neutral, value free approach to that which is other. Yet, by virtue of its willingness to embrace the other,[55] openness actually demands a positive initial acceptance of the other. Openness is therefore present as an attitude, a 'disposition towards' or a feeling. It is Geertz's contention that such feelings 'constitute no more a basically private activity in human beings than does directive thinking'.[56] For Geertz, such feelings do not provide motivation. They are a regulative and interpretative faculty. Motivation in people comes from the experience of stimulus deficit. This occurs when incoming sensory stimuli cause awareness of a difference between the internal symbolic model of the world and perceived reality. We seek information to balance that deficit, usually through modification of that internal model.

Openness then, far from being neutral, is a positive quality which will allow the embrace of that which is other. In theological terms, this means being willing to see things from the other's point of view, at least temporarily. If we close ourselves to other ideas and beliefs by exclusion of 'the other', we prevent ourselves from being involved in any dialectic process.

---

[53] Geertz, *Interpretation*, 81.
[54] Geertz, *Interpretation*, 81.
[55] Note M. Volf's important work on this subject, *Exclusion and Embrace* (Nashville: Abingdon Press, 1996).
[56] Geertz, *Interpretation*, 81.

Moltmann has cleverly married the liberal quality of openness and acceptance with traditional Cappadocian understandings of trinitarian, relational theology, with Bloch's orientation towards the future and with a modified Marxist dialectic. The result is a dynamic theology that manages to emphasise Christ's concern for the outsiders and the responsibility of the community of faith to think and act towards them in an embracing way.

Geertz rightly says that symbols are also 'strategies for encompassing situations'.[57]

> [M]eanings can only be "stored" in symbols ... [which] are felt somehow to sum up, for those for whom they are resonant, what is known about the way the world is, the quality of the emotional life it supports, and the way one ought to behave while in it. Sacred symbols thus relate an ontology and a cosmology to an aesthetics and a morality: their peculiar power comes from their presumed ability to identify fact with value at the most fundamental level, to give what is otherwise merely actual, a comprehensive normative import.[58]

An effective ecclesiology for Deaf people will include the openness that is central in Moltmann's scheme. It is appropriate because Deaf people have been isolated and marginalized, culturally and socially, by hearing society and there needs to be a willingness on the part of the aggrieved party, namely Deaf people, to meet that which is other. For Deaf people, who often live and work in both hearing and Deaf cultures, this openness, or the potential for it, may already be there.

At a time when Deaf people are trying to understand how changes in the traditional ways of the Deaf community are going to affect Deaf culture, openness to the future can be positive. It can be a means of entering into dialogue about the nature and impact of change and the acceptance, or rejection, of it.

In church settings, an adoption of openness can be effective from both an evangelical and an ecumenical point of view. The political implications are to foster a spirit of co-operation and understanding. We need an environment in church, and society, which protects the vulnerable. The adoption of an attitude of openness can provide opportunities for an enriching of experience, as we welcome, rather than fear, the possibility of that which is new.

---

[57] Geertz, *Interpretation*, 141.
[58] Geertz, *Interpretation*, 127.

f. How the Social Trinity, the Doctrine of God and the Kingdom of God in Moltmann's Ecclesiology can help Deaf People gain Freedom from Oppression

To understand the nature of Moltmann's ecclesiology, we need to appreciate the role and function of his doctrine of God. We will look at this through an understanding of the nature of the Trinity and its relation to the kingdom of God. Following from this we can consider the effect which language ability may have on the appropriation and appreciation of his ecclesiology. From this we would ask what forms spiritual well-being and maturity take in Moltmann's scheme, and how lack of acceptance by hearing people of Deaf culture may still restrict the ability of Deaf people to participate in his ecclesial models.

Moltmann powerfully describes the conception of God, which appears in his theology, and contrasts it with very different traditional monotheist understandings and their consequent emulation in the rulers of this world who dominate others.

His argument is that the Western church neglected the emphasis of the Cappodocian Fathers,[59] and that of Orthodox theologians on the plurality of God, emphasising instead the oneness of God.[60]

> Two different categories of analogy have always been used for the eternal life of the Trinity: the category of the individual person, and the category of the community. Ever since Augustine's development of the psychological doctrine of the Trinity, the first has taken precedence in the West; whereas the Cappadocian Fathers and Orthodox theologians, down to the present day, employ the second category. They incline towards an emphatically social doctrine of the Trinity and criticize the modalistic tendencies in the 'personal' trinitarian doctrine of the Western church.[61]

Clerical and political monotheistic models subsequently developed and could claim justification through appealing to the monotheistic view of the Godhead, which had been generally accepted since it was developed by Augustine.[62] Moltmann says, significantly, '[i]t is a typically

---

[59] Basil the Great, Gregory of Nanzianzus and Gregory of Nyssa.
[60] See also Moltmann's discussion on 'Social Likeness to God', in J. Moltmann, *God in Creation. An Ecological Doctrine of Creation* (London: SCM Press, 1985) 234-243. We can note that some theologians will challenge the claim that stressing the unity of God necessarily leads to a *static* model. See also the excellent work on this subject, J.D. Zizioulas, *Being as Communion* (Crestwood, New York: St. Vladimir's Seminary Press, 1993) 17.
[61] Moltmann, *Trinity*, 198-99.
[62] Moltmann, *Trinity*, 198.

Western bias to suppose that social relationships and society are less 'primal' than the person'.[63]

Crucially he comments '[t]he Christian doctrine of the Trinity provides the intellectual means whereby to harmonize personality and sociality in the community of men and women without sacrificing the one to the other'.[64] We see this goal of reclaiming the picture of the reconciliation of the 'oneness' and 'threeness' of God and the 'manyness' of creation mirrored in Colin Gunton's 1992 Bampton Lectures. He says '... the point for our purposes is that much modern social and political thought can be understood as the revolt of the many against the one, and at the same time that of humanity against divinity'.[65] Gunton does not view the reconciliation of all creation as being a part of the Divine plan in the same way as Moltmann. They both note the importance of dialogue. Moltmann speaks of how '... the new ecumenical conversations about questions of trinitarian doctrine in the Western and Eastern churches has a trendsetting importance for the future'.[66]

Moltmann relates the doctrine of God, and the place of the Trinity within it, directly and in a unique way to the kingdom of God in a trinitarian doctrine of the kingdom, drawn from the work of Joachim of Fiore. This he develops and links to our understanding of freedom, showing that *'[t]he trinitarian doctrine of the kingdom is the theological doctrine of freedom'*.[67]

In his closely argued points, he develops the theme of reconciliation that runs through all of his theological work. He does this through an understanding of the different actions and roles of the Father, Son and Spirit. These are seen in the indwelling of people by God himself. 'This gives liberty its bearings and fills it with infinite hope'.[68]

In order to overcome what he describes as 'the torment of choice' Moltmann appeals to '... the moral purposes and values of the realm of the Good [which] transcend the realm of freedom in quality'. He notes that '[a]t the same time, the tendency to the realm of the Good is inherent in the experience of freedom'.[69] He later says,

> ... if freedom means community, fellowship, then we experience the uniting of everything that has hitherto been separated. ... The truth

---

[63] Moltmann, *Trinity*, 199.
[64] Moltmann, *Trinity*, 199.
[65] C. Gunton, *The One, the Three and the Many* (Cambridge: Cambridge University Press, 1993) 27.
[66] Moltmann, *Trinity*, 200.
[67] Moltmann, *Trinity*, 218.
[68] Moltmann, *Trinity*, 213.
[69] Moltmann, *Trinity*, 214.

of human freedom lies in the love that breaks down barriers. It leads to unhindered, open communities, in solidarity. It is only this freedom as community that can heal the wounds which freedom as lordship has inflicted, and still inflicts today.[70]

The development of his argument includes a progression of ways of viewing the created being's relationship to God, other people and the future. Seen simply they are as follows. Firstly, viewing God as 'one' results in a subject/object relationship where the subject God, has lordship over the object, mankind. Secondly, in community mankind experiences the subject/subject relationship. Thirdly, when we bring the kingdom of God into the picture, a subject/project relationship is experienced. Where the project is the future 'coming of God' we transcend the present. We can view these three strata in the concept of freedom as 'property', 'social relationships' and 'creative relationships'. We can view these respectively as 'having', 'being' and 'becoming'.[71] Moltmann can then say that *'God is the inexhaustible freedom of those he has created'*.[72]

Moltmann provides a dynamic ecclesiology that uses a trinitarian viewpoint to construct a model of the church that may not be so easily subject to the abuses of power that hierarchical structures can generate. His dynamic conceptualities retain a dialectic tension and this in itself is symbolic of the creative nature of the economy of God that he is seeking to emphasise. Without objectifying the divine nature, he uses the traditional analogies of the person and community to show how God embodies himself within an ecclesial model, which emphasises and promotes experiences of God through community with others and in worship of his glory. The empowering that follows comes from the relationship with the 'project', which is the kingdom of God.

The concepts he uses provide strong symbols for presenting and experiencing the reality of God and the church. Within the provisionality of all knowledge of God, we see symbols that hint at reality and which in themselves are, in some sense, that reality. There is a positive functional outcome in the use of the model, in that it coheres within itself adequately whilst at the same time relating satisfactorily to the world and the church, as we know them.

Of particular interest to us is the way in which Moltmann uses the concept of 'relating to a project'. This concept is an accepted model within sociology, and we have already noted the way in which people 'relate to myths' in order to produce coping mechanisms, including appropriate belief systems, for dealing with their experiences. What

---

[70] Moltmann, *Trinity*, 216.
[71] Moltmann, *Trinity*, 217.
[72] Moltmann, *Trinity*, 218.

has not generally been noted within theological circles is the way in which an average churchgoer relates to the 'project' which is their church, as well as relating to individuals within it, in a community sense, or to the physical building and its location. We could say that the 'project of the church' consists of all that tangible and intangible substance which makes up the reality of the church, from its doctrinal and creedal statements of belief, to the particular ethos and atmosphere which pervades it. From a phenomenological viewpoint, this is an important and yet neglected idea.

The oppression of the dominant hearing culture may show itself by restricting the ability of Deaf people to conceptualise and understand the model of the church.

For all groups who have a lower level of educational attainment, a sacramental model, or a Pentecostal model, both of which emphasise experience over the cognitive element, would enable them to participate more adequately and conceptualise their relationship to the project of the church. Their belief system would provide them with an acceptable and durable model without their having to be intellectually sophisticated or exceptionally successful academically. Moltmann's model emphasises the core value of experiencing church as community and the freedom that confers on the members. He gives priority, to praxis and to loving, friendship type relationships. By including the missionary and ecumenical aspects of church in his model, he provides a stimulus to keep its members outward looking.

Moltmann uses the term 'the church' interchangeably to refer to the assembled congregation of confessing believers or to the dispossessed and marginalized of the world, the poor of Matthew 25. Moltmann's ecclesiology can supplement established church models in a variety of traditions. Moltmann views God as the social Trinity. From God, love overflows to reach humanity. This outward focus of God potentially allows for a quality of openness between members of the church and between them and people outside the church.

g. Dealing with Loss, Psychologically and Theologically

We will now consider the universal human experience of dealing with the loss of a significant person or thing. Moltmann uses strongly personalised theological models of the church and the self, even though he relies on community-based relational concepts to describe them. How people understand each other, God and the church, and view reality is important to him. At the heart of his model lies the loss that God the Father experienced at the point of crucifixion. In Moltmann's theology this sense of loss is not presented as a theoretical matter which is devoid of emotion but as the central part of being of the Godhead experienced with all the cognitive and emotional impact which would accompany such a loss in the human sphere.

This Godforsakenness is ontologically constitutive of the Trinity together with the promise of the restoration and redemption of all things. Christians can know God as the 'Coming God' who exists in what Moltmann describes as the category *novum*. Psychologically this acts as a counterbalance and as an accompaniment to the Godforsakenness that we would otherwise experience as a despairing emptiness leaving us devoid of hope for the future. By suggesting the possibility of recovery in the future from loss in this way, he grounds hope ontologically in God. This provides a dynamic motivating force in us, at the psychological level, through the power of hope. We receive hope and this enables us to have a perspective of openness towards the future. This openness reflects the openness God revealed to us in the scriptural record of his dealings with creation and includes the Incarnation of Christ, his life, death and resurrection, and the coming of the Holy Spirit. The church and its traditions have validated these, held them to be true and attested to them, in Scripture, in the reciting of creeds and training of catechumens in the central tenets of the faith.

By current standards, a healthy person is one who has a cautiously optimistic attitude to the future based on realistic understandings of current and past experiences. In providing this, Moltmann's theology can produce a psychologically stable and healthy way in which we can perceive the relationship between ourselves and the world.

There is power in the eschatological orientation of Moltmann's theology, with its emphasis on promise and fulfilment and its incorporation of suffering, including that associated with the loss of relationship, that is Godforsakenness, into the very being of God. Together with the dialectical process associated with the Coming God, who will redeem all of creation, it provides an appropriate and satisfactory basis for enabling Deaf sign language users to understand the Christian faith.

It can provide a continuing counterbalance to the psychological pain experienced by some Deaf people, through the oppression of a society and culture that does not try to understand their particular linguistic needs and cultural ways. Where Deaf people have experienced such pain, there may be an experience of loss of what could have been if hearing people had related to them in a non-marginalizing way. It can provide an explanation of, and means of coping with, the distress caused by inadequate mourning for that which has been lost or grieving for that which has never been.

h. Moltmann's Theology is Conducive to Developing Spiritual Maturity

The history of mission and ministry to, and amongst, Deaf people, is one of oppression. Deaf people rightly seek a theology that will avoid a tendency to reproduce the mistakes of the past and enable Deaf people to develop a spiritual maturity of their own.

Deaf people are as varied in their interests and abilities as hearing people and therefore need as wide a range of opportunities. We can expect Deaf people to be able to adopt, adapt and engage with a variety of theologies. They have experienced in the past oppressive and paternalistic approaches. There is always, therefore, the possibility of well-meaning approaches, such as applying new theological ideas to their situation, degenerating into condescending action and producing disempowering structures. This underlines the need for a theological approach, which, at its heart, is biased against these negative possibilities.

If spiritual maturity includes a healthy breadth of understanding of the beliefs, values and attitudes associated with the practice of a faith, then it will also include a healthy approach to dogma and doubt and the possibility of future development, built on past understandings and experience. There will also be a need for the recognition of the place of wholeness and an adequate appreciation of the whole person within the structures of the wider society and within creation itself. A definition of personal wholeness within such a theology would also need to include the 'wholeness' of Deaf people.

Moltmann's theology enables it to encompass that which is 'not yet', and to recognise the potential within it. Even if Deaf people had not experienced restricted opportunities in education and employment and restrictions in their church experiences, there would still be value in them adopting Moltmann's theological approach. In view of their oppressive experiences in these areas, the inclusiveness of his theology is an attractive proposition for this group, for whom liberation from past and present oppression is a matter of considerable concern.

Summary and Conclusion

In this chapter we considered how metaphors, icons and signs are used in communication. We drew parallels between verbal and sign languages using Gunton's assertions that all communication is to some degree metaphoric. We also noted the open nature of that sometimes act as a catalyst in leading the receiver of a communication from one state of understanding to another.

We considered the way in which 'space' can be opened up by certain types of communication, and the spiritually creative effect of this. We sought to see how the 'external space' of sign communication could represent 'conceptual' or 'spiritual space' possibly more effectively than verbal communication. We noted the community nature of metaphor construction and maintenance and the tentative way in which they convey truth. Because of their flexibility, they are an ideal way for us to describe our encounter with the transcendental. They invite us to venture beyond that which our sensory experience tells us is certain.

We next considered the impact of social forces communicated through language on our views of our self and our relationships. We saw how socially constructed understandings of self can cause people to label themselves, or others, restricting them from adequately expressing their real self in the process. We saw how Corker drew attention to the difference between self and identity. We suggested that Moltmann appears to use Kierkegaard's view of self, which employs a perichoretic model, and where mutual indwelling is an essential characteristic. We explored some modern attempts to derive an understanding of self from an understanding of God and a social view of the Trinity. This can enable us to incorporate a relational view of self that exists primarily in self-giving love. We noted Thiselton's warning to exercise caution and to avoid interpreting a social model of the Trinity as legitimating an egalitarian view of society.

We argued that Moltmann's understanding of the being of God is one grounded in history, tradition, Scripture and experience. It incorporates the dialectic of the cross and uses the eschaton as a focus on the interim nature of all being states and so provides a firmer concept of identity than a static non-relational understanding.

Using Moltmann's comments on disabled people and the identity that society gives them, we have shown how he sees the gospels as portraying humanness. This is not in completeness and strength, as in the Greek ideal, but in weakness and sickness.

We saw how Moltmann's methodology can enable a view of Christian existence which acknowledges the real contradictions of our humanity but which offers an expression of it that incorporates the dialectic between hope and suffering. It does this through the messianic view of history and the power of the eschatological to form and transform the present.

We saw that Moltmann's adoption of an open approach to conceptualising the truths of the Christian faith not only have considerable value in encouraging ecumenical endeavours but they also actively discourage discrimination and counter prejudice. We also saw how viewing disabled people as 'not normal' causes marginalization and scapegoating. Following Geertz, we saw that we interact with the public and socially stored values of symbols as they challenge or confirm the inner view of the world that we hold. Moltmann suggests that the best attitude for appropriating such symbols is one of openness. This openness does not encourage neutrality but is in fact a 'disposition toward', a positive quality, which will allow us to embrace that which is other. It involves us in a dialectic that opens us to others whom we view as different. Deaf people already partly experience this when they are willing to accept non-Deaf outsiders into the Deaf community once they have established that they are not a threat. This process provides a political stance which if adopted gives opportunities for a greater understanding of other people. This contrasts with distorted images often held by people in society.

We argued that Moltmann has cleverly married the liberal quality of openness and acceptance with trinitarian relational theology. He has also incorporated a modified version of Bloch's understanding of being, which he founded on a Marxist dialectic and orientation towards the future. The result is a dynamic theology that emphasises Christ's concern for outsiders and also the responsibility of believers to embrace rather than exclude outsiders.

We next considered how Moltmann provides us with tools for understanding the important place of freedom in human relationships. He does this within his ecclesiology through emphasising a view of God as Trinity. This relieves us of the subject / object relationship which derives, he says, from viewing God as one rather than as three persons. He also helps us have a correct view of freedom through the concept of the kingdom of God, which he sees as providing a way that we can transcend the present. This happens as we view it as a project to which we as subjects can relate.

Moltmann uses the term 'project' to describe the kingdom of God. We suggested that this be extended so that the church is also viewed as a 'project'. We suggested that the way many believers relate to their local church is similar to the way in which people relate to 'myths'. This is a functional relationship but our understanding of it may be ill defined. This relationship to 'the project' of the church, which Moltmann views as a partial demonstration of the kingdom of God, makes friendship type relationships more important than confessions of faith, although he does not exclude these. Moltmann's view of the church emphasises the openness of members of the church to the outsider. He also emphasises that the church exists in a messianic relationship to the world and in the eschatological expectation of the coming of Christ. For Deaf people, Moltmann's model of the church means that although they are viewed as 'different', this difference does not prevent them from being fully participating members of the church.

We next considered how Moltmann's ecclesiology produces a psychologically positive effect. We suggested it resulted in a cautious optimism that is based on community understandings of truth. It incorporates into the being of God the reality of 'loss', which is presented in Scripture as the Godforsakenness of God the Father, experienced at the time of the crucifixion. It balances this with the eschatological hope of recovery of that which is lost. We expect God to fulfil his promises based on the previous fulfilment of promises as recorded in Scripture.

We concluded by suggesting that Moltmann's ecclesiology can provide a healthy spiritual maturity through its inclusiveness and its holistic view of what it is to be human, and in relation with God and all of the created order. His ecclesiology also provides an understanding of these relationships viewing them as a process and so encourages the embracing of change, which itself can be a vehicle for liberation.

To summarise then, in this chapter, we have sought to highlight and explore some of the most important characteristics of Moltmann's theology and ecclesiology and show how significant and important they are to Deaf people. These include tentativeness in communication and in understanding matters of faith such as a social view of the identity of self that derives from a trinitarian model of relationship.

We have seen how theological, sociological and psychological factors affect our views on the relationship between knowledge and meaning, language and truth. We have also seen how Deaf people have a particular need for a theological model, which can be met through Moltmann's approach, primarily drawing on the openness that is characteristic of it.

We have seen how the incorporation by Moltmann of loss into our understanding of the being of God and his dialectical understanding of reality provides a dynamic and potentially creative view of the Christian faith that appears to be particularly suited to meeting the perceived needs of Deaf as well as hearing people.

Chapter 4

Moltmann's Eschatological Ontology: The Identities of Man and God in Moltmann's Theology and their Relation to Deaf People

Introduction

The purpose of this chapter is to consider the centrality of Moltmann's eschatological ontology in his theological thought particularly as it relates to the development of his distinctive doctrines of God, man and the church. We will also look at thinkers who have influenced him and some criticisms of his approach. Finally, we will consider the appropriateness and validity of its use at the current time both by hearing and Deaf people in understanding who they are and how they relate to God, creation and others.

We have considered already the way in which Deaf people, who are born Deaf or who lose their hearing before the ability to speak is developed, conceptualise reality differently to hearing people. The language of all Deaf people is of a visual nature and they may therefore conceptualise pictorially more readily than hearing people. Hearing people are more likely to conceptualise abstractly. We will look at research into Deaf people's experience as a means of understanding what is happening at a cognitive and conceptualising level. We will show how Moltmann's doctrines of God, man and the church are relevant to Deaf people.

a. Moltmann's Eschatological Ontology and its Centrality to his Doctrines of God and Man, and his Ecclesiology

Grenz and Olson identify Moltmann's revolutionary eschatological ontology as being central to an understanding of his theology as a whole. They note that of particular importance is his eschatological ontological understanding of the being of God. This leads to an eschatological ontological doctrine of man and has consequent effects on his doctrine of the church.

In their summary and critical evaluation of Moltmann's work Grenz and Olson say,

Moltmann's theology introduced several powerful new images and concepts into late-twentieth-century Christianity. No other theologian has done as much to explore the implications of eschatology and of the cross of Christ for the being of God.[1]

They acknowledge his indebtedness to the theology of Barth in terms of his understanding of the dialectical nature of the revelation of God. They also note how '[h]e reaffirmed Rahner's thesis of the identity of the immanent Trinity and the economic Trinity; yet he interpreted the connection not as absolute identity without distinction but as reciprocity and interdependence'.[2] They note Moltmann 'holds out real hope for theology's ability to speak relevantly to secular people by drawing on revelation's answers to meet their needs and questions'.[3]

We feel that they are rather unfairly critical of the tensions that they maintain exist in Moltmann's theology. They say that

> ... most significantly, in spite of his intention of providing a new approach to the traditional problems of the transcendence and the immanence of God, Moltmann ultimately abandons them to a tension. He speaks of the God of the eschatological future, the 'power of the future,' the God with futurity as a mode of being who *comes* out of the future to contradict and transform the world. But he also talks about the suffering struggling God of history whose unity as Father, Son and Spirit is still future to himself. How exactly these pictures of God cohere Moltmann leaves unexplained.[4]

In response we can note that Grenz and Olson were writing before Moltmann published *The Spirit of Life* and *The Coming of God* each of which were to develop his understanding of the doctrine of God as being primarily messianic and eschatological. In *The Coming of God* in particular he expands, by explaining from the eschatological perspective, the significance of the immanent Trinity for the economic Trinity and salvation history.[5]

Müller-Fahrenholz rightly says that Moltmann 'aims at a theological explication which is as ordered and logical as possible' and that '[p]recisely because his theological trains of thought about God are to

---

[1] Grenz and Olson, *20th Century*, 185.
[2] Grenz and Olson, *20th Century*, 183.
[3] Grenz and Olson, *20th Century*, 176.
[4] Grenz and Olson, *20th Century*, 185.
[5] See Grenz and Olson, *20th Century*, 186. See also R. Olson, 'Trinity and Eschatology: The Historical Being of God in Jürgen Moltmann and Wolfhart Pannenberg', *Scottish Journal of Theology*, 36 (1983), where Olson concludes that Moltmann 'seems to affirm an ontological monarchism himself'.

Moltmann's Eschatological Ontology

become a fanciful "dance" of thought "before" God, he wants to avoid intrinsic contradictions and irrational leaps of thought'.[6]

In a passage in which he seeks to define more clearly the term advent Moltmann traces the root of the word *adventus* to a rendering of the Greek word *parousia*.

> In secular Greek, *parousia* means the coming of persons, or the happening of events, and literally means presence; but the language of the prophets and apostles has brought into the word the messianic note of hope. The expectation of the parousia is an advent hope. For in the New Testament the past presence of Christ in the flesh, or the present presence of Christ in the Spirit, is never termed *parousia*. The word is kept exclusively for Christ's coming presence in glory.[7]

He then goes on to speak of the eschaton.

> The 'eschaton' of an eschatology which works with the concept of God suggested here, and with this advent understanding of the future, is not an eternity which can neither enter time, nor remain *outside* time. This eschaton means a change in the transcendental conditions of time. With the coming of God's glory, future time ends and eternal time begins.[8]

Moltmann's dynamic understanding of the perichoretic nature of the Trinity has, as integral to its being, the potential to generate the category *novum* from which flows his understanding of the being of man that has potentiality as a constitutive factor. Potentiality in God and in man is not just something extra, in the sense in which we would understand it in everyday terms, but a creative possibility that defines our very being. Ontologically, God is as much potentiality as he is reality and we experience this at a perceptual level as a re-aligning of self with the reality of the *coming God*. We experience this as eschatological hope of a messianic kind, defined primarily as a re-understanding of the way in which linear time is broken into by the *coming* kingdom of God. 'Only the idea of the coming God, and the advent concept of time which is in accord with him, open up categories for eschatology'.[9]

As far as this affects Moltmann's ecclesiology we can immediately see that traditional notions of the form of the church need to be re-examined. If we define God and man in eschatological ontological terms we need also to view the church in this way. Its potentiality and messianic being are fundamental to it as are its transience and primarily non-institutional nature. The church exists in a glory producing

---

[6] Müller-Fahrenholz, *The Kingdom and the Power*, 239.
[7] Moltmann, *The Coming of God*, 25.
[8] Moltmann, *The Coming of God*, 26.
[9] Moltmann, *The Coming of God*, 26.

worship experience, and enjoyment of the life of God. The *dance* and S*abbath* of God and its messianic task result in it being task oriented towards all of creation. It brings the *promise* from the Godhead of the ultimate redemption of all things through the historical event of the cross and the resurrection experienced as a proleptic event. The church will therefore involve itself in ecumenical and political efforts to extend and announce the kingdom of God. It will do this through the relief of suffering by joining in the suffering of those it encounters both within the confessing Christian community and outside of it. In practice, there will be a powerful motivating force experienced by the members of the church as they contemplate and become aware of the potentialities and realities of the promises of God and their expected fulfilment.

b. Moltmann's Eschatological Ontology and Immanent Transcendence as the Experience of God

In *The Spirit of Life* Moltmann explains the importance of developing his *holistic* doctrine of God the Holy Spirit states and that one result of it is that '... its effect can be therapeutic'.[10] It can anticipate the reconciliation of all things in creation. He says,

> ... it is literally essential for us to develop *a holistic doctrine of God the Holy Spirit*. ... It must be holistic in at least two ways. On the one hand, it must comprehend human beings in their total being, soul and body, consciousness and the unconscious, person and sociality, society and social institutions. On the other hand it must also embrace the wholeness of the community of creation, which is shared by human beings, the earth, and all other created beings and things.[11]

This doctrine of God has immanent transcendence centrally placed. Moltmann is arguing against the anthropomorphic tendencies in modern philosophies and theologies that place the conscious self at the centre of models of reality. Picking up the immanent realism and phenomenological approach of Husserl and expanding Max Scheler's view of man as being '... endowed with freedom and a meaning that cannot be denied by science'[12] he shows how we can experience God through encounters with the inner self and with the external world. Such encounters, he says, go beyond 'self as subject' perceiving 'other

---

[10] Moltmann, *Spirit of Life*, 38.
[11] Moltmann, *Spirit of Life*, 37.
[12] F. Dunlop, *Thinkers of Our Time, Scheler* (London: Claridge Press, 1991) back cover.

objects'. If we allow for an inter subjectivity, in terms of the person's relationship to reality, we find that

> ... awareness of the self is something that is *constituted*; it is by no means solely constituting in character. ... The experience of God's Spirit is always also the experience of what Schleiermacher calls 'the common spirit', the God who is sociality (Hölderlin's 'gemeinschaftliche Gottheit'), who binds together I and Thou and Us, as Feuerbach said.[13]

Going beyond this socially constructed self and noting the presence of God within the social scene, this self is in constant dialogue with what it perceives as internal and external reality, and constantly modifies itself as a result. Thus, Moltmann develops the idea of the 'possibility of perceiving God in all things, and all things in God, [which] is grounded theologically on an understanding of the Spirit of God as the power of creation and the wellspring of life'.[14]

Moltmann then draws out the different horizons with which reality may be perceived.

> Perception that is related to the perceiving subject asks: 'what does it mean for me?' This is now replaced by the perception which takes its bearings from the all embracing horizon. Things then appear in the light of the boundary encircling them. If this boundary is not annihilating Nothingness, but is God the creator, then things do not fade into that horizon; on the contrary their contours become sharply distinct.[15]

For Moltmann, God is in creation but not in a purely pantheistic way. To put it in anthropomorphic terms, God is experiencing the fullness of all created reality at an emotional as well as a cognitive level. Our experience of God occurs as we experience aspects of the created order and is not limited to our perceptions of the conscious self. There is a perichoretic, interpenetrating and interdependent relationship between us and God and creation. The boundaries or horizons of the possibilities of our existence are extendible to infinite lengths within the overall promises made by God in his covenant relationship with all of his creation. Moltmann develops and provides a coherent and constructive doctrine of God that is eschatologically ontological. There is a strongly 'therapeutic' outcome to the adoption of such a doctrine for it stresses the rights and responsibilities attached to the non-hierarchical relationships within the Godhead and within the created order. A respect for

---

[13] Moltmann, *Spirit of Life*, 33.
[14] Moltmann, *Spirit of Life*, 35.
[15] Moltmann, *Spirit of Life*, 36.

the 'other' and an acknowledgement of privileges and duties also flow from this way of viewing God.

Moltmann has always sought to provide a theology which is praxis centred and has drawn on Bloch's Marxist based philosophy for this linking of action and material reality. Within the wider philosophical field there are similarities with the immanent realism of Ingvar Johansson's 'nested intentionality'. Johansson acknowledges Peter Berger's contribution in this area. He draws on Bhaskar who, like Berger and Johansson, has been partly inspired by Marxism.[16] In particular, Johansson uses Bhaskar's term *'dual character of praxis'* which acknowledges that '... when a social agent produces something he often *re*produces at the same time a certain state of affairs'.[17] He uses the illustrations of currency and language. 'When you buy something you produce private satisfaction ... but at the same time you participate in the reproduction of the currency used. When you talk to someone you produce messages and help to reproduce language'. He also points out that '[t]he dual character of praxis has its counterpart in a *duality of structure*'. Societal realities such as currency and language have the quality of both the medium and the outcome of actions. 'Without currency some kinds of transactions would not be possible, but without actions which make use of the currency the currency would not exist'.[18]

Johansson notes the limitations of existing sociological models. Weber's, Durkheim's and Berger's are able, only to a limited degree, to differentiate between individuals and societal realities and at the same time emphasise their relatedness. Johansson's goal is to unite individuals and society '... with the help of the intentionality category and different types of nested intentionality. Without nested intentionality there would be no societal matter in contradistinction to natural matter'.[19]

Johansson seems to see what he terms 'nested intentionality' as an extension of the category of intentionality and this provides a key to understanding both man and society. A man is made up not only of drives and desires which might on the one hand be biological or personal but also of drives, desires and intentions. These are the result purely of his position as being 'within' society. Linguistic signs, he argues, both facilitate and constrain. Man has a natural, or biological nature, and a social nature. Action can only flow from intentionality,

---

[16] I. Johansson, *Ontological Investigations. An Inquiry into the Categories of Nature, Man and Society* (London and New York: Routledge, 1989) 314.
[17] Johansson, *Investigations*, 313.
[18] Johansson, *Investigations*, 313.
[19] Johansson, *Investigations*, 314.

which is determined by natural sources within a person, or from conventional forces of society. Similarly, some 'states' such as 'shame and pride'[20] require at least two participants. For our purposes we can note that Moltmann's view of 'being' as the state of 'being in relation', requires at least two participants and the 'being' of the regenerate person requires God to be a participant in our 'being'.

Johansson is approaching the matter from an atheistic standpoint, but even so, we can connect his theory to Moltmann's suggested view of God as being immanently transcendent. This provides an opportunity for a third level of interaction and influence as God reveals himself to individuals and affects their perceptions of themselves, and of society, and their intentionality. He is not a transcendent God who is remote from the created order. He is one who exists within it whilst at the same time allowing it to exist within him. He permeates all of created reality whilst at the same time giving it qualities that it does not naturally hold.

God is the 'possibility of the new thing' in that he is the power of the eschatological future in the present and therefore introduces and maintains a freshness and redemptive element to all of reality by the all-inclusive ministry of reconciliation. He influences the moral decision-making will of man both at an individual and societal level. He is able to provide through the anticipation of the fulfilment of his promises a level of experience which is of a heavenly quality. Through his revealed view of man and the created order, seen primarily in the revelation of Scripture, this experience of the kingdom of God is a foretaste of an eternal reality. It includes the holistic doctrine of God acting therapeutically on 'the existing cleavages in human beings themselves ... divisions between human beings, and ... the disjunction between human beings and nature'.[21]

c. Christology and Eschatology and the Identity of Jesus

Bauckham notes the centrality and close linking of Christology and eschatology in Moltmann's work from *Theology of Hope* to *The Coming of God*. Moltmann founds his understanding of the identity of Jesus Christ on his understanding of eschatology. In *Theology of Hope* Moltmann said the following:

> [t]he fundamental event in the Easter appearances then manifestly lies in the revelation of the identity and continuity of Jesus in the total contradiction of cross and resurrection, of god-forsakenness and

---

[20] Johansson, *Investigations*, 307.
[21] Moltmann, *Spirit of Life*, 37-38.

> the nearness of God. ... The sole bridge of continuity between the primitive Christian proclamation and the history and proclamation of Jesus himself is *via* the raising of the one who was crucified. This is a continuity in radical discontinuity, or an identity in total contradiction.[22]

Moltmann notes the way in which early Christological disputes and heresies arose through various other understandings of the relationship between Christ's identity and the cross and resurrection. These failed to see the identity of Jesus '*in* ... cross and resurrection'.

> [The identity of Jesus] must remain bound up with the dialectic of cross and resurrection. ... the contradictions between the cross and resurrection are an inherent part of his identity. ... It is formally a question of a dialectical identity which exists only through the contradiction, and of a dialectic which exists in the identity.[23]

He goes on to explain this, saying '[c]ross and resurrection are then not *modi* in the person of Christ. Rather, their dialectic is an open dialectic, which will find its resolving synthesis only in the *eschaton* of all things'.[24]

Moltmann then refers to the words spoken by the risen Jesus which confirm his identity 'It is I' as being in continuity with the Jesus who had lived and died but which also confer the duty of involvement in his mission. 'His appearances were vocatory appearances by which the men involved were set to follow the footsteps of the mission of Jesus'.[25]

> His enigmatic identity in the contradiction of cross and resurrection has therefore to be understood as an eschatological identity. The titles of Christ which are used to express it anticipate his future. They are therefore not hard and fast titles which define who he was and is, but open and flexible titles, so to speak, which announce in terms of promise what he will be. They are therefore at the same time also dynamic titles. They are stirred and stirring ideas of mission, which seek to point men to their work in the world and their hope in the future of Christ.[26]

We can see then that Moltmann's eschatological ontological understanding of Jesus Christ provides the backbone of his theology in that it is able to provide a link between the apparent discontinuities of the

---

[22] Moltmann, *Theology of Hope*, 199.
[23] Moltmann, *Theology of Hope*, 200.
[24] Moltmann, *Theology of Hope*, 201.
[25] Moltmann, *Theology of Hope*, 202.
[26] Moltmann, *Theology of Hope*, 202.

life and death, and the cross and resurrection of Jesus. It also provides a continuity between history and the present, and the present and the future. This is not at a mythological level, by which the story of Jesus is interacted with and impacts upon the life of the believer, but through an eschatologically based understanding of identity of the self. This is founded on an open dialectic which finds its synthesis in the *eschaton* of all things. This eschatological ontology of the self derives from the eschatological nature of the being of God. It also provides an eschatological ontological understanding of the being of the church. It does this by linking us with the words of the resurrected Jesus which define and commission his disciples. It also inextricably links the being of the church with its mission because it is bound to the promise of the eschatological future of its members and of all things.

d. Moltmann's Conceptions of God and Self and their Impact on Deaf People with Particular Reference to Wholeness and Impairment

Moltmann's understanding of the doctrines of man, God and the church emphasise a holistic approach to reality, which acknowledges the incompleteness of all beings whether they are impaired or not. They stress the redemptive act of God, as it exists in his promise, which will renew all things in creation. They stress the interrelatedness and healthy co-dependence of all creation, both with itself and with its creator. They stress how the reconciliation of all things relates to the mission of the church. This mission is the task of communication of the healing gospel of the creator to all individuals and groups, hearing or Deaf.

To appreciate Moltmann, Deaf people need to go through an awareness-raising and consciousness-awakening process. Deaf people in some Western countries are undergoing a radical re-understanding of how they exist as people and within society. Some have used a process of assertiveness and there has been a rethinking of who they are and how they relate to others. As a result they see themselves as members of a language minority group who have been oppressed, marginalized, exploited, and denied opportunity by hearing people within society.

Within the Deaf community a mood of despair and despondency of previous times has become, for some, a mood of hope based on what appears to be the partial achievement of liberation. The hope Moltmann provides is one that forms a permanent feature of a person's understanding of their being. It tells us who we are and what our purpose is.

Moltmann provides a view of the self that has a right relation to creation and to God. We should view relationships in the light of the eschaton. God promises a sense of acceptance and purpose. As an expression of this, the church can build healthy communities within which abuse against vulnerable minorities by those who hold power is minimised. Liberation from the perspective of the dominant is the first step. Practical deliverance from the power of the oppressors should follow.

e. The Sources of Moltmann's Eschatological Ontology and his Epistemology

Moltmann's theology has its roots in providing a response to the problem of suffering and how we can relate it to our understanding of God. He has tackled this by adopting a new ontology of God and man, based on eschatological events. He picks up Hegel's categorising of concept as event. He also builds on Barth's theology especially the aspect Bradshaw describes as the vision that 'includes both the principle of analogy and that of dialectic. This dialectic retains its characteristic of encounter, confrontation, partnership ... [and so] Barth reflects both the "Hegel-Marx-Bloch" line and the "Kierkegaard-Nietzsche-Heidegger" line'. Bradshaw says of this '[h]e seeks to do justice to both emphases'.[27] Moltmann criticises Barth.

> It is of decisive importance for the doctrine of God whether we start from the Trinity in order to understand the sovereignty of God as the sovereignty of the Father, the Son and the Spirit, or whether we think in the reverse direction, proceeding from the sovereignty of God in order to secure this as being the sovereignty of the One God by means of the doctrine of the Trinity.[28]

Moltmann argues that Barth and Rahner, like Schleiermacher, are both in danger of 'Sabellian modalism – or, to be more precise, Idealistic modalism'.[29]

Moltmann is adopting and adapting Barth who was influenced by Kant and Hegel, among others. It is worth noting what Habermas has said of Kant and Hegel.

> Hegel fashioned his dialectical mode of justification in deliberate opposition to the transcendental one of Kant ... What Kant regarded as a unique (Copernican) turn to transcendental reflection becomes, in Hegel, a general mechanism for turning consciousness back upon

---

[27] T. Bradshaw, *Trinity and Ontology. A Comparative Study of the Theologies of Karl Barth and Wolfhart Pannenberg* (Edinburgh: Rutherford House Books, 1985) 134.
[28] Moltmann, *Trinity*, 140.
[29] Moltmann, *Trinity*, 144.

itself. This mechanism has been switched on and off time and time again in the development of spirit. ... What Hegel calls 'dialectical' is the reconstruction of this recurrent experience and its assimilation by the subject, which is faced with ever more complex structures. In sum, Hegel goes beyond the particular manifestation of consciousness Kant analyzed, focusing instead on knowledge that has become autonomous—that is, absolute knowledge.[30]

Habermas identifies one recent approach which is that of pragmatism and hermeneutic philosophy. This offers an alternative to Kantian and Hegelian attempts, through their philosophies, to provide a universal explanation of knowledge and being

> [which] accords a higher position to acting and speaking than to knowing. But ... [they] play a qualitatively different role from that of self-reflection in the philosophy of consciousness. They have no justificatory function any more save one: to expose the need for foundational knowledge as unjustified.[31]

Moltmann's has drawn on and developed ideas from Hegel, Kant, Barth and others. He emphasises orthopraxis over orthodoxy. He is willing to interact with 'the trinitarian history of God'[32] revealed in the Bible which Conyers says, for Moltmann, '... proceeds from the identity of God's promise with the fulfilment of his promise'[33] and invites us into dialogue with it. There is dynamism within his conceptual framework that is able to take us beyond the search for the identification of universals within any epistemological framework. There are aspects of what Habermas calls a pragmatic and hermeneutic philosophy in his approach.

Pannenberg's theology, like that of Moltmann, dynamically uses the eschaton in developing the doctrines of God and man. Bradshaw accuses Pannenberg of integrating his epistemology and ontology.[34] The question arises as to whether Moltmann has also done this. Bradshaw notes that Pannenberg's 'trinitarian doctrine is ... the foundation for his ontology and epistemology, [which] ...unites for Pannenberg ontology and epistemology ... [and which] distinguishes Pannenberg strongly from Process theology and places him in the more subtle family of

---

[30] J. Habermas, 'Philosophy as Stand-In and Interpreter' in J. Appleby, E. Covington, D. Hoyt, M. Latham and A. Sneider (eds.), *Knowledge and Postmodernism in Historical Perspective* (New York and London: Routledge, 1996) 511.
[31] Habermas, 'Philosophy', 514.
[32] J. Moltmann, *The Future of Creation* (London: SCM Press, 1979) 82.
[33] Conyers, *God*, 52.
[34] Bradshaw, *Trinity*, 249.

Christian idealist thought'.[35] 'Man's openness to the world and his openness to the deity beyond ... is always, for Pannenberg, indirect, that is through his knowledge of the world'.[36] To further understand Moltmann's view of revelation we can consider Conyer's comments.

> ... [F]or Moltmann, revelation is not identified with history (even as seen from its end) but continues to be the 'Word of God,' as in Barth. Except in Moltmann's case, revelation is neither the reception of history as a mirror of God's activity that can be known proleptically from the end of history (Pannenberg) nor the unveiling of the "eternal presence of God in time" (Barth). Rather it proceeds from the identity of God's promise with the fulfilment of his promise. ... The promised future stands in contradiction to the perceived present, and yet, through his promise, God's faithfulness is demonstrated—just as "in all the qualitative difference of cross and resurrection Jesus is the same," and thus God's faithfulness is vindicated.[37]

Conyers notes the part played by Gerhard Von Rad's work 'in the rise of eschatological theology' and of how Moltmann 'never tires of emphasizing that "Christian theology speaks of God historically and of history eschatologically"'.[38]

Moltmann provides an epistemology that utilises the primary categories such as future and hope in the context of the eschaton, adopting a partially process understanding of reality for them to underpin and interpret. As Conyers points out, Moltmann's view contrasts with that of Pannenberg. 'The starting point must therefore be not the assumption of universal history but God's promise and faithfulness *in* history'.[39]

His eschatological ontology sees God as being a subject in relation with man who is also a subject, and this inter subjectivity attempts to avoid objectification. It does this by viewing the three persons of the Godhead as they interrelate. His use of a dialectical understanding of knowledge and perception provide a clear epistemology even though in his scheme he closely links it with, and uses it to interact with, his ontology.

---

[35] Bradshaw, *Trinity*, 332.
[36] Bradshaw, *Trinity*, 249.
[37] Conyers, *God*, 52.
[38] Conyers, *God*, 71.
[39] Conyers, *God*, 73.

f. Current Identity Crises: Falling into the Future

The subject of eschatology has a vast literature and we will not be attempting a survey of it. Following Moltmann, we are not concerned with when the parousia may be expected to occur, but rather how its certainty affects our theological understanding. As Travis has said:

> [NT] [p]assages suggesting imminence indicate a *theological* rather than chronological relationship between present and future. They indicate the certainty, not the timing, of God's completion of what he has begun. ... NT writers are in fact less concerned with the timing and manner of Christ's coming than with its purpose.[40]

The philosophies people adopt emphasise certain aspects of time, and so affect the way in which they perceive reality. People in modern Western society often find themselves romanticising the past and partially idolising it. There is an emphasis on experiencing, and preferably enjoying, the present moment. So central is the emphasis on the present that a person can feel as if they are falling into the future.

Control of a person's destiny is often no longer perceived as being in the hands of an all-powerful deity, but in the fallible hands of each person. People see the apparatus of the nation state and commercial enterprises as strongly influencing personal futures. The hope that people experience is not of the biblical variety and may be limited to material or personal gain or, at the least, an avoidance of suffering. In Marx's thought, the people's enemy is alienation. In Durkheim, it is anomie. This is where 'people are less closely locked into the order of society, so their basic desires may become limitless and confused. At this point, anomie becomes almost a psychological state of disorder and meaninglessness ...'.[41]

People in Western society today typically experience rapid change in many areas of their lives. Accompanying this is a sense of rootlessness. Past certainties have no adequate replacements. At the root of this, say some recent writers such as David Harvey, is the effect of capitalism in shaping 'our sense of time and space in its very operations'.[42]

Harvey has aptly described the way in which in Western society since the 1960s a throwaway society has developed, which 'meant more than just throwing away produced goods ... but also [throwing

---

[40] S.H. Travis, 'Eschatology' in Ferguson and Wright (eds.), *New Dictionary of Theology*, 230.

[41] G. Marshall (ed.), *The Concise Oxford Dictionary of Sociology* (Oxford and New York: 1996) 16.

[42] Editors' preface to D. Harvey, 'The Condition of Postmodernity' in Appleby *et al.* (eds.) *Knowledge*, 493.

away] values, life-styles, stable relationships, and attachments to things, buildings, places, people, and received ways of doing and being'.[43] He also speaks graphically of the effects of the

> ... accelerations in turnover times in production, exchange, and consumption that produce, as it were, the loss of a sense of the future except and insofar as the future can be discounted into the present. ... Past experience gets compressed into some overwhelming present.[44]

Hearing and Deaf people can often feel overwhelmed by quantity. This can be quantity of goods, information, choices or relationships. Traditionally stable categories of duty and honour no longer hold the central place they once did within a person's understanding of self and the relationships that exist with others within society. A strongly narcissistic strand in the make up of a personality is often accepted as normal and has superseded previous emphases that often included an attitude of sacrificial self-giving.

The right of a person to fulfilment through achievement, entertainment or some other activity appears to have replaced respect for others and their property. Some people have responded to their overwhelming feelings by seeking answers in non-Western religions and practices that involve contact with psychic and supernatural realities. These sometimes involve meditative and reflective techniques or unusual approaches to wholeness of being and health.

Harvey's use of the term 'discounting the future into the present' is appropriate. To discount is to '[g]ive or get present worth ... detract from; part with for immediate but smaller good; use up effect of ... beforehand'.[45] In many senses our experience can be that Western consumerism encourages current gain above all else.

Deaf people are also subject to these forces. There are two distinct differences. The first is the consequence of early profound deafness in that it will 'radically change an individual's relationship with the world – there will be much less direct contact with the surroundings. ... A consequence of this may be a loss of personal security and weaker bonds of contact with people'.[46] The second is the fact that they are widely dispersed geographically. The experience of Deaf people is often of 'marginalization' and personal isolation as only one in a thousand of the general population have sign language as their first language. This can mean that their experience of alienation is more

---

[43] Harvey, 'Postmodernity', 495.
[44] Harvey, 'Postmodernity', 498.
[45] *Concise Oxford Dictionary of Current English*, 5th edition.
[46] Church of England, Advisory Board of Ministry Working Party (eds.), *The Church Among Deaf People*, 7.

acute than that of hearing people particularly if they are not part of a supportive Deaf community. Moltmann sees an answer to these crises of identity coming to us as we understand and experience the nature of the church, as revealed by God in Scripture. He views the church as being an accepting and liberating 'community' where we can receive an answer to the forces of disintegration that surround us. We can have a new way of viewing reality, a fresh perspective, and can combat the forces of oppressive hierarchical organisations through our solidarity with other oppressed people. It is through our developing understanding and experience of the church that we experience an increased sense of continuity in our lives. This arises from our knowledge and experience of our covenant relationship with God and one another, into which we enter with the assurance of faith, based on the scriptural record, that he will fulfil his promises to us.

Speaking of the Trinity and how our view of it will affect our interaction with each other and God, Conyers says we may view the Trinity as '...a God for whom history is not only the medium of his self-disclosure, but the mode of his being'.[47]

Moltmann takes one of the biblical ways of talking about God and uses that as his starting point for discussion about the way in which we may understand God today. In the preface to Conyer's book he confirms that 'covenant' forms the basis for much of his thought and that he has derived that from the biblical examples and descriptions of covenant that God entered into at various times with his people.[48]

Following Moltmann, we can say that, our history is in God's experience of the world and us. Our past and future are in him, and his being includes us.

g. Perspectives as the Link between Ideas and Matter: The Need for an Open View and Moltmann's Concepts of Hope and Space

The category of *perspective* is an important tool in Moltmann's theological scheme. It is a hermeneutical tool for establishing and measuring doctrinal realities. Moltmann does theology in an experimental way and uses a method that makes suggestions and invites the reader into dialogue. Perspectives provide the way into the initial presentation of the subject matter for consideration and discussion. Perspectives have at least some of the characteristics of attitudes. From a cognitive viewpoint they depend on previously gained knowledge of facts and their relation to one another as well as their relation to that which is unknown.

---

[47] Conyers, *God*, 4.
[48] Conyers, *God*, ix.

Moltmann uses the term *perspective* to describe a hermeneutical approach, or attitude, which affects a person's understanding of reality, including our understanding of God and self.

Moltmann acknowledges that '[h]ope and planning represent the future in different ways'.[49] We can view them as metaphors or symbols of the future. He says '[t]he field of hope and planning is summarized historically, by means of the "future"; ontologically, by means of "possibility"; and anthropologically, by means of "freedom"'. He notes the way in which planning provides 'anticipatory dispositions'[50] for the future, and influences history through a dialectical process.

The matter of probability then arises because planning is more effective in some areas than others and probability requires us to use hope when planning. This then addresses, or acts dialectically on, the possibility of 'unforeseen developments' and relates to 'those incalculable and unplanned moments in history'.[51] Hope, however, 'comes from the realm of inter-personal relationships'. Moltmann views these as necessarily requiring freedom and says, '[i]n personal relationships, hope presupposes the otherness of the other and his freedom and becomes a hoping trust in which one person promises himself to another for his future'.[52] From this it follows that 'destiny' and 'coincidence' are both matters which are determined more by planning than by hope, and they are dependent on the promise of the other in the context of our relationship. 'Hope then refers much less to that future which is available out of my own powers than to that future which another man places at my disposal. In that case, hope is not the disposition of my future, but the expectation of the future of the other, based on his promise'.[53]

Recognising the 'new thing' which comes from hope Moltmann says 'This 'newness', which the otherness of the future determines, lies on the border between what is possible and what is impossible'.[54] From this he sees that '[h]ope is always born from the emergence of the new. Hope sees the advent of the future and reaches out for it in open expectation. ... At the moment when the new awakes hope, suffering and dissatisfaction with the old are born'.[55]

> Faith ... means that through the history of Christ and the promises of the gospel, God reveals his future to men and has, thereby, granted

---

[49] Moltmann, *Hope and Planning*, 178.
[50] Moltmann, *Hope and Planning*, 178-79.
[51] Moltmann, *Hope and Planning*, 180.
[52] Moltmann, *Hope and Planning*, 180.
[53] Moltmann, *Hope and Planning*, 180-181.
[54] Moltmann, *Hope and Planning*, 181.
[55] Moltmann, *Hope and Planning*, 182.

them freedom. ... The prospect of this future coming from God already opens up here and now an open space of change and freedom which must be shaped by responsibility and confidence.[56]

From this detailed and helpful discussion of hope we can gain greater insight into the way Moltmann views the constitution of hope and how it functions. It is an 'intentional horizon' which shows 'the driving superiority of the real future over the planned future' and it works by allowing suffering generated by love, and 'leads man to the origin of freedom, of what is future and possible'.[57] It is the mechanism, he concludes, by which men 'should recognize meaningful goals, and find the courage to invest human and material powers ...'.[58]

Hope is that which gives us an attitude to the future, which includes our plans and goals, and a disposition towards that which is not yet possible. This attitude is not fatalistic but enables us to anticipate a future that may not seem probable. In this way it introduces us to a way of gaining freedom from the historical necessity of cause and effect. It makes us dependent more on the promises of others than on our own powers. We experience this relationship to the promises of others dialectically so that it leads us out of the fatalism of a world that is dependent on the contingent facts of history.

We can view hope as a power that motivates us by means of the time pressure of the future on the present. It then also creates the potential for suffering as we encounter the possibility of loving others. Loving relationships carry with them the possibility of disappointment because they may change in nature or cease to exist. Hope brings with it responsibility and confidence which may manifest themselves in courage.

The commands and promises of God can influence the way in which we who receive them perceive our relationship to God, one another and the world and the attitude and perspective that we adopt in the face of 'that which is unknown'.[59] In terms of our existential experience of life we then have the possibility of encountering the totally 'new thing' with what might be called 'personal strength'. Our hope is based on the revealed Word of God which itself is attested to, and validated by, past

---

[56] Moltmann, *Hope and Planning*, 183.
[57] Moltmann, *Hope and Planning*, 198.
[58] Moltmann, *Hope and Planning*, 198.
[59] For example, Josh. 1:9: 'Have I not commanded you? Be strong and courageous. Do not be terrified; do not be discouraged, for the Lord your God will be with you wherever you go'. God speaks these words and brings hope in the context of the exodus of the Jewish people from slavery in Egypt and as they are on the brink of taking possession of the land which God has promised to them.

historical events. Our relationship with the future is a dynamic one and provides motivation and strength.

It is our commitment and attachment to hope that provides the possibility of the promised 'new thing' and the resources needed to encounter it. We also face the suffering, or 'existential angst', which accompanies the possibility that the new thing may not happen as promised. We live within the dialectic of this uncertainty and the certainty contained in the type of hope referred to in Hebrews 11:1. This hope, when 'contained within' faith, enables the faith to be described as 'being sure of what we hope for and certain of what we do not see'.[60] We also live within the uncertainty generated by our experiences of encountering new things. This may tell us that things may not always be as they appear, nor work out as it appears they will.

Moltmann uses the category of *hope* as a transcendent category and one that is a bridge for facilitating transcendence through a revised concept of space.

> The ecological concept of space has run up against some misunderstandings, and in order to avoid these I should like to use a *perichoretic concept of space* as a way of apprehending the experience of space as I have described it–space as mutual in-existence. Perichoresis is also called *circuminessio*, mutual indwelling, and mutual *inhabitatio, 'habitation in'*. This offers a better way of describing the warp and weft of life than ecological terms for space. The perichoretic space concept of reciprocal in-existence corresponds on the creaturely level to the concept of the eternal inner-trinitarian indwellings of the divine Persons.[61]

Whilst Moltmann takes issue with Heidegger on a number of points it seems that when he is referring to being, and the relationship of the being to and for others and the category of space, there are some similarities with Heidegger's use of *Dasein*. Macquarrie has noted that '*Dasein* is not synonymous with "human being" but is, in Heidegger's words, "a pure expression of being". He also calls it a "clearing", like a clearing in a forest, the place or the "there" where being is brought to light'.[62] For Moltmann, however, the 'clearing' is a creation of, and a characteristic of, the person who is in relationship.

> Just as through their reciprocal indwellings the divine Persons also form a common space, so community on the creaturely level forms the social space of reciprocal self-development. Created beings have

---

[60] 'Now Faith is being sure of what we hope for and certain of what we do not see' (Heb. 11:1).
[61] Moltmann, *The Coming of God*, 301.
[62] J. Macquarrie, *Heidegger and Christianity* (London: SCM Press, 1994) 4.

to exist side by side and together, and for this they need wide open spaces in which they can move freely. There is no subjective *freedom* without these *free spaces* in social life, spaces opened up by respect and affection, and secured through legal systems.[63]

As we act in love by creating space for others we endow them with freedom within the relationship that exists between them and us. We do this by giving them time, attention, care and affection. For Moltmann space is a non-tangible entity which exists alongside physical realities and allows a *dwelling within* which enhances, and gives substance to, other people. There is an overlapping of spaces as there is within the being of the trinitarian Godhead. The relational space that we create by giving to another creates space in their life. Because of our mutually indwelling relationship with God, this newly created space also exists within God. It is a fascinating illustration and explanation of the way in which we can perceive our existence.

It is important to remember the openness of the space to which we are referring. The infinite giving nature of God to mankind through the person of his Son means that there is a potentially infinite space in which we may exist. In relational terms this means that we limit the potential for our existence only by our fallen nature. When we perceive ourselves through hope as *being in Christ* it is as if we were on the edge of a large clearing in the forest that stretches as far as the eye can see and as far as the mind can think. Our experience of this space is one of being somewhere other than the place where we should be. It is as if we were exiles in a foreign land, and it is only hope that sustains us. 'This hope means that the time of history is experienced as exile, as the far country and remoteness from God, as existence under God's "hidden countenance"'.[64]

Moltmann shows that the foundation of the Christian hope of redemption and eschatological hope is in the outworking of the relationship that exists by the mutual indwelling of the Shekinah glory and creation. '"In Christ" we find a double dwelling: the indwelling of God and the indwelling of believers. This double indwelling becomes the foundation for the eschatological and universal hope of Christians for the new creation of all things'.[65]

We can conclude this section with an acknowledgement that these concepts of hope and space are very important in Moltmann's theological scheme. They form the basis of his understanding of 'being' and 'being within relationships'. They link experience of reality with history and with God's revelation. He views these things primarily at a

---

[63] Moltmann, *The Coming of God*, 301.
[64] Moltmann, *The Coming of God*, 305.
[65] Moltmann, *The Coming of God*, 306.

phenomenological level. He successfully illustrates how we can see the influence of God as dynamic and purposeful yet he allows for promises of freedom and challenge and 'being with' through mutual indwelling.

More importantly his scheme offers a way of viewing relationships that is not idealistic. It allows for the possibility that they may fail. If they fail it allows for their redemption. Perspectives link past, present and future. They link this world with the world that is to come. They allow us to picture God as being here in the present through his mutual indwelling of all creation and also as coming in the power of the future as it influences the present. There is a motivational power in eschatological hope as it dialectically encounters reality. These things together with Moltmann's use of the concept of the transcendent nature of relational space all provide constituents of an eschatological ontology of being, of God and man which are liberating in themselves.

The implications for Deaf people are considerable, as they are for the hearing. The way of viewing our being and our relationships to God, and others, offers a creative and redeeming alternative to the secular modern worldview. Compared to other Christian theological worldviews it offers scope for creativity as we face the possibility of new relationships in the context of community.

h. Being and Doing and Existing in Praxis

The social, political and economic scene has changed dramatically since the 1960s and this has affected theological reflection. Moltmann's theology was developed in the shadow of the cold war, fears of Soviet communist expansion and domination, and a rapidly developing and all pervading consumerism. His groundwork on foundational issues and his ability to respond to the perceived concerns of the age have enabled him to be adaptable and relevant in his theological thought. The priority of orthopraxis needed to be argued for in the 1960s and it need not be discarded now as irrelevant.

Meeks has noted, 'Moltmann has affirmed that the Incarnation has primacy over the *eschaton* when the question of knowledge is concerned'.[66] We have shown that the dialectically developed anthropology produces a doctrine of man that has an eschatological focus but allows for historical interaction with the world in the light of the promises of God and in the hope of their fulfilment. Man exists in this dialectic. The future is a part of his existence. Being 'in God' means he is in the future. God reveals himself through the power of the future, which acts on human beings and creates history. Knowledge of

---

[66] Meeks, *Origins*, 161.

what we are is composed of, in part at least, the dialectic that exists between the 'now' and the 'not yet'. God calls us to be 'for' and 'with' others. 'The Christian lifestyle arises in the field of tension between the silence of contemplation and the struggle of love for the life and freedom of others'.[67] Our being is dependent on relationships with God and others.

Meeks crucially says, '[f]or some time modern theology has known that it had to live with one foot in the church and one foot in modern society. With the "dialectic of reconciliation" this delicate balancing feat is historically possible'.[68] The reality of the church, says Meeks, includes the fact that 'the whole life of the church is defined by and directed towards its mission'.

> [T]he church is not always acting in the world. The church cannot be exhaustively construed as mission. From the perspective of the Incarnation, the proclamation of the Word and the constitution of the congregation out of a new humanity have a certain theological and temporal priority over the act of mission ... the church can be spoken of as a community which is more than missionary existence for the world.[69]

Bauckham noted recently, that in Moltmann's developed model of the church, '[a]ccording to his promises Christ is present now in two forms by identification, both of which anticipate his future presence in person at the parousia'.

> As the exalted Christ he identifies with the church in its apostolic mission of proclamation, and in this way is present in the Gospel, sacraments and fellowship of the church, which anticipate his kingdom in the world. These are, therefore signs of his presence and so where the true church is to be found. But also, as the crucified Christ he identifies with the poor, who anticipate the kingdom, not in active mission but in suffering expectation. The true church is therefore to be found in fellowship with the poor. The church exists in the presence of Christ only when it links the two forms of Christ's presence by missionary presence among the poor...[70]

In contrast to this model the church in the UK sometimes presents a picture of being predominately 'middle class' and concerned more with the maintenance of the status quo rather than being in a dialectical relationship to the world through identification with the poor. Since the 1960s, within the mainstream denominations, there has been much

---

[67] Moltmann, *Open Church*, 46.
[68] Meeks, *Origins*, 163.
[69] Meeks, *Origins*, 162.
[70] Bauckham, *Theology*, 130.

more use made of small groups to help people experience church as community. The house church movement also represents a significant alternative model emphasising the community involvement of its members with one another and those outside the church. Within traditional churches and organisations, such as the Salvation Army, there has been a continuation of slow but faithful attention to the needs of the marginalized in society. Society has provided much more money, relatively speaking, for social welfare programmes and for funding the development of voluntary organisations.

The quality of provision in the church for Deaf people, however, continues to be at a low level. In a debate at the General Synod in 1997, which considered Deaf people in the church, Canon Edward Burns (Blackburn) noted that 'The Church of England had 15 full time chaplains, a third of whom were not fully qualified'. Another difficulty was also noted.

> The problem ... was the theology of language in many churches, which was a "genuine blockage" [to the development of Ministry among the Deaf.] For some, God's truth was very clearly bound up with words, and it was necessary therefore to revisit our theology of God as communicator through the body and all the senses, as well as verbally.[71]

Within society and the church there is a felt need to attend to those who are less well off but the structures appear inadequate for the task. At a theoretical level, the structures rely on a perception of man and his relationship to the world that has economic efficiency high on its list of priorities. We perceive self as an autonomous entity, which has as its goals wholeness, fulfilment, pursuit of pleasure and the avoidance of suffering. We may become aware of the need to relieve people of suffering but this has to compete with hedonistic activities for time and attention. Moltmann invites us to enter into dialogue with others to confront these issues. Only as the importance of his thought and work percolates through our seminaries and ministerial training colleges will people at a local level become aware of it. Then we may see the opportunity for existing structures to be changed.

Alternatively, the church would do well to consider building new structures based on the understanding of self, God and the church, which Moltmann has provided. When the power of the Coming God in the form of the parousia is recognised we may expect and hope for a church and people that identify with the poor as Christ commanded.

---

[71] Elaine Storkey (London) Synod Report, *Signs, Magazine of the National Deaf Church Conference* (Autumn 1997) 4.

Summary and Conclusion

In this chapter, we looked at the implications of Moltmann's eschatological ontology for his doctrines of God and man and the understanding of our identity.

We saw that Moltmann gives priority to the potentiality of the coming of God by focussing attention on the messianic nature of God's saving truth which breaks through the phenomenal experience of time by providing hope. We noted that we are to understand this hope as dynamic, moving or transient and it introduces into our perception of being the possibility of the *new thing*. We gain knowledge and experience of this hope through the dialectical process we are involved in as we encounter the scriptural record of the promises of God and the fulfilment of these promises.

We noted that Moltmann's doctrines of God and man provide an understanding of the kingdom of God which allows for the experience by God of the suffering of man, which Moltmann identifies as being as a result of man's alienation from God and God's creation. He also encourages ecumenical thought and action because he emphasises the acceptance of diversity within unity. We saw how Moltmann's purpose in developing his doctrine of God in this way is to ensure that it has within it the potential for therapeutic application in the form of reconciliation.

We noted that Moltmann sees our reality as perceived against a backdrop of the all encompassing reality which exists *within* God, using the concept of our perceptual horizon. Rather than believing that 'nothingness' exists beyond that which is perceived, which would ontologically threaten us with annihilation, he suggests that our boundaries are defined, more clearly, against the all-filling horizon of God.

This holistic approach to the doctrine of God enables Moltmann to link material reality and action. We noted similarities with Johansson's nested intentionality, which acknowledges the dual character of praxis, whereby actions take place and form, and reform, societal structures. This view links the individual and societal views of being and self. We saw that Moltmann seeks to extend it by introducing theologically a third level, or participant, in the interaction, namely God's revelation of himself and his will. In this way, individual drives and socially produced intentions are affected as God influences the decision making will of man. We may perceive this as the foretaste of the kingdom of God as it acts therapeutically by reconciling disharmonies and differences within and between human beings, as individuals or as groups, and in their relationship with God and his creation.

We saw how the identity of Jesus Christ affects Moltmann's doctrine of God. He reveals his identity in the paradox and total contradiction of his death and his resurrection. His identity is a dialectical identity. This is an open dialectic in that it has its resolving synthesis only in the *eschaton*. From this identity of Christ come the titles of Christ which anticipate his future and which, being open and flexible, announce the promise of what will be. From this is derived the being of the church which is stirred to mission through the anticipations of the future announced in the words, titles and being of Christ. The church itself therefore provides a link, through this theological understanding of God, man, Christ and the church, between the apparent discontinuities in life and particularly between life and death, past and present, God and history.

We looked at how Moltmann's scheme has a number of emphases that we could view as positive in relation to Deaf people and their situation in the world. Firstly, there is his holistic approach to reality, which acknowledges the incompleteness of all beings. Within this approach, there is no reason to treat Deaf people differently from hearing people because of their deafness, other than to accommodate the fact that they speak a different language. Secondly, there is his view of the redemptive and salvific nature of God's revelation, which offers a promise of renewal and release from all oppression. Thirdly, there is his stress on interrelatedness, co-dependence and eventual reconciliation of all people, which it is the task of the church to announce and usher into being.

At a time when Deaf people are beginning to liberate themselves from forces which have oppressed them in the past these aspects of Moltmann's theology can appeal as a way for Deaf people to understand themselves and their relationships.

We looked at how Moltmann stresses the importance of orthopraxis alongside orthodoxy, and uses dialectical understandings of knowledge and perception.

We next examined Moltmann's understanding of the identity of God and man in the context of current identity crises. The eschaton causes us to be concerned with the certainty of Christ's return rather than the timing or manner of it. We looked at the different understandings of time in modern society which cause the individual to place more emphasis on personal fulfilment rather than self-sacrifice. In the modern world, the future has less value, as we have traded it for current 'gain'. We contrasted this with Moltmann's dialectical understanding of the future and God's covenant relationship to mankind. We can see that he fulfils his promises in history and this links us positively with the past and provides strength and motivation in the shape of hope for the future.

We next looked at how Moltmann uses the categories of perspective, hope and space and the value he places on an open view towards all things. Perspectives provide a link between idea and matter itself and are a hermeneutical tool. They function in a similar way to attitudes. They link past experience and knowledge with the future possibilities of existence. We can link perspectives with our plans for the future and they can then produce an anticipatory disposition for the future.

We noted that hope and planning exist as metaphors or symbols by which we can describe our ideas about the future. Hope exists in the realm of inter-personal relationships and presupposes the 'otherness' of the 'other'. It also presupposes trust whereby we may make and keep promises. How we relate to promises in the present can affect our experience.

We saw that Moltmann's view of theological perspectives draws on an analogy with visual perspectives. God creates a new space for being through a dialectical process of our relationship with the promises of others, which releases us from the shackles of the contingent facts of history. For Moltmann, the promises of God in Scripture are a symbolic way of understanding our relationship to God and give us a biblical perspective, which shapes our perception. Hope is an intentional horizon that creates an open space for change and freedom. It is a transcendent category and a bridge to that which is beyond our perception. For Moltmann, respect and affection open up 'free spaces' within social life, like a clearing in the forest and the openness of the 'space' is potentially infinite.

We made a connection between the way in which sign language exists in space and needs movement for its expression with Moltmann's use of these concepts in his theology. We also linked the way in which Deaf people, more than hearing people, hold a concept of self which is dependent on their relationship to other people. We have sought to draw significance from the theoretical understanding of being which in Moltmann's case involves the use of an analogical use of physical space and movement, with the physical reality of sign language, which needs space and movement for its existence.

We noted how over the past 30 years there have been great changes in the emphases of theology, as society has changed its concerns. For Deaf people too there have been significant changes in the way in which they perceive themselves. We saw how the church had adopted some simple notions of the importance of community for church life in the form of an emphasis on small group experiences and the value of personal relationships. We saw how Moltmann developed his concept of the being of the church more fully in this period. We saw that a breaking away from a theology in which God's truth was constrained by words could benefit the wider church as well as ministry to and among Deaf people.

To summarise then, in this chapter, we have carefully considered the way in which Moltmann's eschatological ontology is central to his theological thought and how it affects his doctrines of God, man and the church. We have argued that, by using a method that promotes openness and suggests possibilities Moltmann has provided an ecclesiology that addresses many current concerns of Deaf people.

Chapter 5

The Nature of Communication within Relationships in Moltmann's Ecclesiology and its Relevance to Deaf People

Introduction

In this chapter, we will look at Moltmann's understanding of communication. In his model of the church, which is congregational in nature,[1] he emphasises a non-hierarchical structure and 'friendship type' relationships that exist within a framework of eschatological hope. This influences the way communication takes place within those relationships and its content.

We will look at the processes involved in communication and this will include theories on the functioning of the mind and social factors. We will examine the effect his theological concepts have on communication.

Our argument in this chapter will be that Moltmann's conception of the church facilitates the development of good models of communication for Deaf and hearing people through providing flexible theological concepts. We will show that these have the potential to function well at both the theoretical and practical levels. We will examine the way in which Moltmann uses theological categories and how they operate at a symbolic level and have an iconic function. We will show that they operate creatively within our consciousness by providing a bridge that transcends reality as perceived by our senses and the reality that we can only know by faith. We will examine the processes of dialectical tension in these symbols that echo the dynamic iconic symbolism of some Deaf signs.

We will start with our examination of communication by considering the social trinitarian nature of God and Moltmann's eschatological and relational human ontology. We will see how he views the process by which God communicates to his creation and the way in which intuitive and emotional factors affect the communication process.

---

[1] See Moltmann, *Trinity*, 202: 'The presbyterial and synodal church order and the leadership based on brotherly advice are the forms of organisation that best correspond to the doctrine of the social Trinity'.

We will show that there is evidence within his theological programme to support the concept of pre-existing archetypal internal symbolic representations. In this concept, communication partly uses symbols that pre-exist within us and enables them to be uncovered. This potential may be latent in humans at birth. We will link this with Moltmann's view of God's revelation of himself that is an unveiling of his characteristics. We have the 'shape' of these within us from birth and as God enlightens us he causes them to be 'unveiled' to our understanding.

a. Methods used by Moltmann to Define Communication in Relationships

In this section, we will examine the way in which Moltmann uses certain concepts to define the process of communication. These include trinitarian relationality and suffering, eschatological hope, God's history in the world. We will also look at our attitudes to these.

Moltmann's theology has been a part of a recent trend towards recovering a trinitarian understanding of God and his creation. Moltmann has helped to form the new paradigm by which we may view theological truths as existing within a trinitarian and relationally based framework.[2] Relational categories are central to his work and flow from his foundational theological work on the 'theology of hope'. We will consider the ways in which his eschatological ontology gives us an understanding of how communication takes place, both at the level of person with person, and at the level of person with God.

Moltmann says we should not view God as a subject perceived by man, but as the one whom we encounter through participation in his trinitarian community. This trinitarian community is in relationship with creation itself. Communication therefore takes place in the actual process of living and being. Participation in the lives of those communicating is necessary for the process of communication to occur. This is the experience of life. Communication occurs within a holistic and ecological doctrine of creation so '[t]o be alive means existing in relationship with other people and things. Life is communication in communion'.[3]

Talking of this relationship between human beings and creation Moltmann argues that our doctrine of creation should incorporate 'symbols which mould the unconscious and guide awareness in a way which is unknown to the conscious mind'. He says he wants to integrate into his thinking 'the approaches of poetic perception and

---

[2] Thompson, *Trinitarian*, 4.
[3] Moltmann, *God in Creation*, 3.

intuition' and an '[e]schatologically orientated theology [which] is dependent on a messianic imagination of the future, and sets this imagination free'.[4]

By addressing the question of suffering and linking it with eschatological hope Moltmann brought a fresh dimension to the understanding of communication. The distractions of the temporal world can easily take our attention from eternal matters. Scripture enables us, through its stories of promise and fulfilment, to adopt biblical thought forms and perspectives that enable us to reinterpret our experiences in the light of the promised future as well as in the light of the past. God illuminates our understanding as we perceive a loving God with the nature and characteristics revealed to us in the person of Jesus Christ who shares in our suffering with us.

Moltmann links our interpretation of the past with the future hope of the coming kingdom of God. This provides direction and a correct attitude in the present by linking us with the outworking of God's purposes in our lives. We should note that the word 'attitude' can refer to bodily posture in relation to another. It also has a more psychological use, describing the self's relationship to 'others' and that which is 'other'. Attitudes can arise from within us, through personal reflection, from social forces, or through the affiliations we have with others. Our affiliation to a Christian group will result in us adopting certain attitudes as we share the values and beliefs of the group. We may also adopt certain attitudes as our pragmatic adaptations to the group situation in which we find ourselves.

If we are open to our future attitudes can motivate us. Whilst our future may appear uncertain, our knowledge that there will be an ultimate reconciliation of all things can strongly influence our attitudes. God calls us to be open to him. Our eschatological hope will affect our worldview and the processes by which we perceive, interpret and interact with reality.

If God's hope is communicated by God's Spirit, then the regenerate will receive it at conversion. There will be an ontological change. Ontological hope may lie dormant within us, existing as a potentiality, until God activates it on conversion. This hope then provides us with religious attitudes and practices that, together with our social context and pragmatic reactions to life's events help us to perceive, and cope with, reality.

Upon coming into the new relationship with the Trinity, by the Spirit, we receive hope, or an awareness of it now being within us. The coming God will be in relationship with us by the Holy Spirit, who is the power of the future in the present. Our hope will then be knowl-

---

[4] Moltmann, *God in Creation*, 4.

edge. For Moltmann, it is ontological hope which gives rise to epistemological certainty.[5] Farley describes two aspects of the ontological nature of eschatological hope and our paradoxical experience of it. Referring to it as a 'Deep Symbol' he says that '[hope] tends to reside partly at least in the unconscious, in what we are in our deepest selves. More pertinent is that we experience hope only as something deeply paradoxical. Remove these paradoxes and we remove hope'.[6]

Moltmann says, '[t]here is no present identity of a man without continuity with his past'.[7] We find this continuity through an attitude of openness, which is active in us in the present through its links with the past and the future.

> Openness to the future is conditioned by openness to the past. Constant faithfulness to hope is reciprocally bound up with faithfulness to the earth. Christian faith understands itself as faithfulness to hope as it is mindful of the resurrection of Christ, and as faithfulness to the earth as it is mindful of the cross of Christ. Because it leads man into this history of God, it frees him for an acceptance of human life which is capable of suffering and capable of love.[8]

Moltmann shows how hope leads us to follow the example of Jesus and his teaching about the kingdom of God. This leads us to believe that within it there is to be an inversion of the normal hierarchy of relationships in society. The servant, and particularly the suffering servant, becomes the most appropriate role model for us. God has chosen to communicate himself to his creation primarily through the birth, life, death and resurrection of Jesus Christ and the witness of the Scriptures to these historical events. We communicate to a needy world the liberating power of God through actions and words that reflect our belief in these events.

Moltmann has provided an explanation of how all communication is 'open' in the same way that God is 'open' to the future. He is sovereign over all creation. He has allowed us freedom and as we make wrong choices we will separate ourselves temporarily from God and his ways. Openness in Moltmann's theology allows for the fact that our freewill and the consequences of our wrong decisions will bring suffering into the world.

---

[5] 'So, faith is being sure of what we hope for and certain of what we do not see' (Heb. 11:1).
[6] E. Farley, *Deep Symbols. Their Postmodern Effacement and Reclamation* (Valley Forge, Penn: Trinity Press International, 1996) 98.
[7] J. Moltmann, *The Crucified God. The Cross of Christ as the Foundation and Criticism of Christian Theology* (London: SCM Press, 1974) 311.
[8] Moltmann, *Crucified God,* 313.

Communication in the church should be within non-hierarchical relationships. Hierarchical structures within the church appear to be more prone to develop dominating and oppressive mechanisms. Such hierarchies, says Moltmann, stem from a wrong understanding of the Godhead and relationships within it. He argues that an oppressive patriarchal society and church will develop from an overemphasis on the priority of the Father in the Trinity.

It will help us now to consider how Moltmann uses some broad categories in the conclusion to his discussion concerning the 'Ways towards the Psychological Liberation of man'.[9] After interacting vigorously with Freud, he says 'the logic of the instincts differs from the logic of the understanding and is not always influenced by it'. Moltmann is separating reason and emotion.

> [T]he logic of the understanding needs a corresponding level of instinct and feeling on which it can develop freely. It needs a barrier against anxiety and the threat of death on the level of the feelings also, that is, a love of life which brings intelligence to the understanding and orients it.[10]

He has argued already in the chapter that the problem of man is the repression of the anxiety and fear that man has concerning his own vulnerability and mortality. For man to live effectively, and therefore communicate effectively, he must protect himself from these feelings Moltmann proposes that

> [t]he real problem in neurotic pattern formations and in the alienated religion of idols and ossified rituals seems to me to lie not in the various attempts at explanation and derivation, but in the effect of this religion on man'. ... [W]here men flee to rituals and idols in order to be rid of the burden of grief, the result is apathy, insensitivity, the fixation of life in obsessional repetitions. The law of repressions reduces the liveliness of a man. ... With images he builds a wall between himself and his intolerable experiences.[11]

When considering the balance of reason and emotion in the psychological make up and functioning of a person, Moltmann says '... the logic of the understanding needs a corresponding level of instinct and feeling on which it can develop freely'.[12] He considers that the emotional side of man enables the rational side to think creatively about the future in a different way. He shows that the answer to man's problem does not lie in finding the sources of repressed feelings and attempting

---

[9] Moltmann, *Crucified God*, 314.
[10] Moltmann, *Crucified God*, 314.
[11] Moltmann, *Crucified God*, 300-301.
[12] Moltmann, *Crucified God*, 314.

to deal with them, rather they should be dealt with by applying biblical understandings of idolatry and prophecy to correctly identify them for what they are. Various religious attempts may have been right in identifying the problem. They have not always understood that the answer lies in the power of recognising man's existence as being within God's *pathos*.

> ... Christian symbolism ... does not liberate an apathetic rationality of domination but sympathetic reason. ... The Christian symbolism of the situation of man in the *pathos* of God leads to the loving and suffering knowledge of man. It can therefore only take up the iconoclasm that is critical of religion and the psychotherapeutic liberation of man from his vicious circles and develop its own prophetic criticism of idolatry in parallel to that.[13]

A form of existentially based authentic living lies at the centre of Moltmann's philosophical framework. It is not self-centred and concerned with self-actualisation and fulfilment. It is God-centred and directs us to enjoy God and his creation. It modifies the restricting nature of rational thinking by suggesting that we employ instinct and feelings in understanding reality and it does this by offering an open future. Our worship is liberated and more joyful as we accept the anxiety associated with our thoughts of mortality.

Sociologically, Moltmann modifies a Marxist critique of man's problem within society. He recognises the alienation of man by the processes of modern society. Using biblical imagery he identifies as idolatry the attempts by man to solve his problems through the institutions of society. Man sees these problems as a need for meaning and avoidance of pain, whether physical or psychological. Moltmann makes conscious use of the relativity of values in each cultural context. We can note, for example, his comments concerning psychological health.

> [T]he Christian interpretation of the human situation must nevertheless also question the compulsive idolatry which the concepts of production and consumption introduce ... and develop another form of humanity. Suffering in a superficial, activist, apathetic and therefore dehumanized society can be a sign of spiritual health.[14]

In concluding this section, we can say that for the purposes of developing his ecclesiology Moltmann can rely on simple psychological models of the self because his emphasis is constantly on the dynamic nature of reality. Communication within his scheme also uses biblical

---

[13] Moltmann, *Crucified God,* 314.
[14] Moltmann, *Crucified God,* 315.

thought forms. These emphasise the process of finding truth in the journey travelled. Exodus type narratives have an analogical relevance for the reader. They also produce processes of thought that recognise the 'promise and fulfilment' nature of God's communication to man which has occurred in his history with the world. They are therefore also paradigmatic, prescriptive and normative for our self-understanding and our understanding of our world. For Moltmann, the direction in which we are going is all-important. If we are following the way of Jesus Christ then biblical imagery communicates who we are and what we should do on the journey.

b. The Effect of Symbols, Signs and Icons on the Formation of our Theological Concepts and Perception of Reality

In this section, we will be looking at how Moltmann uses symbols, signs and icons in the formation of theological concepts and the part they play in communication. We will look at how they communicate to us our perception of reality and we will note that Moltmann often uses the inherent dialectic in symbols in his theological categories. Our conclusion will be that by understanding the function of signs, symbols and icons in Moltmann's ecclesiology we will be helped to understand how his view of the process of communication could benefit Deaf people.

At the outset it will help us to note one definition of a symbol.

> A symbol has characteristics of a sign: it stands for, points to (indicates); in short, it signifies something. Characteristic of a symbol, however, is that it draws together facets of meaning of that which it symbolises, concentrating or compressing them in a pregnant fashion. A sign can also function in this way, when it serves e.g. as a token or a portent.[15]

To help us understand the way in which Moltmann uses symbolism in his theology we will consider the work of Dillistone on symbols. For Dillistone the primary significance and importance of a symbol is its ability to connect, and he says this 'focusing of attention on *connection* agrees with the original use of the root verb *symbollein* in Greek'.[16] He also notes the social function of symbols in connecting, including '... all kinds of bodily gestures and activities [that] also possess symbolic

---

[15] R.D. Knudsden, 'Symbol' in Ferguson and Wright (eds.), *New Dictionary of Theology,* 669-670.
[16] F.W. Dillistone, *The Power of Symbols* (London: SCM Press, 1986) 14.

significance'.[17] Symbols *are intimately related to social cohesion* and *to social transformation*.[18]

All symbols will follow two important principles, which are those of analogy and of economy. Symbols will have two essential principles, intensity and metaphorical tension.[19] A symbol, he says, '... is a powerful instrument to extend our vision, to stimulate our imagination and to deepen our understanding'.[20] Its function is to bridge the gap between what we perceive as the symbol and the thing that lies beyond it.

He builds on Berdyaev's proposal that the modern situation has seen the development of technique as being the dominant factor that has led to the development of culture. Paradoxically this threatens the extinction of symbols, without which culture cannot flourish. The answer that Dillistone proposes is to hold social law, which is necessary for culture to survive, in tension with the freedom, which comes from using symbols. Neither must have the overall dominance. '[M]an is for ever involved in the tension or dialectic between order and freedom. ... It is the *symbol* which can hold law and liberty together ...'.[21]

Traditional approaches to the use of symbols have used 'the dialectic of uniformity and diversity of symbols in liturgical history' noted by Tripp, who comments that in this dialectic is a tension that provides a 'creativity which is part of the inherent liveliness of the Church'.[22]

Dillistone's view of symbols agrees in two respects with the view of the early Barth in that both emphasise the dialectic and existential aspects of the Christian faith. For the early Barth symbols mediate revelation. He speaks of the 'Word of God' as being apprehended by us in three ways, the written, the proclaimed and the living 'Word of God, Jesus Christ'. He speaks of these three as 'tokens' of revelation.[23]

Our experience of God is real. He communicates with us as he wills, but our subsequent reflection on it, and communicating to others concerning that experience, will involve the use of these tokens, or symbols, which are secondary items, and which we know as the written and the proclaimed 'Word of God'. This proclamation is the preaching and witnessing by God's people to his being and actions, and the congregation conveying from generation to generation the

---

[17] Dillistone, *Power of Symbols*, 15.
[18] Dillistone, *Power of Symbols*, 15 (his italics).
[19] Dillistone, *Christianity*, 35.
[20] Dillistone, *Power of Symbols*, 13.
[21] Dillistone, *Power of Symbols*, 222.
[22] J. Tripp, 'Worship and the Pastoral Office' in C. Jones, G. Wainwright and E. Yarnold (eds.), *The Study of Liturgy* (London: SPCK, 1978) 523.
[23] J. Baillie and H. Martin (eds.), *Revelation* (London: Faber & Faber, 1937) 62-65.

'truths' about God, through other symbols such as 'credal statements' or sacraments. In addition we can note that there will be a reservoir of local 'stories' or narratives of God's dealings with his people, as well as recorded evidence of these, which may occur in, amongst other things, art, music, writing and architecture.

All of these symbols, whilst having a reality within themselves, perform the function of pointing to a reality which is beyond, and also contain within them a meaning which encompasses that reality. It is this meaning which speaks at a non-verbal and non-literary level of that which is beyond.

Moltmann is in agreement with Dillistone when he says that real life requires the promise of a new future that is entered into freely. The symbol of the theological category of the eschaton and all that it promises invigorates the present and motivates us towards the future. For Moltmann, the symbolic function of 'eschatological hope' is held in dialectical tension with the ordering law of the history of God, as revealed through Scripture and the experience of the church.

For Moltmann, the openness that is intrinsic to a symbol is its key quality. This enables it to function with an element of indistinctness, at least when it is encountered initially. It is a loose, flexible tool to link past worlds with current worlds and current worlds with future possible worlds. We need this in order to avoid viewing life as a sequence of seemingly unconnected world models, which succeed each other in our consciousness. The symbol may become more distinct as we enter into the reality it represents. For it to be most effective it needs to operate alongside, and in dialectical tension with, an ordering system of laws which on the one hand constrain it and on the other hand draw further meaning out of it.

Some symbols, however, convey meaning to us merely by our encounter with them.[24] They may have inner 'secrets' or they may just cause something to happen within us as we encounter them. For example, Christians have used church architecture in this way to draw out a specific type of response of awe or reverence. The sheer size, colour and texture or the context of symbols will influence what they say to us.

Symbols appear to have the same 'vulnerability' as metaphors in that their power may sometimes become less with use. Symbols that appear in the liturgy of the church may change in their significance in the same way that words can change in meaning. New symbols and new ways of using old symbols can be a bridge between the expres-

---

[24] Playwright D. Hare recognises this in his fictional political play, 'The Absence of War', where the main character notes 'Words don't just have meaning, they also have an affect'.

sions of faith of the church and the changing society in which it finds itself. A modern example of this is seen in the understanding of the church, emphasised in the Roman Catholic Church since Vatican II, as being both 'The Body of Christ' and 'The People of God'. Küng has noted, '[j]ust as the real ecclesia is constantly evolving, so the ecclesiology of the ecclesia evolves too'.[25] Between them, these symbols have a dialectical creative tension, which we cannot merge.

Symbols, like metaphors, may change in their meaning. Gunton notes the effect of the community on such changes. For many English people he notes that there are two possible communities in which 'metaphors have taken shape and maintained their currency'.[26] These are Western culture and the church. He highlights the danger of metaphors changing their meaning over time. A practical effect of this may be that church models may not reflect the claims of the Christian faith. There may be 'hollowness' apparent, a dichotomy between the proclaimed faith and the lived faith. Gunton says '[t]he actual shape the church's life and worship have taken is often a practical denial of such claims, making them appear the product of false consciousness'.[27] In so far as that consciousness is operating with inadequate meanings, then clearly it *is* the product of a false consciousness. Those Christian churches that use metaphors and symbols significantly should be aware of this tendency and guard against it.

The symbol of 'emotional currency' is useful to describe our interaction with others. We seem to exchange it as we interact with others, through the medium of our facial expressions, hand movements, bodily gestures and the words we use. In sign language Deaf people not only use facial expressions to convey emotion powerfully but also use them as part of the grammar of the language. 'Signers actually look at each other's faces, not their hands, when communicating'.[28] Emotion may act as a 'carrier' in sign language. The analogy here is of the radio wave that modulates and which uses a constant steady emission as a carrier for these modulations.

Words, spoken and written are part of the way in which we perceive our world. They are the code by which we describe and interpret reality and communicate with others. Deaf sign language users employ a visual and spatial code for these purposes. The fact that it is spatial and visual will affect the nature of the symbols in the minds of those communicating. The shapes and movements associated with particular signs used by Deaf people may incorporate, or mirror, signs and sym-

---

[25] H. Küng, *The Church* (Tunbridge Wells, Kent: Search Press, 1968) 12.
[26] Gunton, *Actuality*, 173.
[27] Gunton, *Actuality*, 198.
[28] Sutton-Spence and Woll, *Linguistics*, 81.

bols which have significance in the life of hearing people, either through their relationship with current experience, or through the memory of what these shapes and movements once signified and meant. Current signs may 'resonate' with the past in the internal world of the person perceiving them. They may 'conjure up' good and bad associations through their imagery.

Our perception of symbols is a part of the way that we form our beliefs and values and establish our 'internal model of reality'. Not only will external influences have shaped that world, but 'self talk' will also modify or help form it. Our hopes and fears, and our anticipations and expectations of future events, will be involved in the process of forming and reforming that internal model. The people with whom we interact will also contribute and provide us with linguistic and symbolic information. We try to 'make sense' of the world using our stored memories and new information. We may perceive the symbolic information we process as being clear to us or not clear. The information may be static and clearly defined like an image on a road sign, or moving and loosely defined like a gesture used to convey some fact or intention. We may also perceive it at a subconscious level. Such symbols might become for us component parts of the 'atmosphere' existing when we are in a place where an event is occurring.

It will be helpful for us, in understanding how Moltmann uses symbols and how sign language uses iconic signs, to consider how symbols differ from icons. Ouspensky and Lossky show how icons have a similar task to that of traditional theology in that 'the task of both alike is to express that which cannot be expressed by human means, since such expression will always be imperfect and insufficient'.[29] They also helpfully compare the methods of those who produce icons with the way in which parables are used in Scripture.

> [T]he methods used by iconography for pointing to the Kingdom of God can only be figurative, symbolical, like the language of the parables in the Holy Scriptures. But the content expressed in this symbolical language is immutable, both in the Scriptures and in the liturgic image.[30]

Also important is the purpose and function of the icon.

> The purpose of the icon is not to touch its contemplator. Neither is its purpose to recall one or the other human experience of natural

---

[29] L. Ouspensky and V. Lossky, *The Meaning of Icons* (Crestwood, New York: St. Vladimir's Seminary Press, 1982) 48.

[30] Ouspensky and Lossky, *Icons*, 49.

life; it is meant to lead every human sentiment as well as reason and all other qualities of human nature on the way to illumination.[31]

Lossky presents the tradition of the church and Scripture as being the vehicles by which it preserves and passes on its faith but presents them as equally representing 'different modes of expression of the Truth'.[32]

Icons, used in the contemplative life, express in earthly materials and forms, that which is heavenly and ultimately inexpressible. They do this just as dogma preserves truth in words that are inadequate. Both are 'witnesses of Tradition ... the narrow door which leads to knowledge of Truth in the Tradition'.[33] Lossky also says,

> [t]he fundamental principle of this art is a pictorial expression of the teaching of the Church, by representing concrete events of sacred History and indicating their inner meaning. ... The image is reduced to a minimum of detail and a maximum of expressiveness.[34]

At the heart of the icon is a mystery that is partly revealed by it and through it. 'The mystery enacted and the mystery depicted are one, both inwardly in their meaning and outwardly in the symbolism which expresses this meaning'.[35]

In the Iconoclastic Controversies (726-843) Theodore the Studite '... argued that the icon was a true representation of the *hypostasis* (i.e. person) of its subject, but that it had a different nature (*ousia*; ... [s]ubstance). An icon of Christ was thus able to bring the believer into direct contact with his person but it was not an idol'.[36] In the icon the third dimension is believed to be the transcendent divine reality.

We believe that the function of the icon can be seen as similar to the function of theological concepts constructed in words and used for dogmatic pronouncements, preaching and teaching. It is also similar to the function of the bread and the wine in the Eucharist. The believer is led to a greater experience of the Divine revelation through the encounter with the icon. The icon is part of the container and conveyer of truth, yet it consists of that truth itself.

Signs, symbols and icons can all contribute to the 'atmosphere' of a situation. It is within this atmosphere that relationships exist and communication takes place. We can consider, for example, the atmosphere

---

[31] Ouspensky and Lossky, *Icons*, front cover, inside.
[32] Ouspensky and Lossky, *Icons*, 15.
[33] Ouspensky and Lossky, *Icons*, 20.
[34] Ouspensky and Lossky, *Icons*, 27.
[35] Ouspensky and Lossky, *Icons*, 31.
[36] G.L. Bray, 'Iconoclastic controversies' in Ferguson and Wright (eds.), *New Dictionary of Theology*, 326.

we experience during a church service, which is formed by a number of symbolic and other factors that include architecture, music and liturgy. The attitudes, relationships and roles of those taking part will also contribute to the way we perceive the atmosphere. Our past experiences and future expectations may also be significant in determining how we perceive the service. In an older church building, the knowledge that worship has taken place there in a similar form for, say, a thousand years, may influence our perception of what is occurring. As we entered, we may have seen the list of vicars who were responsible for looking after the souls of the parish during that time, and heard the bells chiming as they have done for many hundreds of years. In some senses we are participating in a drama being re-enacted and our knowledge of the main constituents in the production of that drama determine our internal world model of that external reality. We also form our expectations within and through that world model.

We may experience a large number of symbols at one time that provide us with information for our internal model. Sometimes these symbols provide information which seems to conflict with that given by other symbols. Our ability to synthesise this information, or not, will result in us gaining a coherent picture of reality or one which has within it discordant elements. Sometimes it may not be possible to synthesise the symbols perceived and the resultant tension may be a creative or destructive one. Moltmann frequently emphasises the creative and transformative function of metaphors. He says '[m]etaphors of the historical future are *movable symbols*, as Ernst Bloch made clear' and 'go beyond what is at hand, and reach out in anticipation to the possible future by imagining what might be'.[37]

The relationship by us, to others taking part in the scene we have described, will also be significant when we try to 'make sense' of what is occurring around us. Confusion may develop when we process conflicting or unusual symbols. Other people, and their interpretation of the scene, may confirm what our sensory input is telling us is 'out there' or not. Confusion may also arise within us when our experience of reality conflicts with internal expectations of what might be expected.

Involved in the construction of the internal model of the world are our beliefs and values. They appear to act as a filter and a hermeneutical tool for us. They help us sort into order and prioritise what we perceive. They are the basis for our attitudes, and yet our attitudes will survive changes in our belief system, as they form part of our character, that is our innermost being.

---

[37] Moltmann, *Experiences in Theology*, 163.

Symbols of the past, existing in our memory, are clearly a part of the process by which we experience reality now. Our memory of events also contains our belief and values system and internally constructed world that existed at a previous point in our life. The past consists, at least in part, of symbols representing the past as we see it now. These symbols can intrude, and sometimes conflict with the world as we know it now, and cause internal dissonance. They may not have fully formed themselves and we may only partially understand them. Symbols that exist in our memory can influence us as much as any current event. Where we cannot relate them to specific known life events, we could view them as potential evidence of archetypal images retained by us, within the conscious and subconscious mind. They may be shared 'group' symbols, which form a part of the 'folk' consciousness of a group.

The symbols used in the biblical narratives can have a very strong influence on our current life as they help form, and interact with, our internal model of the world. They can aid our understanding of what happened many years ago, and help to form our expectations of what will happen. Promise and fulfilment can become a real and active part of our internal world model and processes. The scriptural record will influence strongly our understanding of cause and effect, as will the day-to-day dealings we have with members of the church today. Our relationship with reality will depend heavily on the symbols we use to interpret it. The priority we give to any of those symbols, over others, will occur as our belief system and values process them.

Symbols have a surplus of meaning that is valuable to our understanding of how they function. Moltmann says,

> [e]very experience that happens to us brings with it a context of meaning without which we cannot take in the experience at all. This wider horizon literally 'dis-closes' itself, in its first, daybreak colours, in the individual experience. ... Symbols represent this inherent tension, present in every experience, between the determined and the undetermined – the tension between particularity and totality, present and future. It is this tension that is the ground of the symbol's surplus of meaning.[38]

We should note that this 'surplus of value' in symbols is one of the major factors that enables us to move from one state of understanding to another.

In this section, we have seen how we may perceive reality and the place that symbols, and in particular theological and ecclesial symbols, have in providing details of that reality. We have noted how Moltmann

---

[38] Moltmann, *God in Creation*, 297.

views the experience of reality as being a dynamic process and that he sees both man and God involved in a constant movement within their relationships. We can see that communication needs the tools for transcending not only the realities of the natural and the supernatural worlds, but also for coping with the changing shape of both these realities in the past and the present, as they interact with each other.

c. Moltmann's Linking of Ontology and Communication

If we start from Moltmann's understanding of what it is 'to be' this will provide a way into understanding how he views communication. We have established already that being for Moltmann is eschatological. His ontology of man and ontology of God is eschatological. His epistemology flows from that starting point.

For Moltmann, the relationships within the Godhead and the way they exist and function determines how all other relationships exist and function. 'Being' itself is a relational concept. It is socially constructed and viewed as a dynamic process. Moltmann's approach differs from that of Berger and Luckman and Whitehead. Our perception of 'being' and reality derive from our direct and indirect interactions with God, Scripture and other persons.

We have discussed already how Moltmann uses a strongly dialectical understanding of the development of knowledge and history itself and that dialectical experience is part, at least, of what we experience in our encounters. It comes to us as 'other' and we experience the other, as 'Thou'. We are a person in relationship with another person rather than a subject in relationship with an object.

There is scope within Moltmann's understanding of communication for analogical processes as well as dialectical influences. He emphasises the holistic understanding of being and includes all creation as existing in God. A perichoretic understanding of relationships affects how Moltmann views being.

Moltmann understands God to have communicated to his creation through the real events of history recorded in Scripture. The events themselves happened in the context of a future that was 'open' in the sense that it was not foreknown in detail and predetermined by God. There will be a certain conclusion, however, which will be the reconciliation of all things and this will occur because of God's ultimate sovereignty.

We find ourselves involved in this scheme of unfolding events. We are appealed to through the witness of the gospel message to choose the way that facilitates reconciliation, redemption and peace.

As we have noted in the last section our perception of reality is affected by symbols. We can note that Moltmann speaks of the 'archetypal' nature of some symbols and, in this, draws significantly on Jung.

> Through the movement of their 'meaning more', symbols do not establish facts; they release experiences. Symbols do not define; they 'give us something to think about', and invite us to new discoveries ... They can only be discovered and dis-closed, for they are present in all languages and all traditions of awareness. There are fundamental patterns which lend bearings to human life, and to which language reverts again and again, because they provide an order to the unconscious. We call images which put a fundamental impress on the soul or psyche, 'archetypes'. ... An archetype is a predisposition of the soul which produces and orders concepts, absorbs experiences and gives them expression.[39]

For Christians, the greatest communication of all is the self-giving love of God evidenced in the sacrifice into death of his Son, Jesus Christ, and the taking up into the Godhead of the suffering associated with that death. The loss by God the Father is experienced as a reality by God, the Trinity, as separation occurs within the Godhead itself. God through his love provides a way to redeem all separation, suffering and death. That love also promises to overcome the current experiences of sin by us if we are open to receiving it. It functions in our lives as hope. This hope promises that at a future date all will be well. This hope in the future is the power of God in the present. God communicates an invitation to us, and the Holy Spirit acts as a communicator of that love, through his activity in the world, drawing people to follow God and the way of Jesus Christ.

In practical terms, Moltmann is open to the fact that the communication of God's love may occur through words, written or spoken, drama, song, music, dance and all the many other ways in which people express themselves in the course of their lives according to the abilities God has given to them. Creation also speaks, in part, of God the creator and witnesses to his love and promises.

Moltmann believes that the revelation of the character of God occurs through natural means, as well as through the words of Scripture, and there is now a hope in us of the ultimate redemption of all things. Moltmann's commitment to ecumenism, and even more his commitment to a philosophy that requires the future to be open, can be likened to other theological attempts to reconcile that which appears irreconcilable.[40]

---

[39] Moltmann, *God in Creation*, 297-298.
[40] See Marshall's excellent work in attempting to deal with the sometimes conflicting proposals of Calvinism and Arminianism, by looking at the many

Moltmann is using scriptural ideas not to form a system that coheres and is complete in itself but a theological approach that is open and creative and holds in tension seemingly irreconcilable truths. By these truths dwelling together in tension we find presented and communicated the caring heart of God whose will it is that none should perish.

In this section, we have looked at the way in which theological concepts in Moltmann's theology function as symbols in linking his ontology and communication. Not only do they represent another reality in the way that a sign does but they also have an iconic function in providing a bridge for the person using them to transcend the gap from earthly to supernatural realities. They operate through dialectical and analogical processes and provide a powerful means of connecting, through a fluid and dynamic epistemology, an eschatological ontological understanding of God and man. They therefore fit well within his overall project of having a theology that is open to the future.

d. Effects of Translation on Immediacy and our Experience of God

In this section, we will firstly look at the place vocabulary has in our understanding of God and ourselves. We will then look at the way in which mediation affects concept formation. We will look at how both language and the social contexts within which we find ourselves 'translate' reality for us. Deaf people may not benefit from the background sounds, which provide a great deal of contextual information to hearing people, but they may receive some additional information through interpreters. In his view of communication, Moltmann stresses the need for an attitude of openness and the fact that non-linguistic communication is as important as linguistic. This provides Deaf people, as well as hearing, with a positive reason for adopting his approach.

We have seen how Moltmann stresses the trinitarian basis for relatedness in human experience and how the trinitarian view of God provides a model by which we may understand God better and a model for understanding the true nature of human 'being'.

Gunton has described the early church's development of the doctrine of the Trinity, and the associated vocabulary for expressing the facts concerning it. With the word *homoousion*, for example, it enabled the church to 'establish a new ontological principle: that there can be a

---

references in the New Testament to 'persevere in the faith that you have received'. I.H. Marshall, *Kept by the Power of God* (Carlisle: Paternoster Press, 1995 [1969]).

sharing in being'.[41] This allows for us to retain the 'otherness' of the members of the Godhead whilst acknowledging their co-inherence and the perichoretic nature of their being within our concept of God. Gunton's point here is that it is the development of a modified vocabulary that provides the opportunity for us to form and maintain the conception.

Vocabulary can provide meaning in a direct referential way where it prescribes that to which it refers or an inferential, more indirect process, which enables us to form a concept perhaps by the juxtaposition of terms. In the case that Gunton is describing it was a change in the meaning of a word that gave the means to develop a changed conception. 'It was the function of the *homoousion*, the teaching that the Son is "of one being " with the Father, to express the ontological relation between the Son and God the Father' which the Nicene theologians adapted and so '... introduced a note of relationality into the being of God: God's being is defined as being in relation' he then concludes '[s]uch is the impact of the doctrine of the incarnation on conceptions of what it is to be'.[42]

Moltmann's scheme emphasises the eschatological being of God and man. He acknowledges the dynamic and changing nature of being that corresponds more closely to our experience of reality than fixed conceptions. We may best look on these as useful stepping-stones, enabling us to move to a position whereby we can incorporate dynamic conceptions into our models of understanding.

We are now concerned as to how far mediation occurs in the formation of concepts, how important the mediation is, and how it affects our concepts. Vocabulary is one of the tools of language and it mediates truth to us. Most experience can be reinterpreted in linguistic form and the greater our knowledge of an appropriate vocabulary the greater may be our ability to adequately describe what we have experienced. In Gunton's example we have seen how a word that is given a new meaning can 'stretch' a form of words and this allows us to conceive and understand that which was previously incomprehensible. Gunton speaks of the development of the doctrine of the Trinity.

> The crucial move in the process was to distinguish between two words whose meaning had until then been virtually synonymous, ousia and hypostasis, both meaning 'being'. ... [T]he capacity of a language increases by a process of de-synonymy: that is, the process whereby two words which are in the beginning synonymous take on

---

[41] C. Gunton, *The Promise of Trinitarian Theology* (Edinburgh: T & T Clark, 1991) 8.
[42] Gunton, *Promise*, 8.

different shades of meaning, and are so able to perform different functions.[43]

In this case we allow 'otherness' and 'oneness' to co-exist within the concept of God without the concept experiencing or causing us conflict or tension. The oneness is not mathematical but relational.

We can say we exist separately and we may also be described as being part of a group. Within our conception of the Godhead we need to overcome the 'part' element in the concept, as God is not separable into parts. With our language, it is easier for us to say that 'three particular persons are individuals yet they are also a group'. Grammar, vocabulary and the conventional use of our language make it possible for us to form a concept that proves to be satisfactory to our understanding.

We can say that to a certain extent language mediates reality. It expresses experience and can be adapted to express new experiences. Traditional Christian understandings of Scripture are that it reveals God to us. It does this by acting as a mediator and communicates to us truths concerning God and his dealings with the created order, often through a process of confrontation, by consolation or by conveying these in narrative, poetic, prophetic and other forms. The conceptions it provides inhere together because Scripture itself, through the process of development of the canon, inheres together itself. We could say that eternal truths are 'translated' into forms which we can understand and which we can understand at a range of levels.

Language is working, in the case of hearing people, at an internal level in so far as we receive sound stimuli and process them through our internal language processing mechanism. Vital to the process is the type of relationship that exists with the external world. Additional stimuli provide background information in the case of hearing people. All the environmental noise that accompanies any situation provides a context within which we may understand a specific verbal communication. It also provides validation of the nature of the relationship a person has with the world. This relational aspect of communication is crucial for our purposes. We may perceive a particular social setting as 'friendly' or 'hostile' and this determines the way in which communication takes place.

For sign language users, mediation occurs also through the process of using an interpreter. If the interpreter is adequately skilled, professionally proficient and sympathetic to the parties involved an adequate conveying of facts and concepts may occur. These will, however, be filtered through the mind and body of the interpreter. Knowledge may

---

[43] Gunton, *Promise*, 9.

be perceived in three levels, immediate and experienced, verbally reported and written in words. Concepts can be seen to exist at these levels in the experience of Deaf people except that there are four levels. These are directly experienced, viewed through the medium of sign language, viewed through the medium of an interpreter or recorded on film or videotape.

Moltmann stresses the relational nature of being church so there would appear to be an advantage to Deaf people in his model. The non-linguistic language of communication that occurs between the parties involved in a relationship of love can reduce or eliminate misunderstanding and allow for the development of a rapport that facilitates understanding. Within the less formal setting of relationships founded on Christian love, subtleties of meaning are able to develop more easily as experimental uses of language depend on trust and an openness in the mind of the parties involved.

e. Boundaries and Communication

We will now consider the differences in the experience of boundaries in the lives of Deaf and hearing people and how this affects communication. We will conclude that, as Moltmann emphasises solidarity with those whom society oppresses and marginalizes, because they are considered different, his theology offers the promise of practical improvements in the experience of Deaf people.

Communication, as we normally understand it, involves a reaching across from one thing or person to another. It implies that there is difference, distance and a method to be used. It follows from this that definitions of being, and the boundaries between beings, are crucial when discussing communication. Moltmann brings the future, in the form of a transcendent possible reality, into understandings of being and communication. Moltmann's emphasis in his theology is on a perichoretic understanding of the Trinity and of the place that God's eschatological nature has in our 'being'. He views transcendence not in traditional metaphysical ways but in ways that are concerned with the experience of 'persons' in history. In discussing the relationship between transcendence and immanence he describes how we use the terms.

> We generally use the word 'transcendence' for whatever exceeds the immanence that is present and open to our experience ... [w]e use 'immanence' for what projects into our experience, for the present, for this world. ... The two terms therefore belong together. They define each other mutually and are reciprocally related to one another.

> ... There is only a distinction and a relationship in the experience of 'the boundary'.[44]

As Moltmann presents the relationship between transcendence and immanence, he views each as defining the other in a dialectical way. They need each other to exist. One is the negation of the other. This is in the form of 'possibility' at the boundary between the two. Moltmann focuses on this aspect of theology as being paradigmatic. He effectively moves the concepts of immanence and transcendence from the metaphysical categories of 'this world' and 'the world beyond', to the category of history. He views history as being both this world as currently experienced and also the open nature of the possible future of this world. More specifically 'we understand by history the experience of reality in conflicts. ... [H]istory is rather the impression that man, together with his society and his world, is an experiment; and that not only is he himself a risk – his world is a risk too'.[45]

There is a distinction in Moltmann's thought here between an idea of the future and the 'utopia of the beyond'.

> The 'utopia of the beyond', properly understood, bursts apart all the worldly relations and cohesions we know. ... [T]he vision of a qualitatively new future of history can become a transcendent horizon which opens up and stimulates the process of transcending towards a new historical future.[46]

From this we can see that Moltmann is viewing all our current experience in terms of what we generally perceive as 'history', as being in a dialectical relationship through faith to the future, which is qualitatively different.

> The transcendence of the future of a 'Wholly Other' begins for it dialectically, in the lifting up of those who are 'the others' in a particular present and in particular societies. This is the link which is for faith 'the power of change'; and this is the way faith experiences, in the midst of history, the power of the God who transcends history.[47]

We need to bring these thoughts down to more practical applications when we are considering communication and Deaf people. We usually think of communication as defined in spatial terms, for example, we cannot hear the human voice at a normal conversational level beyond a relatively short distance without electrical or mechanical help. Visual

---

[44] Moltmann, *Future of Creation*, 1.
[45] Moltmann, *Future of Creation*, 14.
[46] Moltmann, *Future of Creation*, 15.
[47] Moltmann, *Future of Creation*, 17.

communication is normally limited to a few miles at the most. Beyond these boundaries, we could say that 'the other' exists.

If we pursue a model involving a socially constructed reality, we find that it is only as we are able to communicate with that which is 'other' and as it communicates with us, that we are able to clearly define ourselves by differentiating between that which is 'us' and that which is 'other'. If we view the boundary as being that point at which we encounter the 'other', then it is apparent that for the Deaf person the edge of reality is closer, in a spatially experienced sense, than it is for a hearing person. From this we could conclude that the possibility of non-existence, which in existential terms is the negating of current existence by the encounter of the 'other', is closer for Deaf people because the 'other' is closer.

If the paradigm, within which reality and our experience of it exists, uses primarily temporal characteristics then the encounter of the boundary between us and the 'other' takes place somewhere else. Moltmann's paradigm does this through emphasising the power of the open future as the eschatological 'coming of God'.

If we identify with those who are 'other' in the form of persons or groups who are viewed for one reason or another as different within our society, a sense of solidarity with them will be possible. This will arise as we accept our oneness with them and come through our openness to the 'otherness' of the eventual hoped for outcome of God intervening in history, in a new way, in the future.

The marginalization of those who are different within our society will be less likely to happen if the model we use to value them, and ourselves, includes the future 'vision' in the event of the eschaton. When this occurs it will transform all known reality, by reconciling all things to one another, and to God, through the shed blood of Christ on the cross at Calvary. This will occur not through the political and religious actions of us now but through the dramatic intervention of God breaking into history and so providing a qualitatively different future. The fact that we believe this to be an event that is going to happen will change our view of the present time and our relationships with others. It will also be reflected in the way that communication takes place between us.

f. Linguistic, Sociolinguistic and Neuropsychological Research

In this section, we will note significant factors from these other disciplines that directly impinge upon the current discussion. Within the confines of this work, we are primarily concerned with theological matters and cannot exhaustively examine the numerous implications, which these disciplines have, for the ways in which language and meaning affect understandings of identity and communication.

Downes shows that social conventions also determine language performance. He maintains that our ability to follow these social rules is not held biologically, as part of our linguistic knowledge mechanism, which Chomsky has argued is inherent in all individuals.[48] Downes sees people as subject to three forces. He describes these as the laws of nature, social laws or conventions, and the internal psychological process that can be described as 'intentionality'. He says '[c]onvention is a crucial part of our ability to make symbols and develop rules for actions. Social rules are, on the whole, conventional rules'.[49] He concludes that '... man exists on all these levels simultaneously'.[50] He challenges Chomsky, whom he says has '... a psychological and ultimately biological view of language'.[51] Besides this, he points out that, language has a textual function that will determine usage. By this he means that the tools of language components, such as parts of speech in a sentence, have specific purposes and the restricted nature of each tool's purpose will restrict the way in which we use it within language discourse. We can note that all three forces combined have the effect of both facilitating and restricting how we may use language to communicate.

For theological purposes, we can note that Moltmann stresses the importance of eschatological hope on a person's experience of self and the world. 'Meaningful action is always possible only within a horizon of expectation, otherwise all decisions and actions would be desperate thrusts into a void and would hang unintelligibly and meaninglessly in the air'.[52] He goes on to differentiate between the forces which society brings to bear on the individual, and the forces that are exerted through the church.

> The Church lays claim to the whole of humanity in mission. This mission is not carried out within the horizon of expectation provided by the social roles which society concedes to the Church, but it takes place within its own peculiar horizon of the eschatological expectation of the coming kingdom of God, of the coming righteousness and the coming peace, of the coming freedom and dignity of man.[53]

---

[48] Pinker has convincingly argued that grammatical ability in language use is also an 'instinct, an inborn, inherent characteristic in human beings'. Pinker, *Language*, 17.
[49] W. Downes, *Language and Society* (London: Fontana Paperbacks, 1984) 360.
[50] Downes, *Language*, 363.
[51] Downes, *Language*, 358.
[52] Moltmann, *Theology of Hope*, 326-327.
[53] Moltmann, *Theology of Hope*, 327.

We can extend the argument to say that the forces on a person from four directions are the forces that create intentionality in a person. These will be the forces of nature, the biological forces arising from within a person (including psychological functioning), social rules or conventions, and the forces that the church exerts through the 'missionary proclamation of the gospel ... God's promise of new creation through the power of the resurrection'.[54] By the proclamation of the gospel, Moltmann means not 'the "churchifying" of the world',[55] nor only salvation of the individual soul, but 'the realisation of the eschatological *hope of justice*, the *humanizing* of man, the *socializing* of humanity, *peace* for all creation'.[56]

Rather than viewing Christianity as a sub culture with its own conventions to maintain, Moltmann sees that it has a responsibility to confront the institutions of society.

> In practical opposition to things as they are, and in creative reshaping of them, Christian hope calls them in question and thus serves the things that are to come. With its face towards the expected new situation, it leaves the existing situation behind and seeks for opportunities of bringing history into ever better correspondence to the promised future.[57]

Psychologically, our understanding of our place within the world will affect our view of ourselves. We can explain that understanding of ourselves in terms of our relationship with what we perceive and know. Moltmann proposes that the basis for our understanding of our own ontology, and therefore our primary epistemological basis, is in our relationship to God viewed through the eschatological hope promised in Scripture. If we view all reality in that way, we will view communication as that which takes place within that framework.

Our interaction with the world, including the church, will reinforce or challenge these things. According to Moltmann the church is able to provide meaning but through mission not through its institutional structure. Thus, the 'force' that has primary influence on a person is that of the church as it carries out its mission. This forms the framework within which we may view existence itself.

Viewed linguistically, we might say that we determine the symbols with which we communicate, as Downes suggests, by the conventions of the culture within which we live. For the Christian, those symbols

---

[54] Moltmann, *Theology of Hope*, 328.
[55] Moltmann, *Theology of Hope*, 328.
[56] Moltmann, *Theology of Hope*, 329.
[57] Moltmann, *Theology of Hope*, 330.

will have their primary basis in Scripture and the tradition of the church.

Moltmann's placing of our understanding of ourselves within the potentially liberating power of the church, is a dynamic and revolutionary move. We understand our being as existing in dialectical relationship to the eschatological hope we have in the coming God. Moltmann says, our liberation also comes from an understanding of tradition that turns us towards the future.

> Promises are transmitted, events of God's faithfulness are recounted, all pointing to the future which has not as yet come about. In this conception of tradition the future which is announced and promised increasingly dominates the present. This tradition of promise turns our eyes not towards some primaeval, original event, but towards the future and finally towards an *eschaton* of fulfilment.[58]

Moltmann makes clear his intention when he says,

> [i]t is therefore the business of a comprehensive analysis of reality to take account of that radical questionableness of reality which provides the general presupposition for the special, Christian questions and statements in theology.[59]

In the light of this, we can say that, for communication to be in line with the new picture of reality he proposes, and for it to be authentic and effective, it will use the method and imagery of promise and fulfilment.

We will next consider, from a psychological viewpoint, how we construct meaning. Recent research in the field of human cognitive neuropsychology has identified areas of the brain that process certain aspects of thought.

Progress in this field is now very rapid but Ellis and Young provided an interesting survey of studies of 'the effects that brain injury in humans can have upon cognitive skills such as perception, language or memory'.[60] Their research has relevance to our study because theological concept formation in Deaf people may occur in a different way to the way it occurs in hearing people. The empirical research presented by them may support this theory.

Ellis and Young work with a model of the mind that has a modular basis. They then use the malfunctioning of one or more of the modules to explain an observed defect in perception, language or memory. By studying people who have suffered brain damage because of strokes,

---

[58] Moltmann, *Theology of Hope*, 298.
[59] Moltmann, *Theology of Hope*, 272.
[60] A.W. Ellis and A.W. Young, *Human Cognitive Neuropsychology* (Hove and Hillsdale: Lawrence Erlbaum Associates, 1988) back cover.

accidents or wounds inflicted by violence, it has been possible to construct models of the internal systems that may exist within the mind. Our minds use these systems to create meaning and process communication. This research proceeds by establishing that certain brain damage has clearly resulted in the loss of certain specific functions within the whole language processing function of the brain.

Some people may have lost the ability to gain access to the word that is, for example, the name of a particular fruit and with it the ability to access all words relating to the semantic sub-category of fruit within the mind. Loss results in the lack of ability to retrieve and say the required word. The person affected may still be able to communicate the meaning of the word by using mime or, in some cases, by using writing. This indicates that an 'image' of that to which the word relates is held elsewhere in the brain.

Concerning sign language, Ellis and Young note that sign language is predominately a left hemisphere specialisation.[61] All language processing is a predominately left hemisphere function, but the symbol aspect of signs, including the iconic, remains, as with hearing people, and in non-linguistic tasks in Deaf people, a right hemisphere function. It would appear that once we process a symbol in the right hemisphere, we pass the information about it to the left hemisphere for linguistic processing. The important point here is that Ellis and Young have shown that a model in which the brain is assumed to work on a modular basis is sustainable. Of significance for our purposes is the fact that retrievable knowledge, in the form of 'imagery', exists separately from linguistic information and is processed in a different part of the brain.

The fact that we hold imagery in a different part of the brain is of particular significance for our study here because the process of *knowing*, for all people, involves the processing of *both* linguistic and other information. We are proposing that we identify and know abstract concepts, such as beliefs, values and Christian doctrines, by using our visual-spatial mental capabilities to decipher the dynamic iconic information relating to them. This enables us to *know* them by their form and movement. Mary Brennan has contributed significantly to research in this area and says 'Iconicity, then, is essentially a potentially perceivable relationship which holds between the form of a sign and its referent. The referent itself may or may not be concrete'.[62] She goes on to say that some analysts of sign language intuitively recognise non-arbitrary relationships between many signs and their meanings. She argues that these signs often appear to use an *indirect* appeal to a visual

---

[61] Ellis and Young, *Human*, 262.
[62] M. Brennan, *Word Formation in British Sign Language* (Stockholm: University of Stockholm, 1990) 16.

metaphor. Signers may employ these creatively and in varying ways, depending on the context of the communication and the subject matter they are communicating. These non-conventional and non-arbitrary visual-spatial signs, also often depicting motion, can more adequately express relationships between the objects, ideas and information being communicated, than would be the case if they were not used. The implication from Brennan's argument is that although verbal languages also use metaphors in a direct way they frequently use indirect appeals to visual metaphors, which create iconic imagery processed in our brains, separately, but in parallel with, the strictly linguistic components of communication.[63]

The practical impact of this for our study is that when thinking of abstract concepts, such as doctrinal beliefs, we can think of them as consisting of, or being able to be understood through, iconic imagery. This leads us to consider the possibility that when we *understand* what we believe to be the truths of God we perceive them as having a *form* which we recognise as a form in the visual-spatial sense. Within Moltmann's method is this indirect appeal to visual, spatial and moving metaphors. His method involves the suggesting of possibilities and this means that he may sometimes only vaguely outline the 'shape' of that to which he is referring. It is this 'hinting at' that can enable us to begin to grasp aspects of God and his revelation that so often elude straightforward descriptions. As the poet is able to use words by their association and juxtaposition to convey meaning far beyond that which they otherwise have, so Moltmann's creative 'suggesting' approach often leads to our being able to comprehend theological concepts in dynamic forms.

As well as holding within the brain information that is essential for communication, signs and symbols, which exist in the material world, 'store' information. We interact with these external symbols by using our internal knowledge and experience of them. An example to illustrate this is of a chef in a restaurant who takes a number of orders. If business is slack, he may store the information in his short-term memory. When it is busier, he may rely on the information on the tickets provided by the waiters. Another way might be for him to place one

---

[63] We should note also Sarah F. Taub's important work in the area of metaphorical iconicity which shows that signs can share both metaphoric and iconic 'mappings', for further details of her approach see her 'Iconic Spatial Language in ASL: Concrete and Metaphorical Applications', paper presented to Mind III: the annual conference of the Cognitive Science Society of Ireland; Dublin, Ireland; Aug. 17-19, and her book, *Language from the Body. Iconicity and Metaphor in American Sign Language* (Cambridge: Cambridge University Press, 2001).

symbolic item for each order on the table in front of him to remind him what meal he is going to prepare. For example, an egg reminds him of an omelette. For our argument, we would also see symbols as being culturally specific, so for example in Hong Kong, the egg may represent egg fried rice.

Objects that are 'culturally specific' also have a status, a social significance, which is symbolic in nature. Social roles have an important symbolic function particularly within formal settings in a society. As Hollander has noted '[t]he biggest difference between formal and informal interaction is that the latter depends more on individual dispositions and satisfactions'.[64]

Expectations of role performance are culturally defined. The symbolic nature of the social role acts as oil in the machinery of society enabling it to run more smoothly. For example, in some circumstances if a chef walked out with the prepared meal, instead of giving it to the waiter to take to the customer, the social convention may have been broken. The exception might be that it would be acceptable for him to do this in a very expensive restaurant in the West, or a poor people's eating-house in the East. In both cases, it might be socially acceptable for the person who has cooked the meal to serve it.

There could be in each person's mind a store of the possible actions required in any given situation to meet the requirements of the conventions of a society. It is likely that social cues produce appropriate action. We learn such action from childhood by participating in '*reciprocal role relationships*'.[65] A store, or lexicon, of actions appropriate for different situations seems likely. The various possible expectations of any social situation are available like a 'vocabulary of action' that can be used according to the 'grammar' of the society in which a person finds himself required to act. These interactions involving symbolic objects and roles, with which we are familiar in society, have an element of *dance* about them. Moltmann has noted how

> The Christian traditions of the patristic church took over the image of the world as dance from the ancient cosmologies, and liked to associate them with eschatological notions about 'the play of the heavenly dance'.[66]

Names of people and the names attached to their social status have symbolic significance and functions also. Social interactions contribute to the development of the individual and symbolically form part of

---

[64] E.P. Hollander, *Principles and Methods of Social Psychology* (New York: Oxford University Press, 3rd edition, 1976) 213.
[65] Hollander, *Principles*, 214.
[66] Moltmann, *God in Creation,* 306.

The Nature of Communication 173

their being with which they communicate. Moltmann views the social dependability of a person as developing from the harmonisation, which a person experiences with himself and his environment. This process is one of 'dependability and faithfulness' which comes from the identity he forms for himself by

> ... his life history [which] is denoted through *his name*. Living together socially consists of a dense web of promises and fulfilments, compacts and dependabilities, and cannot exist without these structures of trust.[67]

Our hopes and fears and our anticipations and expectations of future events will be involved in the process of forming and reforming our internal model. The people with whom we interact and with whom we spend our time will all contribute by providing us with linguistic and symbolic information. We try to 'make sense' of the world by using our stored memories and this new information. In the world of Deaf people such communication may on occasions be more direct, perhaps because so many signs are themselves iconic in nature. We have noted that the relational aspects of communication derived from Scripture, which may exist in non-linguistic form, are important for Moltmann. Deaf people have a greater understanding of their experience of life through the community in which they exist. The community aspect of 'being' and communicating, which derives from Moltmann's understanding of Scripture, may therefore have more significance in the lives of Deaf people than in the lives of hearing people.

g. Communication in the Church

In this section, we are concerned with the fundamental ways in which God communicates with mankind and how Moltmann's ecclesiology views that communication as taking place. We will not be dealing, in detail, with the practicalities of interpreting in a church service or the methods to be used in conducting a church service for Deaf people. These are mainly practical matters that require the application of non-theological administrative and organisational techniques together with an awareness of Deaf culture and pastoral sensitivity.

Care needs to be taken to ensure that the best possible setting exists for Deaf people to experience church. Our task here is to establish a theological understanding of the church that will help those involved in this process. In Moltmann's ecclesiology, he emphasises how the gospel contributes, through hope and openness, to relationships that are liberating and to a faith that brings into being the kingdom of God.

---

[67] Moltmann, *God in Creation*, 262.

Armed with the results of these reflections the caring pastor of a Deaf congregation should be better equipped to minister God's love to Deaf people.

Firstly, we need to note the fact that 'movement' in all perceived reality is important for Moltmann. We cannot understand anything in terms of a fixed reality because all reality exists in the movement of time.

> ... [T]he church can only understand its own position or abode in participation in the movement of the history of God's dealings with the world, and therefore as one element in this movement. Its attempts to understand itself are attempts at understanding the movement of the trinitarian history of God's dealings with the world; and its attempts to understand this movement are attempts at understanding itself.[68]

For Moltmann the desire and ability to communicate and the means of communicating are in the very openness of the being of God that we perceive in the history of God's dealings with the world. Moltmann makes an interesting contrast between the openness of God and the openness of the created being.

> We cannot speak of the love of God as being open to the world and time in the way that we can of the creature, which has to be open to the world and time out of 'deficiency of being', but we can do so on the basis of the divine fullness of being and superabundance of life which desires to communicate itself.[69]

He therefore sees the openness of God as an intrinsic characteristic of the community of the triune God. The overflow of love from this community forms the act of communication by God with his creation. This takes place in the 'history of the Trinity'. About this Moltmann says:

> [i]f we therefore talk about a 'history of the Trinity', we do not mean a history of deficiency and death; we mean the history of the self-communicating livingness of God which overcomes death. This history of the Trinity opens up through the sending of the Son and the sending of the Spirit. But just because of that, the inference drawn from the contemplation of the history of Christ and the sending of the Spirit in the light of their sending does not yet embrace the whole trinitarian history of God's dealings with the world. The origin of this history is comprehended, but not yet its future.[70]

---

[68] Moltmann, *Church in the Power of the Spirit*, 53.
[69] Moltmann, *Church in the Power of the Spirit*, 56.
[70] Moltmann, *Church in the Power of the Spirit*, 56.

As Bauckham has rightly noted:

> it was Moltmann's development of the concept of the trinitarian history of God as an overarching theological context for the doctrine of the church which enabled him to integrate these earlier ecclesiological insights into a comprehensive ecclesiology in *The Church in the Power of the Spirit*.[71]

There is in Moltmann an echo of Hegel's world spirit philosophy but the openness that Moltmann brings to the picture is different from Hegel's more closed view. For Moltmann the ability to identify the church as a happening with an open future is most significant.

> The church participates in Christ's messianic mission and in the creative mission of the Spirit. We cannot therefore say *what* the church is in all circumstances and what it comprises in itself. But we can tell *where* the church happens.[72]

This happening is the communicating of God of himself in and through the activity of the Holy Spirit. 'The church has its true being in the work of Christ. That excludes an independent ontology of the church and permits merely the account of the history of Christ's acts'.[73] It is the communication of God through the proclamation of the kerygma and its history, which are important aspects of the church.

> If then Christian proclamation and the history that communicates it coincide and are one and the same thing, then Christology and ecclesiology can no longer be qualitatively distinguished, for the two meet in the doctrine of the kerygma.[74]

Jesus' mission, and that of his disciples, consists in liberating action as well as proclamation. This liberating action is as important as the proclamation of the gospel and is another goal of mission.

> But mission has another goal as well. It lies in the qualitative alteration of life's atmosphere – of trust, feeling, thinking and acting. We might call this missionary aim to 'infect' people, whatever their religion, with the spirit of hope, love and responsibility for the world.[75]

Christians have as their responsibility the communicating of this through their very being. This is part of their mission for Christ.

> No life can be understood from its own standpoint alone. As long as it lives, it exists in living relationships to other lives, and therefore of

---

[71] Bauckham, *Theology*, 121.
[72] Moltmann, *Church in the Power of the Spirit*, 65.
[73] Moltmann, *Church in the Power of the Spirit*, 69.
[74] Moltmann, *Church in the Power of the Spirit*, 71.
[75] Moltmann, *Church in the Power of the Spirit*, 152.

> time with perspectives of hope. It is these that constitute in the first place a living being's unique vitality, openness and capacity for communication.[76]

Moltmann encourages communication in the form of dialogue with other religions and sees this as a responsibility of the church. Christians in the relationships developed through this dialogue will then have the possibility of continuing Christ's mission in the world by being a liberating influence and confronting the forces that oppress and dominate.

This relating in Christ's name, if honest and open, will not result in a diluting of the characteristics of the church. It will give the church a new way of perceiving itself and of how others perceive it. Moltmann uses this concept to show how the gospel provides a way of encountering all that we may refer to as 'the other' in a way that does not threaten our identity. 'We do not lose our identity, but we acquire a new profile in the confrontation with our partner'.[77]

This 'open friendship' is characteristic of Moltmann's view of the church and models itself on the response of God to man. We give others dignity through this friendship in the same way that God gives man dignity through his friendship with us. 'God shows his friendship by listening to man'.[78]

Hope is central to the development of relationships. Hope is a horizon that determines whether a relationship will live or die. God communicates that hope to his creation by revealing the nature of the relationships within the Trinity. This giving of hope is a giving of freedom that enables us to choose life over death in relationships. These present themselves to us as opportunities for extending God's kingdom in this world.

> But if hope is specific in the relationships of one life to another, then it indicates a line, a tendency or a direction for these relationships: a temporal line, along which these relationships ought to be developed; a tendency which can be missed or followed in the relationships; a direction in which changes in fellowship become meaningful. The formulation of hope's horizon therefore affects both sides, their relationships to one another and the time in which the two appear in relationship to one another. Without this comprehensive framework of hope, the relationships remain without meaning.[79]

---

[76] Moltmann, *Church in the Power of the Spirit*, 133.
[77] Moltmann, *Church in the Power of the Spirit*, 152.
[78] Moltmann, *Church in the Power of the Spirit*, 119.
[79] Moltmann, *Church in the Power of the Spirit*, 134.

As we view the church as something that occurs, or happens, we must not confuse it with the organisations that go under the name of the church. The gospel brings liberation and a sense of hope in the eschatological calling out that it proclaims. The coming kingdom manifests itself as the followers of Christ communicate this hope through their lives. We can then say that the church is 'the social form of hope'.[80] The actions of those who are seen to constitute it declare the exodus message of hope and liberation as they encounter the risen Christ. The new life promised and offered in these actions, which proclaim the kingdom of God is one that confronts '[t]he idolatry of power, the fetishism of money and "things", as well as political messianism …'.[81] Kingdom of God in this context 'does not mean God's rule over the world in general through creation and providence, but the ultimately liberating, all-redeeming and therefore eschatological kingship of God over his creation'.[82]

When we use a term like the kingdom of God, we use it to represent something that is beyond. The term is a symbolic representation of that to which the word refers. In a similar way, Moltmann notes how the New Testament several times refers to Christ as the 'image of God',[83] and he also refers to '… the comprehensive Christian horizon of life by the symbol "the kingdom of God"'.[84]

Communication in the church, as far as it concerns our understanding of reality, requires the shattering of images, which follows the confrontation of them with faith received through the gospel. Moltmann says '… the successor of the prophets true faith acts iconoclastically against the idols and fetishes of timorous man'.[85] God calls the church in its messianic mission to that confronting of false images. As the church confronts them and shows them for what they are, it communicates the truth of the gospel. Those who see the confrontation and are involved in this 'happening' then form the church. We find the church where Christ is experienced through the preaching of the Word, in the sharing of the sacraments, in fellowship and in reaching out to the poor.

With Küng, Moltmann is seeking to avoid a Platonic dualist understanding of the visible and the invisible church. There is a tendency towards idealism in his thinking on the church though he decries such idealism at times. In some respects, Moltmann might concede that the

---

[80] Moltmann, *Church in the Power of the Spirit*, 85.
[81] Moltmann, *Church in the Power of the Spirit*, 90.
[82] Moltmann, *Church in the Power of the Spirit*, 99.
[83] Moltmann, *Church in the Power of the Spirit*, 101.
[84] Moltmann, *Church in the Power of the Spirit*, 134.
[85] Moltmann, *Church in the Power of the Spirit*, 154.

church could be seen to have an essential nature, though this would be stretching his understanding of the church. Moltmann agrees with Küng when he says '[t]he one Church, in its essential nature and in its external forms alike, is always at once visible and invisible'.[86] He agrees on the essential temporary and provisional nature of the church and sees the church as 'the eschatological community of those who believe and love'.[87]

Verbal and written images in Western languages traditionally use a method that emphasises the construction of ideas that build on one another, and use reason and logic as their prime methods of communication. In literature and theatre it is sometimes more common for images to be set off against one another in order to communicate a message but in general discourse this is not the method used.

Moltmann uses images, in the form of theological concepts contained in metaphors, to represent the church. He shows that these images need to dialectically confront false images that represent the world of self-interest and lack of concern for the other. The real nature of the world is then revealed. As we confront the false views of the other, we follow Scripture and Christ's command to love others. Our courage to love in this way becomes possible because of God's promised protection from annihilation. It is as Christians communicate within these healing and transforming relationships that God extends his kingdom.

Summary and Conclusion

In this chapter we explored the nature of communication within relationships noting the eschatological impact of Moltmann's theology. We noted how his theological categories operate at a symbolic and iconic level. We suggested that we could explain these as pre-existing archetypal internal symbolic representations of reality in our minds. These resonate with the externally perceived representations of categories whether we see these in sign language or hear them in words. Sign language, we suggested, is more able to convey these.

We examined the trinitarian base of his congregational concept of church community life where he sees it as communication in communion. We noted how he approached the problem of suffering using eschatological hope and how he uses biblical models of narrative to reinterpret life's events in the light of God's promises and the fulfilment of those promises. We noted how he uses a post-Hegelian dialectical approach to the development of knowledge and being itself. He argues

---

[86] Küng, *Church*, 38.
[87] Küng, *Church*, 103.

for approaches to communication which involve poetic perception and intuition and which utilise a messianic imagination of the future.

We considered the way in which 'attitude' is an important component in the communication process. We saw how Moltmann sees ontological hope as leading us into God's history through the cross and the resurrection, enabling us to open ourselves to the future.

We next looked at how Moltmann uses broad categories in his understanding of the problem of mankind when it is viewed from a psychological angle. We have anxiety and fear concerning our own vulnerability and mortality. As a protection against such feelings, Moltmann says we sometimes build religious ritual and imagery into our life and this then forms a wall between life and us. Communication through this barrier then contrasts greatly with the communication that exists within a loving accepting community.

Moltmann highlights how wrong communication can stem from psychological attempts to assuage the pain of suffering and grief and how these take the form of idolatrous practices. These practices actually further distance us from those with whom we want to communicate. Solidarity in suffering with others and with God produces an understanding of self that enables communication to proceed in an open way.

We saw that symbols and signs act as metaphors for reality and allow us to differentiate one thing from another. They may accumulate within the collective unconscious of a society and form archetypal images within us. Signs may bind us to others within society as we use them to bring order to our existence. Symbolic representation is more productive in encouraging us to be open to possibilities as it often holds seemingly incompatible things in creative tension.

We saw that symbols have the power to construct 'chains of being' which enable progress to be made to wholeness. They bridge the tensions that exist within people between wanting order and unity in life and the conflicting need for newness and freedom in creativity. Theological concepts can operate at this symbolic level. They contain dialectical tensions between order and unity and openness to the future and the 'new thing'. Symbols such as theological categories have a reality within themselves and they perform the function of pointing towards a reality that is beyond. They also contain within them a meaning that encompasses that reality.

We next looked at how icons differ from symbols and how Lossky saw them as preserving and passing on faith. We recognised the inadequacy of art, like words, to convey the reality of supernatural realities. As with church architecture, icons involve us in a mystery that we cannot otherwise express and often consist of a refined imagery that has a minimum of detail and a maximum of expressiveness.

We saw that Moltmann uses theological categories in symbolic ways and through the dialectic inherent in symbols produces a dynamic and open theology. His use of the eschaton as the primary symbol causes the future to be a dynamic element in our experience of the present as we hold it in tension with the history of God's dealings with the world. Moltmann's categories, such as that of the eschaton, are like icons that both reveal and depict a mystery.

We noted how icons, like metaphors, sometimes have a reduced effectiveness as a result of changes in community practices and the development of different understandings of reality. Moltmann describes how we apprehend a new experience represented by symbols. In the tension that exists between them, there is a surplus of meaning. We drew a parallel with the way in which sign language, in addition to using referential signs, uses a variety of gesture-type signs to convey meaning similar to the way in which actors are taught to convey an emotion by simple gestures, movements or bodily positions. We suggested that both means of communication, acting and sign language, use emotion as a 'carrier' in a much greater way than spoken language. We noted that Moltmann stresses how we employ our emotional and intuitive capacities when dealing with theological concepts.

We saw that through analogical and dialectical processes, which demonstrate the eschatological ontological nature of our being, we encounter a surplus of meaning in symbols. This surplus of meaning creates tensions that lead us on to the experience of new things.

We saw how language, in mediating concepts to us, facilitates the holding of new concepts. We also saw how within a loving relationship communication flows more easily and can convey much more than in a relationship based on contract or formality.

We noted how Moltmann's relational understanding of being affects perceptions of personal boundaries. We noted also the different perceptual boundaries experienced by Deaf people. In terms of the closeness of that which forms the boundary of our perceived world, we concluded that Deaf people have a closer horizon and that we could therefore say that any existential fear of encountering 'the other' is closer. Moltmann's theological approach, which encourages an approach of being open to the other, could therefore benefit Deaf people.

We saw how biological, social and psychological forces impinge on communication. Moltmann's scheme modifies these so that the eschatological horizon provides a backdrop against which we may observe human intentionality and attitudes.

We saw that the brain usually processes language in the left hemisphere and visual imagery in the right hemisphere. We suggested that archetypal iconic imagery, normally processed in the right hemisphere, pre-exists in people and is the means by which we identify and process theological concepts. These theological concepts have a shape and form that we identify in the visual processing sector of the brain.

We next explored the way in which social role expectations and performance and external objects used in a conventional and symbolic way could act as 'vessels' for containing and passing on concepts. Reciprocal role relationships could be seen to be learnt by us from childhood onwards and with them the 'cues' learnt by which the 'steps' in the 'dance' of life may be performed. Social cohesion follows from a dense network of interwoven dependencies, which require a pattern of promise and fulfilment for their existence.

Viewing communication, as Moltmann suggests, as taking place between 'persons in community' and noting the significant percentage of iconic signs in sign language, we proposed that Deaf people might more easily understand the nature of reality, and communication within it, in Moltmann's scheme.

We next looked at the place of movement in perceptions of reality and saw that Moltmann views all reality as flowing from the movement of the 'trinitarian history of God's dealings with the world'. He views the desire and ability to communicate, and the means of communicating as existing in the openness of the being of God. The church does not have a separate ontological identity as such but is 'a happening' with an open future.

The nature of relationships is crucial in Moltmann's understanding of communication. God's promise of deliverance from annihilation enables Christian relationships to develop which welcome the one who is 'other'. Our horizon of expectation depends on Christ's eschatological promises of ultimate deliverance and reconciliation. It is within a perspective formed by eschatological hope that we may view communication and it is within this that all relationships exist and develop.

We saw that traditionally Western languages use a method of constructing ideas using reason and logic. By contrast, as is sometimes the case in the theatre and literature, the juxtaposition of images can communicate more powerfully. For Moltmann, 'being' is communication and we extend the horizon of reality by the incorporation of eschatological hope into our very being.

To summarise then, we have in this chapter examined in detail the nature of communication within Moltmann's theology and as it is experienced in both hearing and Deaf people. We have shown that Moltmann uses symbolic understandings of theological categories in order to generate a concept of the open nature of the future in God's history with Mankind. We have shown how Moltmann stresses the centrality of communication for his understanding of life itself. For him, 'being' is communication. We have shown how unmediated experiences are an ideal that Moltmann holds, but that normal communication involves mediation through the means of symbols and iconic encounters. We have shown this to be particularly relevant to sign language users as they commonly use iconic signs. We have shown Deaf people may be more able to accept unresolved and seemingly contradictory information and incorporate it into their understanding of the world. Finally, we saw that Moltmann's view of the church and communication uses the dialectical relationship between images that represent ways of understanding reality.

Chapter 6

The Concept of Relationship in Moltmann's Theology and its Appropriateness for Deaf People

Introduction

In this chapter, we will be examining the concept of relationship as Moltmann understands it. We will consider the nature of relationships between people within the church and their relationships with people outside. We will also be looking at his understanding of our relationship with God.

Moltmann gives prominence, in his understanding of reality to the ontological significance of eschatology and applies this to relationships. He also sees relationality as primary in understanding reality. He says '… everything real and everything living is simply a concentration and manifestation of its relationships, interconnections and surroundings'.[1]

We will start this chapter by noting how he views the political, economic, cultural and psychological aspects of being church and how these affect relationships. We will see how he emphasises the messianic element in the 'being' of the church and how he views all godly relationships as having a liberating function. We will see that he views it as necessary for liberation to occur in the political, the economic and the cultural relationships of life, and in the relationship the church has to the state. We also note how he explains psychologically and by using categories from social psychology how our relationships with disabled people are an asset to us. Theologically we will note how he draws on the category of anticipation to frame an understanding of the way in which relationships with those who are 'different' can bring about an expectation of enrichment rather than a sense of burden to the believer.

Our primary need is a change in our way of thinking, says Moltmann, and this comes through the eschatological impact of the messianic message of the gospel.

> Integrating, and integral, thinking moves purposefully in this social direction towards the goal of an inclusiveness that is many-sided, and ultimately fully comprehensive. …[and] serves to generate the

---

[1] Moltmann, *God in Creation*, 3.

community between human beings and nature which is necessary and promotes life.[2]

This is his answer to the alienating impact of '[m]odern thinking [which] has developed by way of an objectifying, analytical, particularizing and reductionalistic approach'.[3]

In addition, we will consider how we may view relationships through his understanding of culture and community; in-groups and outsiders; promise and fulfilment; and the dialectical tension between what is and what is to come in the future. We will also note Moltmann's use of perspective and how we determine our conceptions through our perceptions, which come from attributions and attitudes. We will look at certain distinctive characteristics of Deaf relationships, the need for Deaf to be involved in organisations that do not oppress, marginalize or exploit; authority structures in the church and the wider world and the effect of society on relationships. We will note the value of 'friendship type' relationships in the Deaf context, the importance of trinitarian relationships in Moltmann's ecclesiology, and the dialectic of anxiety and hope in Christian relationships.

Our conclusion will be that for Moltmann relationships in the church and with God will tend to embody a message of liberation that is at the heart of the proclamation of the kingdom of God and that for Deaf people this is the type of relationship which is well suited to their particular situation.

a. Political, Economic, Cultural and Psychological Aspects of Being Church and how these Affect Relationships

In this section, we will be considering Moltmann's observations on political, economic, cultural and psychological relationships, their affect on the structures of the church and their significance for both Deaf and hearing communities.

We will first consider the political relationships of the church with society. Moltmann defines[4] the way in which he sees Christianity being joined to and dependent on 'the world's life' and in this way affecting it for good through the messianic message of hope that the gospel brings to confront and direct that which it encounters. Moltmann says he chooses to use the term Christianity here rather than the word church.

---

[2] Moltmann, *God in Creation*, 3.
[3] Moltmann, *God in Creation*, 2.
[4] In the 4th section of chapter IV of *The Church in the Power of the Spirit*, entitled 'Christianity in the processes of the world's life'.

> The word "church" always suggests the official church, or the regular organisation; but here responsibility clearly lies with responsible Christians in their secular professions.[5]

Here we see a juxtaposing by Moltmann of divine ideas of eventual reconciliation and redemption of all things over against those ideas that stem from normal individual human responses. Human responses we see psychologically defined as defensive mechanisms of the individual. These we know as the 'fight or flight' responses. Normal responses, argues Moltmann, are for, and stem from, defensiveness inherent in human nature which offers protection against destruction and death.

> We are really concerned with historically mobile and interdependent areas of activity where it is important not to preserve a fore-given 'order' but to regulate ordering processes. We shall therefore talk about processes instead of orders, processes in whose conflicts and trends Christianity is involved, and has to be involved today, more consciously than ever before.[6]

Moltmann says that '[t]he messianic concept represents a categorical mediation between the kingdom of God and history'.[7] This category introduces anticipation of a Christian nature. 'It is Christian when, and to the extent in which, its mediations take their bearings from the history of Jesus and his mission'.[8] This anticipation, in a messianic context, is of liberation. It is a foretaste of what is to come. It is in one sense a 'not yet' but in another sense it is 'an already'.

Moltmann says:

> The democratising process of politics does not relieve the people of responsibility and decision, but is actually an imposition, the imposition of freedom and participation. It is an imposition which is nothing less than the imposition of human existence, rights and duty.[9]

Following from this he says, 'The political task of Christianity is not merely to live in an already existing political order, but actually to take part in forming it'.[10] He champions the cause of democracy and human rights and sees these as the basis on which society may give dignity to man. 'One of these is the right to resist illegitimate and illegal rule'.[11]

---

[5] Moltmann, *Church in the Power of the Spirit*, 164.
[6] Moltmann, *Church in the Power of the Spirit*, 164.
[7] Moltmann, *Church in the Power of the Spirit*, 193.
[8] Moltmann, *Church in the Power of the Spirit*, 193.
[9] Moltmann, *Church in the Power of the Spirit*, 177.
[10] Moltmann, *Church in the Power of the Spirit*, 178.
[11] Moltmann, *Church in the Power of the Spirit*, 180.

This is part of a duty to ensure a restriction exists on power given to others by the political process.

> Because popular sovereignty and the self-government of a political community are really inconsistent with the assignment of sovereign rights to men to rule over other men, they can only be realized in the open process of the constant limitation and control of the exercise of power.[12]

There is an interesting contrast between Moltmann's views on the place that the political organs of the state have and the way in which they should function and his views on the church. The political mechanisms he enthusiastically recommends are designed to protect the vulnerable and give them freedom and dignity. He is clearly against traditional hierarchical church organisational structures even though they may have been developed over many years with the intention of protecting the vulnerable from abuses by ecclesiastical powers. He argues, and not without good reason, that these hierarchical structures have developed primarily in order to ensure that those in power and who have privileges maintain their positions and power. The counter argument is clearly that without maintaining that power there may be less protection for the poor and oppressed against abuse. Lane has accurately summed up the natural response of many people to Moltmann's view of political action when he said '... Moltmann's application of his theology is stimulating and challenging but might be said to lack political realism'.[13]

We should therefore be cautious and realistic when applying Moltmann's theology to the situation of Deaf people or others. In the church we should be less concerned with whether, or to what extent, we can follow the teaching of the Sermon on the Mount but rather see that, in it, Jesus emphasises that what we *do* determines who we are. Moltmann says '[i]t says that everything depends on "doing"'.[14] We should also keep in mind that Moltmann's *ideal* of the church is also influenced by his view of the pre-Constantine church, which, he says, '... offered a real and livable alternative to the systems existing in the world of those days'.[15]

The significance for the church and Deaf people of realistically applying Moltmann's theology is that we will focus on our responsibility to subject church authority and power structures to evaluation. This we

---

[12] Moltmann, *Church in the Power of the Spirit,* 177.
[13] A. Lane, 'Review of The Way of Jesus Christ. Christology in Messianic Dimensions' in *Themelios* 17 Number 2 (January/February 1992) 33-34.
[14] Moltmann, *Way,* 126.
[15] Moltmann, *Way,* 135.

will do in the light of the teaching of the Sermon on the Mount with the intention of ensuring that they do not cause oppression and abuse. In this way, the church directs its attention away from itself to the common people *(ochlos)*, that is the poor, the sad and those who suffer. As one writer, commenting on Mt. 5:39, has helpfully said 'The context shows that *Do not resist one who is evil* (39) means that one should not seek justice for oneself. There is no suggestion that by inaction or silence we should encourage injustice to others'.[16]

Concerning the protection of the vulnerable in the church, Meeks points to the centrality of gifting in the nature of the church, and of the difficulties in expressing itself that the church faces in today's market orientated society. He offers an interesting view of the alternative 'economy' that the church can experience through its fellowship and particularly that which is experienced at the Eucharist. There the 'table manners' of the church ensure a quality of relationship that is dependent only on love expressed as mutual giving, thus preventing 'violence' and the inclusion of 'the stranger' at the meal whose face, though causing us to experience 'shock' enables us to discover our selves as we encounter that which is 'not ourselves'.[17] It is derived from Moltmann's trinitarian based and gift centred view of the church and we consider that it offers an exciting challenge to the notion that hierarchical forms of power are the only means by which the vulnerable may be protected.

Concerning the economic processes of the world Moltmann sees the need for Christian involvement. He says of '[t]he economic process, which is acted out in economic struggles and the exploitation of nature. Here the economic liberation of man and nature from man's exploitation is essential'.[18] This is not just an acknowledgement of how economic exploitation is causing damage to the world. He clearly sees the connection that frequently exists between ecological exploitation, often for economic ends, and the human exploitation that accompanies it. Moltmann recognises the way in which, in modern society, mankind's relationship with economic systems through money is one of being a source of 'labour and as a purchaser'.[19] He sees that ruling over the earth brings with it responsibility.

> Christians who take this seriously will break with those values and requirements which are the driving power behind our modern econ-

---

[16] H.L. Ellison in G.C.D. Howley (ed.), *A New Testament Commentary* (London: Pickering & Inglis, 1969) 146.
[17] M.D. Meeks, 'The future of Theology in a Commodity Society' in Volf *et al.* (eds.), *Future*, 261-263.
[18] Moltmann, *Church in the Power of the Spirit,* 165.
[19] Moltmann, *Church in the Power of the Spirit,* 169.

omy. They will choose the path that leads away from the ruthless satisfaction of demands, to community; away from the struggle for existence, to peace in existence; away from the will to supremacy, to solidarity with others and with nature.[20]

As part of their wider programme of influence in society Moltmann believes that Christians should not only intervene actively in politics, economics and culture but also welcome suffering people into the church, where they may discover therapeutic relationships with other people. 'For it is solidarity and fellowship alone that makes even suffering and the necessary curbing of the natural desires bearable'.[21]

Moltmann sees that 'socialism' is the form that people's relationships with other people and nature should take.[22] For Moltmann there are very strong links between our attitude and actions towards our environment and the ecological systems of the world and the attitudes and actions we have towards one another and with our inner being.

> Changes in the social relationship of people to one another will therefore bring in their wake changes in the relationship between human societies and nature. Conversely, the change in man's relationship to nature from exploitation to co-operation, and from suppression to symbiosis, will bring radical alterations to the social structure in its train.[23]

Willis refers to Moltmann's view of the necessity of political action and indicates the connection Moltmann makes between reflection and practice in the life of faith.

> To be relevant to the present situation theology must develop a political hermeneutic, it must become political theology. This does not mean that theology is to become political in a narrow sense ... [it] must be done in the consciousness of its consequences for the practical political sphere ... [and] must be based on this reflection on practice.[24]

We believe that it is a characteristic of Moltmann's approach, which seeks to be open towards conceptual and theological matters, that it is susceptible to misrepresentation and misunderstanding. He undoubtedly brings criticism upon himself because of a lack of clarity on occasions. Walton, in his criticism of Moltmann's Theology of Hope, rightly sees that Moltmann views the church as existing of and for the

---

[20] Moltmann, *Church in the Power of the Spirit*, 174.
[21] Moltmann, *Church in the Power of the Spirit*, 175.
[22] Moltmann, *Church in the Power of the Spirit*, 175.
[23] Moltmann, *Church in the Power of the Spirit*, 174.
[24] Willis, *Theism*, 136-137.

poor. In our view, however, he misrepresents Moltmann's view of the church as consisting only of the 'economically poor'. In fact Moltmann, whilst giving priority to 'the poor' in the constitution of the church, does not exclude those who are not 'economically poor' as stated by Walton. In our view, Walton is being harsh when he concludes that 'indeed there is little charity in his theology'.[25] Walton views the intention of Moltmann's model to be a vehicle by which the church, which is a sect-like organisation, according to Troeltsch's categories, intends to smash the church-type. He says '[t]here is something very frightening about Moltmann's reductionist political theology and ecclesiology'. But, Moltmann says, 'the mainstream churches and the discipleship groups remain dependent on one another in a kind of double strategy until the community principle can be realized'.[26] Moltmann understands the two groups as existing in a dialectical and necessary relationship to one another. The church-type has the advantage of being open to the world, and accessible to it. It is always in danger of losing its identity because of its openness and because it admits members by infant baptism, but it has an important ministry in the realm of social service. The sect-type is constantly calling the church-type to reform and a pietistic form of spirituality. It offers a closeness of fellowship, a strong sense of its own identity as being separate from the world and personal involvement that the church-type is unable to match. We can definitely read into Moltmann's view of the church the sense that the community, consisting of the fellowship of friends in the sect-type, is the ideal to which we should work. The reality is that, in Moltmann's view, both types will co-exist. In the dynamic of the dialectical relationship between them, the church will constantly be reformed, and the kingdom of God extended.

In a section on cultural life, Moltmann looks at how racism and sexism are examples of culturally based conflicts. He then considers the cultural basis for attitudes to disabled people. Of relevance to our study are his observations on '… the relationship between the handicapped and the healthy'.[27] Moltmann can be criticised here for using the term 'healthy' to describe non-handicapped people[28], but we can note that he later modifies the term to 'non-handicapped, healthy'. We should

---

[25] R.C. Walton, 'Jürgen Moltmann's Theology of Hope' in R.H. Nash (ed.), *Liberation Theology* (Milford, Michigan: Mott Media, 1984) 175.
[26] Moltmann, *Church in the Power of the Spirit*, 326.
[27] Moltmann, *Church in the Power of the Spirit*, 185.
[28] This is in the light of scholarship since the 1970's such as the work done by Mike Oliver (see chapter 1) which has shown that it is not necessary to define handicap primarily as a medical condition.

note that he is writing in 1975 and his point is to show how society disables through the actions and reactions of non-handicapped people. The term 'the handicapped' can suggest that handicapped people are a homogeneous group. By virtue of the indiscriminate way in which handicap occurs, this is not usually the case. Handicapped people are normally as diverse and different from one another as people who are not handicapped. Moltmann clearly recognises this in his following argument concerning the source of our identity, which he describes as not resting in our *having* but in our *being*.[29] To describe people as *healthy* concentrates attention on the health that they *have* and differentiates them from handicapped people who are then primarily identified as not *having* health. Moltmann makes the important point that the primary defining category we should use comes from our equality of *being* before God. This comes from our *being* justified by God. In this, the only difference we experience and need to acknowledge is that between creator and created. The distinctions that we otherwise use to create the identities of others, such as whether they *have* health or not, are often shown to be insignificant, inappropriate or unhelpful.

Moltmann starts by talking of how 'the defence mechanisms of psychology and social psychology come into play in our society, making the situation of the handicapped unendurable, and robbing them of their human dignity too'.[30] He traces the reason for the difficulty that arises for the handicapped person to the fear that 'healthy persons' sometimes experience when they encounter a handicapped person. 'The world surrounding the handicapped views him as a threat, an insecurity and disturbance of its sense of its own value; people develop defence reactions which are coupled with suppressed feelings of guilt'.[31]

As far as social psychology is concerned Moltmann acknowledges that 'It is true that these social consequences would not exist without the handicap but the handicap could well be there without the social results'.[32] It is the fate of being 'put up with' rather than being welcomed which is such a social burden for the handicapped to bear.

Theologically Moltmann concentrates on the fact of justification of the person, healthy or not, and the equality of justified persons in the

---

[29] Moltmann, *Church in the Power of the Spirit*, 186.
[30] Moltmann, *Church in the Power of the Spirit*, 185. For more of Moltmann's views on human dignity see also J. Moltmann, *On Human Dignity. Political Theology and Ethics* (Philadelphia: Fortress Press, 1984).
[31] Moltmann, *Church in the Power of the Spirit*, 185.
[32] Moltmann, *Church in the Power of the Spirit*, 185.

sight of God, tracing a doctrine of equal rights for all from the declaration in Gal. 3.28.[33]

Moltmann believes our main problem is a fear of non-being. 'This follows from a deep-lying primal fear of nothingness and is joined with a hate of one's own existence. Because of this it is never possible to substantiate oneself without depreciating the other'.[34]

The Christian fellowship is then, for Moltmann, a place where 'like' can live together with 'unlike'. The dignity and rights of the other person will be recognised. 'In cultural conflicts Christianity will live the I-identity of faith, freed from the ego, and will demonstrate recognition of the other as a person in his dignity and his rights'.[35] This will correspond to and anticipate the kingdom of God and its righteousness.

Theologically, the important aspect in these observations on Moltmann's ecclesiology is the mediating category of *anticipation*.[36]

We can see that Moltmann is hoping that the church will provide psychological and social answers to the social barriers and stigma that the handicapped experience. The handicapped person experiences a form of handicapping from the social consequences of handicap. In the church, there is often not the liberating experience Moltmann describes, partly because the church has not moved at the same pace as society in making itself more 'user-friendly' to the handicapped.[37] Mainly, though it would seem to be because the 'freedom to live defenselessly'[38] has not been realised within most church structures because they do not conform to Moltmann's pattern.

In this section, we have shown how the distinctiveness of Moltmann's understanding of the church in its political, economic, cultural and psychological aspects can affect the possible experiences of relationships in the church by Deaf people. We have shown that liberating structures can define the handicapped in an inclusive rather than an exclusive way and can note that theological views of reality, which emphasise non-hierarchical and non-judgmental structures, follow from his ecclesiology. These can have positive benefits for Deaf People in defining them not according to their handicap but according

---

[33] Moltmann, *Church in the Power of the Spirit*, 188.
[34] Moltmann, *Church in the Power of the Spirit*, 187.
[35] Moltmann, *Church in the Power of the Spirit*, 189.
[36] Moltmann, *Church in the Power of the Spirit*, 193.
[37] Theatres, businesses and local authorities are often more aware of the ways in which their physical structures, buildings and access and organisational processes can made be less disabling. Church buildings are often old and therefore more difficult and costly to modify tastefully (approximately 5000 Church of England buildings were built before 1500) and funds are often not available for this.
[38] Introduction by M.D. Meeks to Moltmann, *Dignity*, xiv.

to their relationship with God and other people viewed in a reality which is eschatologically orientated.

b. Openness in Relationships, Eschatological Hope, Promise and Fulfilment

In this section, we will consider how Moltmann views openness in relationships as being foundational for understanding them. We will see how important dialogue is to him, whether it is churches speaking to other churches, countries to other countries, or people with other people. We will see that at the heart of his concerns is the nature of a person's relationship to God. This affects all other relationships. Openness is for him a fundamental characteristic of God and when we find openness in his creation this is a sign that God is present. This openness is openness to the future and ultimately to the eschatological future. In any relationship there is always this process of development and evolution even when it is in the direction of decay and disintegration such as can occur towards the end of a relationship. Accepting the future, whether we expect it to be positive or negative, is a healthy attitude for all people in relationships and over-riding this can be the positive effect of the eschatological future which promises a reconciliation of all things.

Moltmann speaks in a way that encourages hope within groups of people whether they are churches or countries. The hope is for a future that consists of reconciliation and harmony rather than defensiveness and discord.

> The embodiment of the messianic promises to the poor and the quintessence of the hopes of the alienated is that the world should be "home". This means being at home in existence – that the relationships between God, human beings and nature lose their tension and are resolved into peace and repose.[39]

When a person or a group encounters an outsider it is threatened and the natural response is to feel that the very 'being' of the group or the person is under threat. The culture and community of any group consists in the degrees of likeness shared by its members. When we meet a 'stranger' with openness a threat to our 'being' exists. If the foundation of our 'being' is secure then there is capacity, or space, to engage. If not then engagement is less likely.

Openness, for Moltmann, is a concept that requires certain factors, such as time and space, pain and suffering, joy and peace, to operate in dialectical tension with each other. Time and space are the contexts

---

[39] Moltmann, *God in Creation*, 5.

within which relationships exist. Pain and suffering are a part of all relationships and these occur in time and space. We can experience joy and peace within relationships but they do not exist without their negative counterparts of sadness and disharmony.

Openness provides space within time and this provides time for which plans do not exist. In this Moltmann is clear, planning is part of the technique of the modern project. Jesus had time for the unplanned as well as the planned. He 'made' space for what we call interruptions. Openness to others means being willing to welcome interruptions. Interruptions are nothing more than encounters of the 'other'. In practice, in the modern world, this may mean building in contingency time or space for them. This may not be enough to cope with the interruption and when an encounter seriously disrupts our lives then a complete re-planning may be necessary. This occurs most evidently when we 'encounter' major loss. The openness Moltmann speaks of extends to 'losing' the relationship we have with someone. This encounter with loss means that we are open to the ultimate other which is death itself. If it is not physical death, it may be the death of a relationship. In practice all relationships as they change are symbolically dying and being reborn as the process of 'being in the relationship' takes place.

The distinction between what we may call 'in groups' and 'out groups' is one that it is useful to make and one that will help us in understanding the nature of relationships particularly those involving Deaf people and hearing people. We can view our 'self' as the subjective self. We often understand the subjective self as that within us that is reflecting upon, evaluating and observing the outside world and all that which is not 'self'. Our 'self' is subject to forces or 'drives' which make us want to seek harmony and new experiences. These new experiences bring with them, initially, a sense of disharmony. Only as we accommodate them into our mental framework, with its balances and tensions, can we achieve again the harmony that we seek.

Meeting new people brings such disharmony accompanied by our 'self' wishing to re-establish a sense of harmony. Even anticipating new relationships can bring a sense of disharmony. This will come from the unknown future effect of the new person on our 'self'. Moltmann draws attention to this fundamental experience of all mankind in the context of an eschatological view of reality.

> Present and future, experience and hope, stand in contradiction to each other in Christian eschatology, with the result that man is not

brought into harmony and agreement with the given situation, but is drawn into the conflict between hope and experience.[40]

This conflict is the source of so much distress in our world, and it is for dealing with this conflict that Moltmann proposes a solution. Separation and estrangement as experienced between persons is the earthly equivalent of the separation that has occurred between mankind and God following 'the fall'. Our human solution to this is to form relationships which are exclusive in the sense that they are dependent on the characteristics or qualities of the person with whom we are in relationship. Moltmann says that what seems natural in society is the bonding of like with like.

We create our 'in groups', that is persons who are our friends. In contrast to these are persons, or groups of persons, who are 'other'. They are outsiders because we have not yet made them insiders. What Moltmann offers is the opportunity to view all who are 'other' as friends who, through the eschatological hope which we allow to work in us, will become part of what we consider to be our 'in group'.

The operation of eschatological hope would seem to need to allow the 'subjective self' to acknowledge differences, such as differences of language and custom or culture, yet not consider these to be a barrier to a friendship type relationship formed and maintained in the power of the Holy Spirit. The environments that we create around us, including our attitudes to ourselves and others and the language we use, have an important effect on our perception of others.

Hearing people can make better relationships with Deaf people if hearing people make the effort to learn and use sign language. It has been observed in a study of Deaf and hearing people working together that there is a close connection between the 'signing [language] environment', which in the observed case was a working environment with a policy that hearing people should always sign when in the presence of a deaf person, and ' ... being involved ... [and] being valued and respected'. It was noted that with respect to making relationships '[c]rucially, hearing people signing enabled the possibility of personal and social relationships to develop between deaf and hearing staff'.[41] This research finding shows that if someone is speaking the same language as us we will be more inclined to feel good about them and we will be more likely to build positive relationships with them.

The same study noted that:

---

[40] Moltmann, *Theology of Hope*, 18.
[41] A. Young, J. Ackerman and J. Kyle, *Looking On, Deaf People and the Organisation of Services* (Bristol: Policy Press, 1998) 16.

when the signing environment broke down and hearing staff spoke in the presence of deaf colleagues, then deaf staff felt unconfident, excluded, struggled to make relationships with hearing people and fundamentally did not feel respected or valued. They easily became angry or frustrated.[42]

It would appear that the 'common language' of persons who are in relationship is crucial for the healthy maintenance of those relationships. Attitudes towards 'others' and attribution of characteristics to them by the 'self', which in some cases is a form of stereotyping, will determine the type of relationship that is possible. The language and the culture accompanying any relationship will often have built-in tendencies and prejudices that it may be difficult to overcome.

Moltmann suggests eschatological hope and openness as being constitutive of Christian relationships. Conflict will not disappear for he has already noted that this is the very seedbed in which hope itself arises. Our reaction to conflict-ridden situations will be determined by the extent to which we 'defend' ourselves or make ourselves vulnerable. If we are secure in our sense of being then we will more easily 'embrace' that which is 'other'.

Any study of relationships involving God must incorporate an understanding of being. Understanding God's personhood as existing in his relationships both inner-Trinitarian and with his creation moves us from the traditional view of God's being as existing in a form of pure essence. We may understand God's nature and being as a result of his actions and his interactions with us in the same way that experiencing love enables us to understand what human love is and what it does. Pure love, which is the biblical description of God himself, is not perceivable as essence but as effect. It shows itself as loving actions take place. Only in relationships can love be expressed, or exist, even if it is the individual's love for himself which is expressed as self love. Love is normative for all relationships. It forms them. Love may be broadly defined as concern for, or interest in, that which is other even that which is other within the self.

It follows that there are obviously degrees of 'loved-ness' that characterise each relationship. In Moltmann's scheme, loved-ness expresses itself in terms of promise or commitment that proves itself by the fulfilment of that promise or carrying out of that commitment. The ontological basis for relationships, for Moltmann, exists in the power of the future forming the present. This follows from the promises we make. The gospel is the revealing of the promises of God. He

---

[42] Young, Ackerman and Kyle, *Looking On*, 17. We should note that knowing a language well also involves knowing the culture that accompanies the language itself, for without that it is difficult to understand meaning correctly.

invites us to commit ourselves to him in faith based on these promises. He also invites us to commit ourselves to other persons, on this basis. The love of God shown in the reconciling work of Christ on the cross frees us from the fear that normally prevents us forming relationships in this way.

c. Moltmann's Use of Perspective and how Perceptions are Determined by Conceptions that come from Attributions and Attitudes

In *The Coming of God* Moltmann emphasises how perspective forms the basis for his theological reflections. He does not just concentrate on a single perspective but many.

> *The Aim: Integrating Eschatology:* With this eschatology, I am aiming at an integration of perspectives which so often diverge: the perspectives of 'individual' and universal eschatology, the eschatology of history and the eschatology of nature too.[43]

Included in the perspectives that he attempts to integrate is a study on the relationship between God and creation. He views this relationship in the context of the traditional understandings of the nature and will of God. Moltmann, in dialogue with Whitehead, Rosenzweig and Urs von Balthasar develops the category of God's imagination which he uses as a vehicle for enabling the fullness of God to be understood.

> Inappropriate though human analogy is bound to be, in thinking of the fullness of God we can best talk about the inexhaustibly rich *fantasy* of God, meaning by that his creative imagination. From that imagination life upon life proceeds in protean abundance.[44]

Moltmann had earlier, in his dialogue with Bloch's conceptions of 'Messianic hopes and concrete utopias', identified the way in which God's imagination, or fantasy, is that which transcends time.

> In life all only repeats itself,
> Only fantasy is eternally young. What has never ever been,
> That alone never grows old (F. Schiller).[45]

We can enhance the human perspective on divine activity and ontology, believes Moltmann, by incorporating the notion of God's imagination into our understanding of God. He develops Whitehead's differentiation of God's nature into his primordial nature and his con-

---

[43] Moltmann, *The Coming of God*, xiv.
[44] Moltmann, *The Coming of God*, 338.
[45] J. Moltmann, *History and the Triune God. Contributions to Trinitarian Theology* (London: SCM Press, 1991) 149.

The Concept of Relationship 197

sequent nature. He sees this as 'an interesting conception'. 'When we look more closely at this doctrine about God's two natures, we find that as far as his consequent nature is concerned, the process of reality really does make God ever richer'.[46]

Moltmann is rightly critical though of Whitehead's concept of the consequent nature of God 'as representing a God who, resembles an unfeeling monitor, which registers and records everything, rather than a human memory which can transform, forgive and forget'.[47]

Central to Moltmann's understanding of the fullness of God is the category of joy which he characteristically describes in doxological language.

> The fullness of God is the rapturous fullness of the divine life; a life that communicates itself with inexhaustible creativity; an overbrimming life that makes what is dead and withered live; a life from which everything that lives receives its vital energies and its zest for living; a source of life to which everything that has been made alive responds with deepest joy and ringing exultation.[48]

Causing this joy is God's interaction with his creation. He is in relationship with his creation in a dynamic way. Flowing from him, and specifically from his 'imagination', are the *charis* that transform life here for us as God takes us up into his life.[49] We are involved in his life and he communicates the energies that are his life to us through our involvement with him. This occurs as we live in our primary relationship with him as part of his created order. He enhances this through our personal relationship with him as we acknowledge his sovereignty over us.

God expresses his joy to us through his divine imagination that enables us to appreciate 'the open fullness of God'. This is not a simple communication of 'the positive' and 'the good', by God to mankind, but is a transfiguring of that which is not good. Moltmann notes: 'We are therefore heeding Hegel' and he does this by incorporating 'the seriousness, the suffering, the patience, and the labour of the negative'.[50]

---

[46] Moltmann, *The Coming of God*, 331.
[47] Moltmann, *The Coming of God*, 332.
[48] Moltmann, *The Coming of God*, 336.
[49] See also J. Moltmann, *Theology and Joy* (London: SCM Press, 1973) where he examines the place of joy in the Christian life and its potentially transforming power. He says, for example, '... Christian congregations should not use their allotted portion of the time free of labour and domination entirely for educational and socio-ethical activities ... [but] Christians should experiment with the possibilities of creative freedom' (85).
[50] Moltmann, *The Coming of God*, 383, footnote 37.

We can extend Moltmann's thoughts on these matters to our perceptions of God. We can note that by using the concepts of perspective, imagination and divine communication of the essence of God through his relationships, firstly within the Trinity and secondly with his creation, Moltmann's approach allows us to view God as forming our concepts of him in us as we acknowledge his active involvement with us.

We can appreciate his ability to provide a bridge for us to the timeless 'zone' of eternity through the idea of his kingdom coming to pass as he transforms that which we are and do whether it involves negative or positive attributions by us to these things in our lives. Moltmann's scheme allows the messianic nature of God's ontological existence to be involved in our changing lives without it taking anything away from our concept of God or it needing us to view God simply as an impersonal but efficient processor of events in his creation.

We form our attributions and attitudes to God by the relationship that we understand to exist between God and ourselves. This is an open and developing relationship in which there are covenant commitments on both sides. This redeeming and creative relationship results in the consummation of all things at the eschaton in a joy and fullness that Moltmann describes in the human terms of 'dance' and 'laughter'.[51] This emphasises freedom and yet involves commitment and accountability.

d. Relationships Involving Interpreters and the Issue of Trust

In this section, we will look first at the ways in which Deaf people's experience of relationships is similar to that of hearing people. Deaf people have been subject to many of the same changes and challenges as hearing people in the modern world. Modernity has been recognised by many, including David Wells, as being 'an interlocking system of values that has invaded and settled within the psyche of every person ... [i]t is, to put it in biblical terms, the worldliness of Our Time'. David Wells has highlighted the impact of modernity on the modern evangelical church and one of its great deceits is that it convinces us 'that God himself is secondary to organization and image'. The result of this is that sometimes the answer to the problems that the church is facing is seen to be that the church

> ... is not *efficient* enough ... or ... not *appealing* enough, because it has not adapted itself adequately to the inner needs of those in the

---

[51] Moltmann, *The Coming of God*, 339.

modern world. ... [and] many are attempting to heal the church by tinkering with its structures, its services, its public face.[52]

It is important to consider, in the modern world, the nature of the relationship Deaf people have with hearing people mediated through an interpreter. Napier has referred to the way in which trust is an intrinsic element in Deaf people's experience of the relationship with interpreters. This may depend on the way in which the interpreter seeks to 'keep in' with the Deaf client by perhaps using lip patterns accompanying signs so that the Deaf person can check the accuracy of the sign. This may provide a bolster to confidence but veers away from the bi-cultural and bi-lingual approach to interpreting which provides the interpreter with more freedom, where adequate trust exists, to more accurately translate the content of a message. Napier says

> that the majority of BSL interpreters use a form of literal translation, as opposed to a 'free' translation, as this is the safest way to embrace their cultural understanding within the interpretation, but still allows them to 'mouth' the English words in co-ordination with the signs, as required by many Deaf clients.[53]

One of the issues here is the need to convey a message and the need to generate a level of trust that would allow a 'free' translation to take place. This would allow the interpreter to '... focus entirely on the meaning, to ignore the form of the message, and ensure that any piece of information is made equally relevant to all parties involved'.[54]

Ideally, the interpreter, who has knowledge of the cultural values of Deaf people, mediates words and concepts in the correct way. The problem is that cultural values are an imprecise way of describing a whole range of emotions, attitudes and attributions that may vary considerably from one person to another or from one group to another. There is a need to avoid treating Deaf people paternalistically. The lack of trust that comes from oppression and paternalistic attitudes in the past may cause them to be sensitive to these issues. This can reduce the level of trust that must exist between interpreter and Deaf person and there may be insufficient freedom allowed to the interpreter to convey the meaning of the message properly. In practice we think it must be acknowledged that the necessary imprecision of defining what is termed cultural values, means that an interpreter can never be 100% effective. Trust is inherent in all communication. The level of trust

---

[52] D. Wells, *God in the Wasteland* (Grand Rapids: Eerdmans, 1994) 30.
[53] J. Napier, 'Free your mind – the rest will follow' in *Deaf Worlds* 14 Number 3 (November 1998) 21.
[54] Napier, 'Free', 15.

required of Deaf people is higher when a third person, the interpreter, is involved in the communication process.

An important element in this discussion concerning relationships involving interpreters is the way in which, in the modern world, the relationship of the Deaf person with the interpreter is often a professional one arranged by contract. This is a general feature of many relationships in the modern world. Moltmann has said concerning these matters that

> [f]ree persons live together socially in a dense weave of promises made and kept, of agreements and trustworthiness; such coexistence cannot exist without trust. It is not predetermined *membership*, but rather *covenant* that is the paradigm of a free society and this covenant is based on social consensus.[55]

The very nature of the relationship the Deaf person usually has with the interpreter can mean that trust does not exist automatically. Within a pre-modern society where relationships were more organic in nature the Deaf person would be more likely to know and trust the interpreter and we might expect communication to be more accurate because of this. Moltmann asserts that it is in such a community that freedom is found.

> Where do I feel personally free? ... [I]n a community in which I am accepted, and in which others know and thus affirm me as I am ... For me, true freedom is realised through mutual acknowledgement and reciprocal acceptance; that is, it is realised personally through friendship, and politically through covenant.[56]

Even today in a smaller community the name of the interpreter may be known and there will be a level of trust based on the interpreter's reputation and past performance.

For Deaf people the existence of a lack of trust which exists in their relationship both with interpreters and with a hearing world, a world which has often misused and abused them in the past, takes away from them that mutual enrichment which could come from the experience of 'difference' in their everyday lives.

Within a church based on the type of relationships that Moltmann's ecclesiology recommends this trust would be more likely to exist. Trust by hearing people in the reliability or otherwise of the message presented to them within a church setting depends also on the trust they have in the messenger. The hearer will either have established this

---

[55] J. Moltmann, 'Christianity and the Values of the Western World', transcript of a lecture at St Paul's Cathedral in September 1998, 13.
[56] Moltmann, *'Christianity'*, 13.

through the building of a trusting relationship through contact and interaction over a period of time or through another person vouching for the reliability of the messenger. Alternatively it may have been established through the institutional processes of the church providing that reassurance by having in place systems and procedures which ensure that the messengers are adequately trained and supported in their ministry according to certain standards which are published for all to see.

e. Defining the Difference between Hearing People and Deaf People

As we consider the relationships that are possible between Deaf people and hearing people we should seek to understand how we define these groups.

The certainty with which one group understands another group or what causes them to differ from themselves is not as clear as it at first seems. Differences of kind have been used in the past to justify oppression and these have been based more on presuppositions than facts. Generalisation is our usual way of extending the particular to the many, and it is clearly an imprecise and, at best, metaphoric use of language. Hearing people believe they have an idea of what Deaf people are like, but they are unable to define this with accuracy.

We can learn from the way in which Turner, in the context of arguing for an apophatic approach to understanding God, describes how Meister Eckhart faces concepts of sameness and difference. '"[D]ifference" is detectable only against a background of "sameness". With individuals it is easiest to say how they differ when they are individuals of the same kind'.[57] '[A]ll words are left behind in the silence of the apophatic'.[58] The inadequacy of our descriptions of difference between categories means that we are led to assume a similar apophaticism towards understanding people groups.

Turner's conclusion about Eckhart's theological use of language is that it is unable to describe the otherness of God. Similarly, using language, we find difficulty in describing the differences that exist between Deaf and hearing people. We believe that an apophatic approach is more able to reveal differences. That is, describing what is *not* different about them leads us to an understanding of what *is* different.

---

[57] D. Turner, 'The Art of Unknowing – Negative Theology in Late Medieval Mysticism' in *Modern Theology* 14 (1988) 477.
[58] Turner, 'Art of Unknowing', 479.

Although his discussion concerns the ecumenical movement Moltmann also describes a way of viewing differences.

> In the ecumenical movement we began with a comparison of different church doctrines and spirituality and orders with the purpose of finding out what separates us and we discovered, in one conference after another, that the differences in theological doctrines and spirituality were not great enough to justify the separation of the churches. On the contrary, we discovered that we could be mutually enriched by our different conceptions.[59]

Any descriptions may be imprecise as they may emphasise one aspect over another, ignore other aspects or the words used may simply be inadequate. Not only is the nature of talk of God metaphorical but we can agree with Brümmer concerning 'the fundamentally *metaphorical* nature of all human thought and experience'.[60] We can conclude from this that it is less possible than is commonly thought to describe aspects of any group that show how it is different from another.

f. The Effect of Society on Relationships

In this section, we will focus on the way the world in which both Deaf and hearing live affects their understanding of themselves and their relationships.

Many writers have noted the almost all pervading influence of consumerism on understandings of self and relationships. Giddens notes that 'commodification' arises from '[a] market system [which] ... generates a variety of available choices in the consumption of goods and services'.[61] One of the traits associated with this concentration on image is narcissism. He notes that in a society, such as ours, where these characteristics exist '[a]ll self-development depends on the mastering of appropriate responses to others; [and that] ... an individual who has to be "different" from all others has no chance of reflexively developing a coherent self-identity'.[62]

Deaf people must establish their own individual difference at the same time as emancipating themselves from the definition that society

---

[59] J. Moltmann, 'Christianity on the Threshold of the Third Millennium – What to preserve and what to leave behind', transcript of a lecture at St Paul's Cathedral in September 1998, 21.

[60] V. Brümmer, *The Model of Love* (Cambridge: Cambridge University Press, 1993) 8.

[61] A. Giddens, *Modernity and Self-Identity* (Cambridge: Polity Press in association with Blackwell Publishers, 1991) 200.

[62] Giddens, *Modernity*, 200.

has given them because of their disability. Giddens says, in the modern era 'ideas of emancipation' have generated

> [e]mancipatory politics [which] involves two main elements: the effort to shed shackles of the past, thereby permitting a transformative attitude towards the future; and the aim of overcoming the illegitimate domination of some individuals or groups by others.[63]

Moltmann's insistence on the church as being, among other things, political encompasses this notion of emancipatory politics, for he has designed his project to encapsulate the gospel message of the releasing of the captives.

> Emancipatory politics works with a hierarchical notion of power: power is understood as the capability of an individual or group to exert its will over others ... [and] to reduce or eliminate *exploitation, inequality* and *oppression*.[64]

In the case of the church, we may view the power exerted as the 'power of God' although that may sometimes be a euphemism for power exerted by human beings, individually, or as a group.

We must acknowledge that emancipatory politics involves an act of judgement, or discrimination, by which one person defines others by labelling them 'the exploited, unequal or oppressed'. By this very act and the use of language to signify that they are 'different' they are not only identifying them but they are also separating themselves from those who are 'different'. The very use of this method creates 'an oppression that exists in difference' by virtue of the categories it generates. In this way, it is working against one of the other characteristics of Moltmann's ecclesiology, which is ecumenism. The intention of ecumenism is to seek to deal with and overcome the problems associated with difference.

We can illustrate this by reference again to one of Moltmann's favourite texts, (Mt. 25:40). It could be argued that Jesus is using the category of 'the least of these' to refer theologically to 'all men who are your brothers in this life in some sense of the word'. When we encounter these people they appear to us to be the poor but this does not mean that we should define them in this way. Defining someone can separate us from them. It can also allow us to exploit them. The question may be asked who gives us the right to judge these others as 'different'? The answer comes through 'loving our neighbour'. In identifying with, and being with, those whom we have initially identified as different we cancel our original classification whereby we

---

[63] Giddens, *Modernity*, 210.
[64] Giddens, *Modernity*, 211.

viewed them as 'different'. The view we have of ourselves in relation to others changes. We may still note that differences exist but the hierarchical relationship with those who are different has disappeared. Any sense of superiority dissolves as we become one with those whom we had earlier considered to be inferior.

g. The Value of 'Friendship Type' Relationships in the Deaf Context

In this section, we will consider how Moltmann's emphasis in his ecclesiology on 'friendship type' relationships can be of value to Deaf people.

John Inge has made the point that 'friendship is the model upon which we should concentrate as we try to understand what it means to be human and what it means to be Christian'. It has so much potential as a fundamental model 'which is not exclusive of anyone ... [and] should in addition be an essential ingredient of all ... relationships'.[65] He follows Lash who has argued that God has made us capable of friendship and this distinguishes us as humans. It makes us capable therefore of 'effectively resisting the degradation of relationship into bonds of ownership and exploitation, dominance and violence and unconcern'.[66] He says, as a Christian, 'I have been taught that I must try to learn to place my fundamental loyalty with no people, no possibility of friendship, more restricted than the human race'.[67]

Inge asks the pertinent question 'Could it be that friendship is the normative Christian relationship?'[68] Both Inge and Lash are in favour of an understanding of the 'friendship type' relationship, to which Jesus calls all his disciples, as being one that does not discriminate against particular individuals or groups. They also stress that such a friendship is not one where God calls us to a morality that results in selfless action necessarily, but one where a degree of reciprocity is evident. Inge says of Jesus' washing of his disciples' feet, '[t]he emphasis is on reciprocity where our generosity and love are encouraged and supported by that of others'.[69] This emphasis allows for our inability to act always without concern for ourselves, either consciously, or otherwise.

---

[65] J. Inge, 'Friendship and Christian Relationship' in *Theology* 101(1998) 425.
[66] N. Lash, 'Hoping against Hope or Abraham's Dilemma' in *Modern Theology* 10 (1994) 242.
[67] Lash, 'Hoping', 242.
[68] Inge, 'Friendship', 425.
[69] Inge, 'Friendship', 424.

There are particular problems that we face as we endeavour to build relationships in the light of our Christian faith. These are rooted in our tendency to 'include' some portion of mankind as being more favoured in our thinking than others and our tendency to be idealistic and disregard our constant inability to live up to our own expectations. The result of these two tendencies is that we tend to discriminate against certain people or groups of people and to be unrealistic in our expectations as to what is achievable in our relationships with others. The potential of 'friendship type' relationships, which Moltmann sees as central to our experience of church as community, and as recognised by Inge and Lash, is that we are called to a wide inclusivism as an ideal. We exhibit and experience vulnerability as we enter into these types of relationship that carry the risk of failure with them. By giving control of the relationship partially to 'the other', we act in faith that God will protect and guide us as we proceed. This contrasts with other types of relationship that allow control by one party or the other to be the norm. We can view friendship type relationships as non-hierarchical in the sense that one person is not 'over' another. Control of the relationship comes from the norms of the Christian group or groups to which the parties belong. Christian 'friendship type' relationships therefore differ from non-Christian friendships by virtue of the fact that the norms of behaviour, such as self-giving, serving the other, etc. may have a more consciously prominent place in the relationships.

For minority and oppressed groups, such as Deaf people that have suffered discrimination, a model of relationship that is fundamentally non-discriminatory has its attractions. Other alternative relationships which can exist within a church setting would all seem to involve a hierarchical approach whereby subordination is called for in the interests of the common good. Whilst these can operate effectively and have apparent advantages in combating the brokenness and damage incurred by the inner self of a person who has suffered discriminatory practices, Moltmann believes a friend alongside is to be preferred to one who ministers from a position of assumed superiority.

It would seem that adopting such a model results in us thinking about other people in a certain way, which determines our attitudes to them and these affect our future actions. This type of relationship involves God by allowing the norms of Christians, whether based on Scripture, tradition or experience to be the determining factor. God is therefore present in the intentions of those involved in the relationship as they acknowledge his values in their beliefs about themselves and the future.

We are suggesting here that the 'friendship type' model of relationship is beneficial in reducing prejudice.

Prejudice is a quality of an individual ... a generalized feeling towards members of a group that disposes a person to think or act unfavourably towards the members of that group.[70]

Fitzpatrick notes that two important aspects in the development of prejudice are *the categorizing of objects of knowledge* and *the formation of stereotypes* and that prejudice 'perpetuates itself through imitation, acculturation or socialization'.[71]

We have sought to show that by urging the giving of priority to relationships, which will by their nature preclude the development of prejudicial attitudes, hearing and Deaf people will be able to interact more successfully. For these relationships to be based within a Christian church community the experience of Deaf people will be less likely to include the experience of prejudice which they encounter as a matter of course in their relationships in their daily lives.

h. Trinitarian Relationships in Moltmann's Ecclesiology

In this section, we will consider the way in which Moltmann has used his understanding of the relationships within the Trinity to act as a model for the type of relationships he believes are normative for people within the church. We will question whether this is a theologically sound approach and whether the project stands up to criticism. Our purpose in doing this at this stage is to show the grounding for 'friendship type' relationships in Moltmann's ecclesiology.

As Gavin D'Costa has said, in his review of Volf's recent book, 'Volf, following Moltmann, argues for pure egalitarian relationships within the Trinity such that no subordination or hierarchy are possible'.[72] D'Costa says that 'like Moltmann, Volf introduces a conceptual and substantive distinction between the constitution of the persons and their relations'.[73] For D'Costa, Volf's ecclesiology, like Moltmann's, is in danger of presenting an ontological monarchistic view of the Trinity. D'Costa in his criticism of Volf, which we can extend to aspects of Moltmann's understanding of the Trinity, separates the proleptic experience of the church, eschatologically understood, from the ontology of Trinity. As we have seen, central to Moltmann's theology is an eschatological ontological understanding, not only of

---

[70] J.P. Fitzpatrick, 'Prejudice' in ed/s *New Catholic Encyclopedia*, Vol XI (New York: McGraw-Hill Book Company, 1967) 728-729.
[71] Fitzpatrick, 'Prejudice', 729.
[72] G. D'Costa, '"On Trinitarian Ecclesiologies", a review of "After Our Likeness. The Church as Image of the Trinity"' by M. Volf in *Reviews in Religion and Theology* Number 3 (August 1998) 9.
[73] D'Costa, 'On Trinitarian', 10.

humankind but also of God himself. The difficulty D'Costa also encounters is with attempting to view in a static way, the dynamic, almost process, views of ontological reality that Moltmann employs. For Moltmann, God is God ontologically in his relations with his creation, as well as with his inner-trinitarian relations. This makes the created order 'part' of God, and so the view is panentheistic. Speaking of the activity of the Spirit, Moltmann says '... creation is a trinitarian process: the Father creates through the Son in the Holy Spirit'.[74]

> It is always the Spirit who first brings the activity of the Father and the Son to its goal. ... Everything that is, exists and lives in the unceasing inflow of the energies and potentialities of the cosmic Spirit. ... Through the energies and potentialities of the Spirit, the Creator is himself present in his creation. He does not merely confront it in his transcendence; entering into it, he is also immanent in it.[75]

If we view God in a static way we either see his inner-trinitarian relations as being 'prior' to his relations with his creation or we see them as a form of modalism. Moltmann's alternative is to view the future, as we perceive it, as being our experience of God. Our understanding of him is not as a subject, remote but graspable, and describable in human terms by analogy, but as a dialectical influence on us which is a fundamental part of our being. He is a God who is always 'coming towards us' out of the future and thus is constitutive of us as well as himself in this dynamic, almost process way of understanding.

We can reasonably ask whether it is valid to extend explanations of trinitarian ontology to the relationships that exist within the church. Volf has argued this convincingly in his recent book. He acknowledges the limits of using the analogy of the Trinity to understand the church[76] but argues that the early church used the Trinity as a way of reconciling its divergent understandings of our relationship to God and to each other. He says that this '... correspondence is grounded in Christian baptism [which] leads believers simultaneously into both trinitarian and ecclesial communion' and that '[i]f Christian initiation is a trinitarian event, then the church must speak of the Trinity as its determining reality'.[77] Significantly, he acknowledges that *Scripture* must determine how we use our analogies when he says '... thinking about the

---

[74] Moltmann, *God in Creation*, 9.
[75] Moltmann, *God in Creation*, 9.
[76] M. Volf, *After Our Likeness. The Church as the Image of the Trinity* (Grand Rapids and Cambridge: Eerdmans, 1998) 198.
[77] Volf, *Likeness*, 195.

Trinity and about social relations in light of the Trinity must be shaped primarily by the scriptural narrative of the triune God'.[78]

Moltmann's answer seems to be that our epistemology needs to reflect the 'eschatological view of reality' as he believes the New Testament presents it to us. Thus, God is always the 'coming God'. Future possibility, in terms of human freedom and potential for relationships, both between humans and with God, is seen as the primary determining factor in Moltmann's epistemology which is closely linked with his ontology.

LaFollette has said that 'whilst most people would deny that they think relationships are static ... our language belies that claim ... [d]ynamic systems, by their very nature, tend to cease unless they are constantly energized ... [l]ikewise for personal relationships ... they survive only if something is done to sustain them, only if the two parties continually relate in meaningful ways'.[79] LaFollette builds an argument that classifies emotions as habits 'emotions are habits, and habits are not under our direct control'.[80] These are important matters when considering 'friendship type' relationships. Initially, he draws on Aristotle's description of friendship as given in Nicomachean Ethics.

> Aristotle divides friendship into three categories: friendships of utility, friendships of pleasure and complete friendships [which are] ... the ideal form ... [A] complete friendship is built on the care for each other as particular, embodied people of good character. It is not a circuitous way of making each person feel better or of satisfying her interests.[81]

Aristotle in Book X of Nicomachean Ethics identifies and emphasises the equalising character of friendships in that both the parties to the friendship gain directly or indirectly from the relationship. 'In all friendships between dissimilars it is, as we have said, proportion that equalizes the parties and preserves the friendship'.[82] He links justice with the process of friendship, but says

> equality does not seem to take the same form in acts of justice and in friendship; for in acts of justice what is equal in the primary sense is that which is in proportion to merit, while quantitative equality is

---

[78] Volf, *Likeness*, 194.
[79] H. LaFollette, *Personal Relationships. Love, Identity, and Morality* (Oxford and Cambridge, Massachusetts: Blackwell, 1996) xi.
[80] LaFollette, *Relationships*, 34.
[81] LaFollette, *Relationships*, 14.
[82] J. Barnes (ed.), *The Complete Works of Aristotle, Volume 2* (Princeton: Princeton University Press, 1984) 1839 (1163b28f).

secondary, but in friendship quantitative equality is primary and proportion to merit secondary.[83]

Aristotle says we cannot view God as a friend because he is too far from us. '[W]hen one party is removed to a great distance as God is, the possibility of friendship ceases'.[84]

Moltmann wants to avoid a concept of hierarchy in the being of God and in his relationships with his creation. This is to avoid the dominance of one over another. His reasoning is that the inner-trinitarian relationships that we perceive God to have and the relationships he has with his creation will be prescriptive for the relationships his created beings have with one another. The assumption is that the power exerted in hierarchical relationships will have the potential for evil. Moltmann views our reconciliation with God as having drawn us into a close relationship with him, and through his emphasis on the perichoretic nature of our existence with God, there is now no 'distance' between us and so friendship type non-hierarchical relationships are possible. The relationships we understand as existing within the Trinity are a model for our own human relationships.[85]

i. The Dialectic of Anxiety and Hope in Christian Relationships and Moltmann's Use of Process Thought

We have considered the way in which, for Moltmann, the ideal relationship within the church is a close 'friendship type'. This model has its roots in inner-trinitarian relationships. In this section, we will consider the way in which the dialectic of anxiety and hope is central to such relationships and how this particularly affects Deaf people.

Moltmann in his chapter on 'The Anxiety of Christ' says, '[i]n anxiety and hope we go beyond existing reality and anticipate the future, so as to make a correct decision about the present'. These two attitudes allow us to transcend the present. Anxiety enables us to anticipate possible danger and hope gives us the courage to face danger or we will 'be numbed by anxiety and totally engulfed by it'.[86] Moltmann makes the point that '[Kierkegaard's] "concept of dread" and [Bloch's] "principle of hope" are not opposites at all. They are quite capable of complementing one another'.[87] That each of these come from God our

---

[83] Barnes, *Aristotle*, 1831 (1158b29-32).
[84] Barnes, *Aristotle*, 1831 (1159a4f).
[85] Moltmann does not deny that God is greater than his creation and rules over it. What he wants to avoid is earthly notions of ruling and subjection that bear no resemblance to the God of the Bible.
[86] J. Moltmann, *Jesus Christ for Today's World* (London: SCM Press, 1994) 52.
[87] Moltmann, *Jesus Christ*, 53.

creator as part of his redemptive process is evident when Moltmann answers the question, *'Who is Christ for me?'* with the answer 'The Christ for me is the crucified Jesus'.[88]

> All human anxiety and fear is fundamentally – which means from birth onwards – fear of separation. ... In our anxiety we participate in Christ's anxiety; for in his suffering Christ went through the very fears and anxieties which men and women encounter too.[89]

Moltmann says '[w]hatever pain, weakness and loneliness people experience in their fear of separation culminates in the experience of being forsaken by God'.[90] The release from fear that we need comes from Christ.

> In the image of the crucified Jesus our indefinable anxiety takes on a form with which we can identify, because in that image we discover our own total wretchedness. It is part of ourselves, our own identity, our own grief. This is the conformity christology of the 'Christ with us'... .[91]

Theologically, Moltmann is using the Christology of 'Christ with us' to explain how reconciliation with God and with other people is achieved. The problem is separation and the answer is conformity with Christ that occurs through us identifying with the *image* of the Christ Jesus crucified. Both anxiety and hope are valid parts of our experience on the way to that point of reconciliation. The fear of separation produces grief in us. God assuages this grief by the hope that accompanies the knowledge of, and experience of, the resurrection. Accompanying this is 'Christ's vicarious suffering of fear and pain'.[92] We have noted previously that God's promise of redemption is ours by faith in his faithfulness.

All relationships exist with the possibility that they may cease. They are vulnerable to the fear that accompanies this possibility. Moltmann shows that their stability and continued existence is dependent on a dialectic of anxiety and hope.

For Deaf people there is a constant awareness of separation, whether they live partly, or fully, in the hearing world. The barriers to communication that exist for them in the hearing culture separate them from important information. Their experience is of a fragmented world, in the sense that it is partial, and they are aware, at least in part, of their

---

[88] Moltmann, *Jesus Christ*, 2-3.
[89] Moltmann, *Jesus Christ*, 53.
[90] Moltmann, *Jesus Christ*, 54.
[91] Moltmann, *Jesus Christ*, 55.
[92] Moltmann, *Jesus Christ*, 55.

non-participation in that world. They will sometimes want or need information from the hearing culture in which they exist and they may experience more fear and anxiety because of this.

Moltmann's recognition that alienation and fear are at the heart of the 'human problem' makes his theology particularly relevant. The experience of Deaf people is not just one of marginalization and oppression. It is also one of fear due to the separation that exists between them and the information conveyed by sound in hearing culture. As evidence of how Deaf people can live with hearing people in a culture that does not cause alienation in this way we can note the famous account of Deaf people on Martha's Vineyard, Massachusetts by Nora Groce. She found

> ... towns .. which for over two hundred years had a high incidence of hereditary deafness. The residents compensated for this condition by inventing or borrowing an efficient sign language which was used by almost everyone, hearing and deaf alike ... She shows the extraordinary degree to which deaf people were integrated into the community, for Vineyarders did not consider deafness to be a handicap. [93]

We have noted earlier that in Moltmann's understanding of what constitutes being and the problem of possible separation, there are elements of process thought. Cobb has provided a useful review of contemporary political theology of three German theologians, J.B. Metz, Dorothy Sölle and Moltmann in the light of process theology.[94] Noting Moltmann's commitment to the need for liberation in an ecological sense as well as a personal and political sense, Cobb quotes substantially from a passage in *The Crucified God*[95] noting that '[t]his is a beautiful summary of guiding images for practice for which a process theologian can only be grateful [he notes that] ... [c]ommitment to these symbols must be related more concretely to political theory and practice'.[96] Cobb has already noted that, for Moltmann, 'the political is not the one horizon for all theology'.[97] He also notes that the political theology which he advocates is one which calls 'for criticism and could support revolution'[98] rather than simply sanctioning the *status quo*.

---

[93] N.E. Groce, *Everyone Here Spoke Sign Language* (Cambridge, Massachusetts and London: Harvard University Press, 1985). Foreword by J.W.M. Whiting.
[94] J.B. Cobb, Jr., *Process Theology as Political Theology* (Manchester: Manchester University Press and Philadelphia: Westminster Press, 1982).
[95] Cobb, *Process*, 90-91.
[96] Cobb, *Process*, 91.
[97] Cobb, *Process*, 12.
[98] Cobb, *Process*, 3.

Cobb notes the way in which some of Moltmann's emphases and methodologies show an influence of process thought and how, '[w]hen process theology does reflect on this central question, [between theory and practice] it finds it can learn much from the sources on which political theology draws'.[99] In arguing that '[t]heologians, of all people, should not underestimate the importance of great beliefs' Cobb seems to over-equate praxis with relevance and states that '[p]ractice is always theory laden, and the relevance for which this model [the praxis model] calls is relevance to a situation which is already perceived through established concepts'.[100] He then goes on to say that 'the praxis model does not work well in the interaction of diverse communities informed by different experience, different practice, different theory and different horizons of meaning' and that process theology has a contribution to make.

> Growth occurs when the conflicting beliefs are converted by creative thought into what Whitehead calls a contrast. That is, their distinct integrity and power are retained in their mutual tension. But a new understanding or perspective is attained in which the truth of each can be realised along with the limitation of each other ... [so] [w]e attain a new basis for a new praxis.[101]

In summary he says:

> There are apparent similarities between growth through contrast and the dialectical process of the Hegelian and Marxist traditions. Indeed, in some of the formulations of the dialectic, the results may be identical. Nevertheless, the usual understanding and application of the dialectic do not lead to the radical openness that is needed, the readiness to encounter the unexpected or the tradition that has developed out of quite alien assumptions.[102]

We understand Moltmann to be proposing just this openness to other traditions and interaction with them. There is an expectation that the unexpected may occur, and the acknowledgement that although we may gain a better perspective from our interaction, we leave others with the right to retain their independent and different understanding of what is. In this way, it would appear that Moltmann has adapted process thought into his understanding and application of his dialectic. For

---

[99] Cobb, *Process*, 58.
[100] Cobb, *Process*, 59.
[101] Cobb, *Process*, 61.
[102] Cobb, *Process*, 62.

The Concept of Relationship 213

him praxis is able to create concepts of truth, and he is committed to the value of theoretical as well as practically based truth.[103]

Moltmann shows that his understanding can be developed and enhanced by his use of process thought and yet he has retained his firm commitment to the primacy of the Christian faith.

Summary and Conclusion

In this chapter we looked at the concept of relationship in Moltmann's ecclesiology and its appropriateness for Deaf people. We noted how Moltmann emphasises the messianic element in the being of the church and how he views all godly relationships as having a liberating function. He uses the *messianic* as a category to mediate between the kingdom of God and history. It is the function of the church to facilitate liberation in the economic, political and cultural areas of life. Moltmann views direct action not simply as intervention but as solidarity and fellowship with others. This enables us to take on their suffering to alleviate it and build community and relationships, which to Moltmann is life itself. This solidarity and fellowship with others also protects the liberated people from becoming the future exploiters.

We saw how Moltmann sees very strong links between our attitude and actions. These may be attitudes and actions towards one another or towards our environment and the ecological systems of the world. He proposes a change in our attitudes and actions from exploitation to co-operation.

With regard to social settings, Moltmann shows how the values of psychology and social psychology operate to produce defensive mechanisms when we encounter an impaired person. We should view all people, impaired or not, in the light of their justification before God. We may then view the Christian fellowship as a social form of justification.

We next saw openness generates a sense of security and reduces tension in relationships. Assurance concerning the nature of our being and our future enable us to be open to encounters, which would otherwise be threatening. Openness facilitates the creation of relational space, which enables the formation of new relationships.

Our understanding of relationships formed by eschatological hope is that they are relationships of love based on commitment, and this involves promises of fulfilment. God's covenant relationship with us

---

[103] Evidence of his faith in this can be seen in his dialogues with other traditions in the World Council of Churches, and with Jewish and Marxist thinkers, which were entered into in the hope of an increased understanding of commonalities.

acts as a model for human relationships. His covenant involves the evidence of past promises now fulfilled, including the death and resurrection of Christ, and the future promise of the eschaton that in experiential terms is always 'coming towards us'.

We looked at how Moltmann employs a variety of perspectives to view relationships and develops the category of God's imagination as a vehicle for understanding the fullness of God's creative activity. From this we can increase our understanding of God's being because imagination allows for both *the new thing* and a transcending of time. The fullness of God in his creative activity is seen in joy transfiguring that which is not good, taking up suffering and all that is negative. It flows from God to us and exhibits itself in the form of *charis* that transform our life.

We concluded that, due to the metaphorical nature of all human thought, an apophatic approach to our understanding of the differences between people groups is preferable.

We looked at the effect of society on relationships and noted the influence in modern society of consumerism, concentration on image and 'commodification' also extends to belief systems emphasising individual choice. These limit the ability of disabled people to fully develop a coherent self-identity. We saw that emancipatory politics, which pre-supposes a hierarchy of power and involve acts of judgment and discrimination, can stigmatise some people such as 'the poor' by categorising them as different.

We looked at friendship type relationships and saw that Moltmann views these as normative for Christians. They are inclusive and emphasise reciprocity and by their very nature work against discriminatory practices and prejudice. We saw how Moltmann models these types of relationship on an understanding of inner-trinitarian relationships and how we experience freedom in the possibility of future relationships. We saw how the exchange of emotions that takes place in relationships sustains friendship and acts as an equalising factor. Within friendships 'justice' is secondary, because 'equality' takes precedence.

To summarise then, in this chapter we saw that the distinctive views of Moltmann on relationships of friendship can be of great value to Deaf people. In particular he offers a theologically sound explanation of why this type of relationship should be preferred over others and stresses the appropriateness of interdependence, equality and co-operation. More importantly he does not deny the difficulties that can arise from the tensions within such relationships but actually identifies this as the source of power that can transform us. The dialectic of anxiety and hope that exists within Christian relationships is the bridge that enables us to transcend the present and 'reach into' the future. As we identify ourselves wholly with Christ, who is with us in our suffering, we see ourselves as reconciled to God and this gives us a new perspective and openness that enables us to form new and liberating relationships.

Summary and Conclusion

We stated at the outset that, in this book, our aim was to provide a practical understanding of the ecclesiology of Jürgen Moltmann and to show its relevance for Deaf people. We put forward the theory that Moltmann's ecclesiology is especially appropriate for Deaf people because his method has parallels with their way of living and being, including how they understand their identity, the way they communicate and how they view their relationships. We said that his theological method is to provoke dialogue and thought by *suggestion* and that he often does this through the creative use of metaphor and by emphasising a relational perspective. This has parallels with the way Deaf people make sense of their lives by using sign language creatively, involving iconic signs and sign-metaphors and emphasising a relational perspective as they establish meaning and develop concepts.

We concluded that the problems Deaf people encounter in relation to the church including those relating to language, culture, disability, power, politics and a history of oppression and marginalization could be adequately addressed by Moltmann's ecclesiology. We found subtle but definite connections with his approach and the way in which Deaf people conceptualise. This includes his way of creating the possibility of new conceptual and relational space through the skilful use of iconic metaphor and by using a dialectical approach that allows for unresolved tensions in concepts and relationships. Through his unique approach to eschatology he provides a dynamic relational understanding of what it is *to be*.

In practical terms we have shown that Moltmann's ecclesiology can be helpful for Deaf people when dealing with poor self image, marginalization by the wider church, prejudice and discrimination, paternalism and oppression, stigma and isolation. He encourages open attitudes, dialogue, a non-judgemental acknowledgement of differences, and action to challenge the social, economic and political causes of oppression.

We saw that perceptions of language and power are dependent on attributions by us of values gained from society and culture. The resulting perspectives affect our attitudes, form intentions and lead to action. There are similarities between the way in which sign language uses perspective in storytelling, that appeals to visual imagery, and Moltmann's view of biblical methods of conveying truths about our relationship to God. Sign language also uses a rich combination of visual-spatial metaphors and iconic signs within a context where the relationship of the parties being referred to, those being signed to and the stance each has towards the other, is crucial for a correct understanding of what is being conveyed. The perichoretic nature of Deaf people's way of being and communicating in Deaf sign language corresponds well to Moltmann's view of life including the way in which creation of metaphorical meaning is a function of the community and involves a certain tentativeness. Some sign language constructions and some iconic metaphors are like boundaries that invite us to venture beyond that which we know and in this sense they are predictive rather than simply descriptive.

We saw that there are links between the way in which we accumulate knowledge and Moltmann's social understanding of being, and his view of time and the future. In particular we saw that he views acquisition of knowledge as including non-linguistic, visual spatial information at the conceptual level. We saw how our reaction to new information is crucially affected by our attitude and how Moltmann, facilitates the embracing of that which is unknown by us, through the use of a conception of the future that includes attitudes of hope, anticipation and openness.

We saw how he uses biblical thought forms and mythical categories that function dialectically as symbols to define seemingly opposing realities. This mirrors the way in which sign can creatively construct meaning by the juxtaposition of seemingly opposing or contradictory imagery. Moltmann's view of God as one who is always coming towards us creates anticipation and his view of humanity is one which, using a dialectical view of hope and suffering, allows for human incompleteness or difference, weakness or sickness.

Moltmann's ecclesiology addresses the fear of loss by incorporating it into his understanding of the being of God and through his interpretation of the impact of the cross on the persons of the Trinity. His relational understanding of being positively affects perceptions of personal boundaries and this could benefit Deaf people, who have a closer personal horizon, as his approach has the effect of dispelling fear of the unknown. The eschatological horizon of the kingdom of God provides a backdrop in the form of a visual spatial symbol against which human intentionality and attitudes are formed and held. Against this, Moltmann's view of communication is based on the identity of persons as coming from their existence in community and has connections with the way of understanding being and communication of Deaf people, which similarly has its basis in relationality.

Moltmann's view of perspectives draws on an analogy with visual perspectives. Hope is an intentional horizon that creates an open space for change and freedom and has links with sign language that uses physical symbolism and space creatively. There can be value in breaking away from a theology in which God's truth is constrained by words. Moltmann's use of openness is not in a neutral, passive or descriptive way but as an active tool that encourages ecumenicity. Freedom flows from a cautious optimism that is based on the inclusive and holistic nature of Moltmann's ecclesiology. Liberation of the oppressed is seen to be a natural responsibility of all and his stress on non-hierarchical relationships means that abuses of power can be avoided.

Moltmann emphasises the liberating nature of godly friendship type relationships that are based on his ideal of non-hierarchical trinitarian relationships. They allow for a dialectic of anxiety and hope and lead us to freedom that is not afraid to encounter that which is new.

We have some limited reservations concerning the applicability of Moltmann's ecclesiology to the situation of Deaf people. These include a recognition that there is a danger of idealism attaching to his view of interpersonal relationships even those that are non-hierarchical. Any practical set of relationships, even if informal in nature, require an awareness by those involved of moderating sanctions if dominance and oppression are to be avoided. We feel that some people would have difficulty in adapting to Moltmann's non-hierarchical approach to church and would favour a strong, but accountable, loving paternalism within a hierarchical structure. This may in fact be more appropriate for some people who lack the ability to function well in friendship type relationships for example people with learning or behavioural difficulties. There may also be people in churches that have an institutional structure, perhaps chaplains serving Deaf people, who find Moltmann's approach seemingly too dismissive of the way in which they have experienced church. They will need tenacity and perseverance if they are to adopt the new ways and forms of church experience that he suggests.

Some people, perhaps because of their political persuasions, may have difficulty in adopting Moltmann's socialist approach and analysis of the problems of humanity.

There may be a reluctance to adopt some of Moltmann's ecclesiological views because he does not provide a blueprint or pattern for the way in which we should *be church*. This can be frustrating for those used to the modern way of applying techniques and ready-made solutions. His way is challenging and requires effort if we are to grasp the need to modify our view, attitudes and perspectives in the ways that he suggests. To follow his way of understanding what it is *to be* and *to be church* requires us to recognise that the genuine forms of the Christian life require a response to his invitation to dialogue and an involvement that may be too demanding.

We have found that Moltmann's many faceted method of dealing with theological matters suggests possibilities, encourages dialogue and provides a well-developed and cohesive theology that is systematically sound. His ecclesiology is particularly able to adapt to the changing concerns of society, as it is holistic in nature. His eschatologically based ontology with its well developed dynamic Christology promises much for Deaf people. He provides a new liberating perspective on life and encourages good models of the church.

We consider that Moltmann's ecclesiology offers Deaf people a way of achieving equality of access, with dignity, to all that the church has to offer as it conveys the simplicity and beauty of our hope in God's promised future.

Bibliography

Alker, D., 'The Changing Deaf Communities' in International Ecumenical Working Group (ed.), *The Place of Deaf People in the Church. The Canterbury 1994 Conference Papers* (q.v.) 178-182.
Appleby, J., Covington, E., Hoyt, D., Latham, M. and Sneider, A., *Knowledge and Postmodernism in Historical Perspective* (New York & London: Routledge, 1996).
Baillie, J. and Martin, H. (eds.), *Revelation* (London: Faber & Faber, 1937).
Barnes, J. (ed.), *The Complete Works of Aristotle, Volume 2* (Princeton: Princeton University Press, 1984).
Bauckham, R., *The Theology of Jürgen Moltmann* (Edinburgh: T & T Clark, 1995).
— 'Eschatology in *The Coming of God*' in R. Bauckham (ed.), *God Will be All in All. The Eschatology of Jürgen Moltmann* (q.v.) 1-34.
Bauckham, R. (ed.), *God Will be All in All. The Eschatology of Jürgen Moltmann* (Edinburgh: T & T Clark, 1999).
Berger, P.L., The Heretical Imperative (London: Collins, 1980).
Berger, P.L. and Luckmann, T., *The Social Construction of Reality: A Treatise in the Sociology of Knowledge* (New York: Doubleday, 1966).
Biesold, H., Crying Hands. Eugenics and Deaf People in Nazi Germany (Washington, D.C. : Gallaudet University Press, 1999).
The Book of Common Prayer The (Glasgow: Collins, undated).
Bosch, D.J., *Transforming Mission. Paradigm Shifts in Theology of Mission* (Maryknoll, New York: Orbis Books, 1991).
Bowlby, J., *Attachment and Loss, Volume III. Loss: Sadness and Depression* (Harmondsworth: Penguin, 1981).
Bradshaw, T., *Trinity and Ontology. A Comparative Study of the Theologies of Karl Barth and Wolfhart Pannenberg* (Edinburgh: Rutherford House Books, 1985).
Braine, D., *The Human Person, Animal and Spirit* (London: Duckworth, 1993).
Bray, G.L., 'Iconoclastic controversies' in Ferguson and Wright (eds.), *New Dictionary of Theology* (q.v.) 326.
Brennan, M., *Word Formation in British Sign Language* (Stockholm: University of Stockholm, 1990).
Brümmer, V., *The Model of Love* (Cambridge: Cambridge University Press, 1993).
Bullock, A. and Stallybrass, O. (eds.), *The Fontana Dictionary of Modern Thought* (London: Collins, 1977).
Cherry, C., *On Human Communication* (Cambridge, Massachusetts & London: MIT Press, 1980).

Church of England, Advisory Board of Ministry Working Party (eds.), *Ministry Paper No. 14. The Church Among Deaf People, A Report prepared by a Working Party of the Committee for Ministry among Deaf People for the General Synod of the Church of England's Advisory Board of Ministry* (London: Church House Publishing, 1997).

Cloud, H. and Townsend, J., *Boundaries* (Grand Rapids: Zondervan, 1992).

Cobb, J.B. Jr., *Process Theology as Political Theology* (Manchester: Manchester University Press & Philadelphia: Westminster Press, 1982).

Conyers, A.J., *God, Hope and History* (Macon, Georgia: Mercer University Press, 1988).

Corker, M., *Counselling — The Deaf Challenge* (London and Bristol, Pennsylvania: Jessica Kingsley Publishers, 1994).

— *Deaf Transitions* (London & Bristol, Pennsylvania: Jessica Kingsley Publishers, 1996).

— 'Deaf people and interpreting – the struggle in language' in *Deaf Worlds* 13 Number 3 (November 1997) 13-20.

Cotton, I., *The Hallelujah Revolution* (London: Warner Books, 1996).

Crystal, D. (ed.), *The Cambridge Encyclopedia of Language* (Cambridge: Cambridge University Press, 1990).

D'Costa, G., '"On Trinitarian Ecclesiologies", a review of "After Our Likeness. The Church as Image of the Trinity" by M. Volf' in *Reviews in Religion and Theology* Number 3 (August 1998) 9-11.

Deane-Drummond, C., 'Jürgen Moltmann on Heaven' in A.N.S. Lane (ed.), *The Unseen World* (Carlisle and Grand Rapids: Paternoster and Baker Book House, 1996) 49-64.

Denmark, J., 'Back to the future' in Laurenzi and Ridgeway (eds.), *Progress through Equality* (q.v.) 5-9.

Dillistone, F.W., *Christianity and Symbolism* (London: Collins, 1955).

— *The Power of Symbols* (London: SCM Press, 1986).

Dimmock, A., 'Sport and Leisure' in J.V. Van Cleve (ed.), *Gallaudet Encyclopedia of Deaf People and Deafness, Volume 3* (New York: McGraw-Hill Book Company, 1987) 330-331.

Douglas, M., *Implicit Meanings* (London, Boston and Henley: Routledge & Kegan Paul, 1975).

Downes, W., *Language and Society* (London: Fontana Paperbacks, 1984).

Dulles, A., *Models of the Church* (Dublin: Gill and Macmillan, 2nd edition, 1988).

Dunlop, F., *Thinkers of Our Time, Scheler* (London: Claridge Press, 1991).

Ellis, A.W. and Young, A.W., *Human Cognitive Neuropsychology* (Hove and Hillsdale, Michigan: Lawrence Erlbaum Associates, 1988).

Ellison, H.L., in G.C.D. Howley (ed.), *A New Testament Commentary* (London: Pickering & Inglis, 1969).

Erikson, E., *Identity: Youth and Crisis* (London: Faber, 1968).

Farley, E., *Deep Symbols. Their Postmodern Effacement and Reclamation* (Valley Forge, Pennsylvania: Trinity Press International, 1996).

Farrow, D.B., 'In the end is the beginning: a review of Jürgen Moltmann's systematic contributions,' *Modern Theology* 14 (1998) 425-447.

Fergusson, D. and Sarot, M. (eds.), *The Future as God's Gift. Explorations in Christian Eschatology* (Edinburgh: T & T Clark, 2000).

Ferguson, S.B. and Wright, D.F. (eds.), *New Dictionary of Theology* (Leicester and Downers Grove, Illinois: IVP, 1988).

Fitzpatrick, J.P., 'Prejudice' in *New Catholic Encyclopedia*, Vol XI (New York: McGraw-Hill Book Company, 1967).

Friedrich, C.J. (ed.), *The Philosophy of Hegel* (New York: Random House 1954).

Fowler, H.W. and F.G. (eds.), *The Concise Oxford Dictionary of Current English* (London: Oxford University Press, 5th edition, 1964).

Freedman, M., 'Myth' in Bullock and Stallybrass (eds.), *The Fontana Dictionary of Modern Thought* (q.v.) 407.

Geertz, C., *The Interpretation of Cultures* (London: Fontana, 1993).

Giddens, A., *Modernity and Self-Identity* (Cambridge: Polity Press and Blackwell Publishers, 1991).

Giddens, A., *Sociology* (Cambridge: Polity Press and Blackwell Publishers, 2nd edition, 1993).

Goffmann, E., *Stigma* (Harmondsworth: Penguin, 1968).

— *The Presentation of the Self in Everyday Life* (Harmondsworth: Penguin, 1969).

Gregory, S. and Hartley, G.M. (eds.), *Constructing Deafness* (London: Pinter Publishers in association with The Open University, 1991).

Grenz, S.J. and Olson, R.E., *20th Century Theology* (Carlisle: Paternoster Press, 1992).

Groce, N.E., *Everyone Here Spoke Sign Language* (Cambridge, Massachusetts & London: Harvard University Press, 1985).

Gunton, C., *The Actuality of the Atonement* (Edinburgh: T & T Clark, 1988).

— *The One, the Three and the Many* (Cambridge: Cambridge University Press, 1993).

— *The Promise of Trinitarian Theology* (Edinburgh: T & T Clark, 1991).

Habermas, J., 'Philosophy as Stand-In and Interpreter' in Appleby *et al.* (eds.), *Knowledge and Postmodernism in Historical Perspective* (q.v.) 509-519.

Hart, T., 'Imagination for the kingdom of God' in Bauckham (ed.), *God Will be All in All* (q.v.) 49-76.

Harvey, D., 'The Condition of Postmodernity' in Appleby *et al.* (eds.), *Knowledge and Postmodernism in Historical Perspective* (q.v.) 493-507.

Helm, P., *The Divine Revelation* (London: Marshall Morgan & Scott, 1982).

Hillman, J., *Archetypal Psychology. A Brief Account* (Dallas: Spring Publications, 1983).

Hitching, R.D., '*Do we need Moltmann's Radical Church? – A Critique of Jürgen Moltmann's Ecclesiology in the Pastoral Context*' Dissertation for MTh King's College, London, 1991).

Hollander, E.P., *Principles and Methods of Social Psychology* (New York: Oxford University Press, 3rd edition, 1976).

Horne, B., 'Theology in the Narrative Mode' in P. Byrne and L. Houlden (eds.), *Companion Encyclopedia of Theology* (London & New York: Routledge, 1995) 958-959.

Hunt, V., 'My Story' in International Ecumenical Working Group (ed.), *The Place of Deaf People in the Church. The Canterbury 1994 Conference Papers* (q.v.) 20-34.

The Hutchinson Encyclopaedia (Oxford: Helicon Publishing, 1996).

Inge, J., 'Friendship and Christian Relationship' in *Theology* CI 804 (1998) 425-426.

International Ecumenical Working Group (ed.), *The Place of Deaf People in the Church. The Canterbury 1994 Conference Papers* (Northampton: Visible Communications, 1996).

Johansson, I., *Ontological Investigations. An Inquiry into the Categories of Nature, Man and Society* (London & New York: Routledge, 1989).

Johnson, R.A., *Rudolf Bultmann. Interpreting Faith for the Modern Era* (London: Collins, 1987).

Jung, C., 'Approaching the Unconscious' in C. Jung (ed.), *Man and his Symbols* (London: Picador/Pan Books, 1978) 1-94.

Kerwin, J., *Building Bridges ... Between the Deaf and Hearing Cultures* (Dutton Park, Australia: Brisbane Catholic Education, 1996).

Knudsden, R.D., 'Symbol' in Ferguson and Wright (eds.), *New Dictionary of Theology* (q.v.) 669-670.

Kuhn, T., *The Structure of Scientific Revolutions* (Chicago: Chicago University Press, 1970).

Küng, H., *The Church* (Tunbridge Wells, Kent: Search Press, 1968).

Kyle, J.G. and Woll, B., *Sign Language. The Study of Deaf People and Their Language* (Cambridge: Cambridge University Press, 1988).

Ladd, P., 'The Modern Deaf Community' in D. Miles (ed.), *British Sign Language. A Beginner's Guide* (London: BBC Books) 27-43.

LaFollette, H., *Personal Relationships. Love, Identity, and Morality* (Oxford and Cambridge, Massachusetts: Blackwell, 1996).

Lane, A., 'Review of The Way of Jesus Christ. Christology in Messianic Dimensions' in *Themelios* 17 Number 2 (January/February 1992) 33-34.

Lane, H., *The Mask of Benevolence. Disabling the Deaf Community* (New York: Vintage Books, 1993).

Lash, N., 'Hoping against Hope or Abraham's Dilemma' in *Modern Theology* 10 (1994) 233-246.

Laurenzi, C., and Ridgeway, S. (eds.), *Progress through Equality* (London: BSMHD Publications, 1996).

Lewis, C.S., *A Grief Observed* (London: Faber & Faber, 1961).

Lewis, H., 'The Deaf Challenge to the Churches', Paper presented to the Deafhood Conference, London 12 July 2001.

Macquarrie, J., *Heidegger and Christianity* (London: SCM Press, 1994).

Maffei, G., 'Archetypal Structures, Primal Repression and the Therapeutic Relationship with Psychotics' in R.K. Papadopoulos and G.S. Saayman (eds.), *Jung in Modern Perspective. The Master and his Legacy* (Bridport, Dorset: Prism Press, 1991) 119-134.

Marshall, G. (ed.), *The Concise Oxford Dictionary of Sociology* (Oxford and New York: 1996).

Marshall, I.H., *Kept by the Power of God* (Carlisle: Paternoster Press, 1995 [1969]).

McDonnough, P., 'A Deaf Priest's View' in International Ecumenical Working Group (ed.), *The Place of Deaf People in the Church. The Canterbury 1994 Conference Papers* (q.v.) 35-54.

— 'Deaf and Made in the Image and Likeness of God. Deaf and Made Like God: Deaf People Communicating the Gospel'. Swanwick Conference Paper, June 1998.

McGrath, A.E. (ed.), *The Blackwell Encyclopedia of Modern Christian Thought* (Oxford: Blackwell Publishers, 1993).

Meeks, M.D., Introduction to J. Moltmann, *On Human Dignity. Political Theology and Ethics* (q.v.).

— *Origins of the Theology of Hope* (Philadelphia: Fortress Press, 1974).

— 'Foreword' in J. Moltmann, *The Experiment Hope* (London: SCM Press, 1975).

— 'The future of Theology in a Commodity Society' in Volf et al. (eds.), *The Future of Theology. Essays in Honor of Jürgen Moltmann* (q.v.) 253-266.

Miller, L., and Grenz, S.J. (eds.), Fortress Introduction to Contemporary Theologies (Minneapolis: Fortress Press, 1998).

Moltmann, J., *'Christianity and the Values of the Western World'*, a lecture at St Paul's Cathedral in September 1998.

— *'Christianity on the Threshold of the Third Millennium – What to preserve and what to leave behind'*, a lecture at St Paul's Cathedral in September 1998.

— *Experiences in Theology. Ways and Forms of Christian Theology* (London: SCM Press, 2000).

— *God for a Secular Society. The Public Relevance of Theology* (London: SCM Press, 1999).

— *God in Creation. An Ecological Doctrine of Creation* (London: SCM Press, 1985).

— *History and the Triune God. Contributions to Trinitarian Theology* (London: SCM Press, 1991).

— *Hope and Planning* (London: SCM Press, 1971).

— 'Hope and Reality: Contradiction and Correspondence' in R.Bauckham (ed.), *God Will be All in All. The Eschatology of Jürgen Moltmann* (q.v.) 81.

— *Jesus Christ for Today's World* (London: SCM Press, 1994).

— *On Human Dignity. Political Theology and Ethics* (Philadelphia: Fortress Press, 1984).

— *The Church in the Power of the Spirit. A Contribution to Messianic Ecclesiology* (London: SCM Press, 1977).

— *The Coming of God. Christian Eschatology* (London: SCM Press, 1996).
— *The Crucified God. The Cross of Christ as the Foundation and Criticism of Christian Theology* (London: SCM Press, 1974).
— *The Experiment Hope* (London: SCM Press, 1975).
— *The Future of Creation* (London: SCM Press, 1979).
— 'The Liberation of the future and its anticipations in history' in R.Bauckham (ed.), God Will be All in All. The Eschatology of Jürgen Moltmann (q.v.) 265-289.
— *Theology and Joy* (London: SCM Press, 1973).
— *Theology of Hope. On the Ground and the Implications of a Christian Eschatology* (London: SCM Press, 1967).
— *The Open Church. Invitation to a Messianic Lifestyle* (London: SCM Press, 1978).
— *The Power of the Powerless* (London: SCM Press, 1983).
— *The Source of Life. The Holy Spirit and the Theology of Life* (London: SCM Press, 1997).
— *The Spirit of Life. A Universal Affirmation* (London: SCM Press, 1992).
— *The Trinity and the Kingdom of God. The Doctrine of God* (London: SCM Press, 1981).
— *The Way of Jesus Christ. Christology in Messianic Dimensions* (London: SCM Press, 1990).
Monaghan, L., 'From Strength to Strength: the Future of Deaf Communities', Paper presented to The Deaf Futures Conference, University of Central Lancashire, June 1996.
Montgomery, J. and G., *No Lesser God* (Edinburgh: Scottish Workshop Publications, 1997).
Moorhead, D., 'Meanings of Deafness' in *Deaf Worlds* 13 Number 1 (March 1997) 2-8.
Morgan Jones, R.A., 'Family Life, Hearing Impairment and the Church' in International Ecumenical Working Group (ed.), *The Place of Deaf People in the Church. The Canterbury 1994 Conference Papers* (q.v.) 104-120.
Morris, J., *Pride against Prejudice. A Personal Politics of Disability* (London: The Women's Press, 1991).
Müller-Fahrenholz, G., *The Kingdom and the Power. The Theology of Jürgen Moltmann* (London: SCM Press, 2000).
Napier, J., 'Free your mind – the rest will follow' in *Deaf Worlds* 14 Number 3 (November 1998) 15-22.
Neill, S., *The Interpretation of the New Testament. 1861-1961* (London: Oxford University Press, 1973).
NIV Study Bible, The (London: Hodder & Stoughton,1987).
Oliver, M., *Politics of Disablement* (Basingstoke: Macmillan and St Martins Press, 1990).
— *Understanding Disability* (London: MacMillan Press, 1996).

Olson, R., 'Trinity and Eschatology: The Historical Being of God in Jürgen Moltmann and Wolfhart Pannenberg' in *Scottish Journal of Theology* 36 (1983) 213-227.

Otto, R.E., *The God of Hope: The Trinitarian Vision of Jürgen Moltmann* (Lanham/London: University Press of America, 1991).

Ouspensky, L. and Lossky, V., *The Meaning of Icons* (Crestwood, New York: St. Vladimir's Seminary Press, 1982).

Pannenberg, W., *Systematic Theology, Volume 1* (Grand Rapids: Eerdmans, 1991).

Parasnis, I. (ed.), *Cultural and Language Diversity and the Deaf Experience* (Cambridge: Cambridge University Press, 1996).

Parratt, D. and Tipping, B., 'The State, Social Work and Deafness' in *Journal of the National Council of Social Workers with the Deaf* 2 Number 4 (1986) 8-11.

Phoenix, S., 'Identification Processes and Staff Training in Family Intervention Using Total Communication' in Laurenzi and Ridgeway (eds.), *Progress Through Equality* (q.v.) 43-49.

Pinnock, C.H., 'Evangelical Theologians Facing the Future: An Ancient and a Future Paradigm', Keynote Address for the 33rd Annual Meeting of the Wesleyan Theological Society Nov 7-8, 1997.

— *The Scripture Principle* (London: Hodder & Stoughton, 1985).

Pinker, S., *The Language Instinct* (Harmondsworth: Penguin, 1995).

Ridgeway, S., 'Deaf People and Psychological Health – Some Preliminary Findings' in *Deaf Worlds* 13 Number 1 (March 1997) 9-18.

— 'Teddy Bear ... Teddy Bear ...' in Laurenzi and Ridgeway (eds.), *Progress through Equality* (q.v.) 25-30.

Sacks, O., *Seeing Voices* (London: Pan Books, 1990).

Shrine, R., 'Challenge and Opportunity. What are the Deaf Ways of Being Church?' (unpublished paper, undated).

Shrine, R., 'Interview' in *Signs, Magazine of the National Deaf Church Conference* (Spring 2001) 9.

Storkey, E., '(London) Synod Report' in *Signs, Magazine of the National Deaf Church Conference* (Autumn 1997) 4.

Sugden, C.M.N., 'Poverty and Wealth' in Ferguson and Wright (eds.), *New Dictionary of Theology* (q.v.) 523-524.

Sutton-Spence, R. and Woll, B., *The Linguistics of British Sign Language. An Introduction* (Cambridge: Cambridge University Press, 1999).

Taub, S.F., *Language from the Body. Iconicity and Metaphor in American Sign Language* (Cambridge: Cambridge University Press, 2001).

Thiselton, A.C., *Interpreting God and the Postmodern Self* (Edinburgh: T & T Clark, 1995).

Thompson, J., *Modern Trinitarian Perspectives* (New York: Oxford University Press, 1994).

Travis, S.H., 'Eschatology' in Ferguson and Wright (eds.), *New Dictionary of Theology* (q.v.) 228-231.

Tripp, J., 'Worship and the Pastoral Office' in C. Jones, G. Wainwright and E. Yarnold, *The Study of Liturgy* (London: SPCK, 1978) 510-532.

Turner, D., 'The Art of Unknowing – Negative Theology in Late Medieval Mysticism' in *Modern Theology* 14 (1988) 473-488.

Volf M., *After Our Likeness. The Church as the Image of the Trinity* (Grand Rapids and Cambridge: Eerdmans, 1998).

— *Exclusion and Embrace* (Nashville: Abingdon Press, 1996).

— 'Theology, Meaning and Power' in Volf *et al.*(eds.), *The Future of Theology. Essays in Honor of Jürgen Moltmann* (q.v.) 98-113.

Volf, M., Krieg, C. and Kucharz, T. (eds.), *The Future of Theology. Essays in Honor of Jürgen Moltmann* (Grand Rapids and Cambridge: Eerdmans, 1996).

Vygotsky, L.S., *Thought and Language* (Cambridge, Massachusetts and New York: MIT Press and John Wiley & Sons, 1962).

Walton, R.C., 'Jürgen Moltmann's Theology of Hope' in R.H. Nash (ed.), *Liberation Theology* (Milford, Michigan: Mott Media, 1984).

Weir, M., 'Made Deaf in God's Image' in International Ecumenical Working Group (ed.), *The Place of Deaf People in the Church. The Canterbury 1994 Conference Papers* (q.v.) 1-10.

Wells, D., *God in the Wasteland* (Grand Rapids: Eerdmans, 1994).

Willett, J., 'Gestus' in Bullock and Stallybrass (eds.), *The Fontana Dictionary of Modern Thought* (q.v.) 265.

Willis, W.W. Jr., *Theism, Atheism and the Doctrine of the Trinity. The Trinitarian Theologies of Karl Barth and Jürgen Moltmann in Response to Protest Atheism* (Atlanta: Scholars Press, 1987).

Woodward, J., 'How You Gonna Get to Heaven if You Can't Talk With Jesus: The Educational Establishment vs. The Deaf Community' in *How You Gonna Get to Heaven if You Can't Talk With Jesus. On Depathologizing Deafness* (Silver Spring, Maryland: T.J. Publishers Inc., 1982) 11-19.

Young, A., Ackerman, J. and Kyle, J., *Looking On, Deaf People and the Organisation of Services* (Bristol: Policy Press, 1998).

Index

alienation xviii, 5, 8, 31, 150
Alker, D. 5
American Sign Language 25, 42, 171
analogy 68, 75, 79, 143, 151, 159, 161, 196, 218
Anglican evangelicalism 31
Anglicans 38
anthropology 87, 99, 134
anthropomorphism 123
anticipation 53, 71, 191
aphasia 47, 66
Aquinas 41
Aristotelianism 73
Aristotle 208, 209
Arminianism 3, 160
atonement 82, 95
Augustine 109
Australian Sign Language 25
autobiography 83, 84, 91

Barth, K. 63, 68, 85, 99, 100, 104, 120, 128, 129, 130, 152
Bauckham, R. 8, 61, 76, 77, 125, 139, 175
being 136, 159
Bellugi, U. 47
Berger, P.L. 98, 124
Bible, The xix, 3, 45, 79, 86
Bloch, E. 63, 105, 108, 116, 124, 128, 157, 196, 209
Body of Christ 20, 29
Boff, L. 100
Bowlby, J. 51, 52, 53, 57
Bradshaw, T. 128, 129
Braine, D. 40, 41, 42, 56
Brennan, M. 170
Brethren 4
British Deaf Association 22

British Sign Language xvii, 6, 24, 25, 26, 29, 33, 34, 40, 42, 56, 69, 70, 94, 97, 199
Brümmer, V. 202
Bultmann, R. 3, 74
Burns, E. 140

Calvinism 160
Cappadocian Fathers 108, 109
chaplains 23, 26, 27
Charismatic churches xx, 3
charismatic experience 4
Cherry, C. 94
Childs, B. 85
Christology 59, 82, 85, 125, 126, 175, 210
Church of England 2, 26, 27, 31, 34, 35, 36, 140
church xviii, xx, xxi, 2, 3, 7, 9, 11, 12, 13, 19, 21, 22, 26, 28, 30, 31, 35, 36, 45, 49, 54, 55, 56, 58, 59, 61, 70, 71, 72, 73, 76, 77, 78, 80, 81, 90, 105, 109, 111, 112, 116, 119, 121, 122, 127, 133, 139, 140, 142, 144, 145, 149, 153, 154, 156, 158, 161, 164, 167, 168, 169, 172, 173, 174, 175, 176, 177, 178, 179, 182, 184, 185, 186, 187, 189, 191, 203, 217, 219, 220
church-type 189
class structure 44
Clements, R.E. 85
Cobb, Jr, J.B. 211, 212
communication xxi, 5, 24, 25, 30, 32, 34, 36, 41, 46, 47, 48, 49, 50, 56, 58, 70, 93, 94, 115, 117, 145, 148, 146, 149, 150, 151, 159, 160, 161, 163, 164, 165, 166,

167, 170, 171, 173, 174, 175, 176, 177, 178, 179, 180, 181, 182, 218
conversion 147
Conyers, A.J. 78, 79, 80, 129, 130, 133
Corker, M. 96, 97, 98, 115
cosmology 82, 108, 178
Council for the Advancement of Communication with Deaf People 26
covenant 79, 82, 142, 200, 214
creation 59, 60, 64, 75, 82, 83, 84, 91, 110, 113, 119, 123, 146, 148, 160, 209
culture 1, 4, 5, 6, 55, 72, 87, 107, 217

D'Costa, G. 206, 207
Deaf Missioners 21
deep symbol 148
Denmark, J. 23
dialectic xviii, xix, 43, 48, 51, 58, 59, 64, 66, 67, 68, 74, 78, 88, 89, 90, 91, 92, 99, 104, 107, 108, 115, 116, 117, 120, 126, 127, 128, 130, 134, 136, 138, 139, 142, 143, 145, 153, 154, 159, 161, 165, 169, 178, 179, 182, 184, 189, 192, 207, 217, 218
Dillistone, F.W. 151, 152, 153
Dimmock, A. 21, 22
disability xviii, 1, 5, 6, 9,10, 11, 12, 14, 15, 39, 45, 55, 77, 84, 217
discrimination xviii, 7, 15
disintegration 32
divine communication 198
doctrine of man 29, 50, 119, 127, 141
Douglas, M. 87, 89
Downes, W. 167, 168
dynamic xvii
ecclesiology xvii, xviii, xix, xx, xxi, 1, 2, 3, 4, 7, 9, 12, 15, 35, 50, 57, 59, 61, 76, 78, 80, 89, 91, 109, 111, 112, 117, 121, 144, 151, 154, 173, 175, 184, 189, 191, 200, 203, 206, 213, 217, 218, 219, 220
Eckhart, M. 201
ecology 82, 136, 187, 188, 213
ecumenical dialogue 3
ecumenism 203
education 16, 17, 33
Ellis, A.W. 169, 170
emancipation 203
Enlightenment 60, 85
ephphatha 29
epistemology 129, 130, 159, 168, 208
Epsicopal Churches 2
equality 208, 214
Erikson, E. 97
eschatological hope xviii, 7, 8, 52, 53, 57, 61, 62, 64, 65, 137, 138, 145, 146, 147, 148, 153, 167, 168, 169, 181, 194
eschatological ontology 14, 64, 65, 66, 67, 84, 90, 119, 121, 126, 127, 130, 138, 141, 144, 146
eschatology xvii, xix, 8, 14, 50, 59, 60, 64, 65, 66, 67, 76, 80, 84, 86, 99, 102, 103, 120, 121, 125, 126, 127, 128, 130, 138, 142, 147, 153, 159, 162, 164, 166, 167, 169, 172, 177, 180, 183, 192, 193, 196, 206, 208, 217, 218, 220
esperanto 24
Eucharist 156, 187
eugenics 39
evangelism 22
events 93
existentialism 3
experience 3
exploitation 31

federalism 79
Fitzpatrick, J.P. 206

Index 231

free churches xx
freedom 110, 111, 112, 134, 135, 137, 138, 143, 148, 152, 185, 200, 214, 218, 219
Friedrich, C.J. 74
friendship 204, 205, 209, 219

Gallaudet College of Higher Education xvii
Geertz, C. 105, 106, 107, 115
gestures 24
Giddens, A. 32, 91, 202, 203
God 14, 18, 20, 21, 29, 46, 48, 50, 51, 52, 53, 55, 58, 60, 61, 62, 63, 64, 65, 67, 68, 69, 70, 71, 74, 75, 76, 77, 79, 80, 82, 84, 87, 90, 91, 94, 95, 96, 99, 100, 101, 102, 103, 104, 109, 110, 111, 113, 115, 116, 117, 119, 120, 121, 122, 123, 124, 125, 126, 127, 128, 129, 130, 133, 134, 135, 138, 139, 140, 141, 142, 143, 144, 145, 146, 147, 149, 150, 151, 153, 159, 160, 161, 162, 163, 166, 168, 169, 171, 173, 174, 175, 176, 177, 179, 180, 181, 183, 190, 191, 192, 194, 195, 196, 197, 198, 201, 204, 207, 208, 209, 210, 213, 214, 215, 217, 218, 219, 220
God the Father 62, 68, 75, 76, 110 112, 120, 160, 162, 207
God the Son 75, 76, 110, 120, 137, 160, 162, 174, 207
Godforsakenness 113, 117, 125
Goffmann, E. 72
Grenz, S.J. 61, 62, 119, 120
Groce, N. 211
Gunton, C. 84, 85, 91, 95, 96, 100, 110, 114, 154, 161, 162

Habermas, S. 128, 129
handicap 12, 39, 189, 190
Harvey, D. 131, 132

Hegel, G.W.F. 64, 68, 73, 74, 90, 128, 129, 175, 197
Heidegger, M. 128, 136
Helm, P. 67
hermeneutics xvii, 48, 49, 50, 52, 57, 129, 133, 143, 157
Hick, J. 3
hierarchy/non-hierarchy xix, 2, 9, 13, 34, 35, 38, 61, 62, 69, 78, 79, 80, 90, 123, 133, 145, 149, 186, 204, 205, 209, 219
high church tradition 31
Hillman, J 54
Hollander, EP. 172
Holy Spirit 48, 59, 74, 76, 90, 101, 102, 110, 113, 120, 121, 122, 123, 147, 160, 174, 175, 194, 207
hope 3, 59, 63, 103, 121, 135, 136, 137, 141, 143, 146, 176, 177, 195, 209
Horne, B. 88
house churches xx
Hunt, V. 19, 20

Ichthus 3
iconic signs xviii, 24, 25, 51, 94,, 145, 161, 170, 171, 178, 180, 182, 217, 218
iconoclasm 85
icons 151, 155, 156, 179
identity 93
ideology 84
image of Christ 100
image of God 18, 20
imagery 155, 170, 217
images 24, 55, 56, 158, 177, 178, 182
imagination 198
incarnation 138
inclusivism 205
independent churches xx
individualism 80
infant baptism 77, 189
Inge, J. 204, 205

integration 33
interdependence 214
interpreter(s) 33, 34, 199, 200

Jesus Christ xix, 8, 9, 10, 13, 14, 15, 36, 37, 55, 59, 62, 63, 65, 67, 68, 76, 80, 82, 83, 90, 100, 108, 113, 120, 121, 125, 126, 127, 137, 139, 140, 142, 147, 148, 151, 152, 156, 160, 166, 174, 175, 176, 177, 178, 181, 185, 193, 196, 203, 204, 209, 210, 214, 215
Joachim of Fiore 110
Johansson, I. 124, 141
Johnson, R.A. 73
Jung, C. 54

Kant, I. 60, 128, 129
Kasper, W. 100
Kerwin, J. 28, 37
kerygma 175
Kierkegaard, S. 68, 98, 115, 209
kingdom of God xviii, xix, 38, 49, 59, 60, 63, 75, 76, 78, 80, 94, 103, 109, 110, 111, 116, 121, 122, 125, 139, 141, 147, 148, 155, 167, 173, 176, 177, 178, 184, 185, 189, 198, 213, 218
Küng, H. 154, 177, 178
Kyle, J.G. 5, 6, 22, 24, 32, 42, 56, 94

Ladd, P. 5
LaFolllette, H. 208
Lane, H. 16, 18, 19, 32, 186
language 1, 4, 5, 6, 7, 21, 24, 34, 36, 37, 38, 40, 41, 42, 43, 44, 45, 46, 47, 48, 51, 55, 56, 57, 66, 70, 87, 89, 91, 93, 94, 95, 109, 114, 124, 140, 142, 155, 161, 162, 164, 167, 169, 170, 171, 173, 178, 180, 181, 194, 195, 197, 201, 208, 217
Lash, N. 204, 205

learned responses 71
Lessing, G.E. 60, 70
Lewis, C.S. 85
liberation xviii, xix, xxi, 9, 12, 14, 15, 21, 23, 47, 52, 57, 61, 69, 82, 89, 91, 117, 127, 128, 150, 169, 184, 185, 187, 211, 219, 220
liberation theologies 4
Lindbeck, G. 86
linguistic information 1
linguistic signs 124
lip-reading 16
lip-speaking 28, 33
liturgy 28, 29, 30, 33, 36, 37, 49, 71, 103, 153, 157
Lossky, V. 155, 156, 179

Macquarrie, J. 136
Maffei, G. 54
marginalization 19, 132, 211, 217
Marshall, I.H. 160, 161
McDonnough, P. 27, 29, 70
McGrath, A.E. 68
meaning 93
Meeks, M.D. 104, 139, 187
memory 158, 169
messianic ecclesiology 76
messianism 15, 202
metaphor(s) xvii, 49, 57, 87, 93, 94, 95, 115, 134, 143, 154, 157, 171, 179, 214, 217, 218
metaphorical iconicity xvii
metaphysics 65
Metz, J.B. 211
Milan Congress, 1880 16, 17
ministers 2
ministry 2, 4, 21, 36
missionary work 23
missioners 22, 23
Moltmann, J. xvii, xviii, xix, xx, xxi, 1, 2, 4, 5, 7, 8, 9, 12, 13, 14, 21, 31, 35, 36, 38, 42, 45, 46, 47, 48, 50, 52, 53, 55, 56, 57, 58, 59, 60, 61, 62, 63, 64, 65, 66, 67, 68,

Index 233

69, 70, 71, 73, 74, 75, 76, 77, 78, 79, 80, 81, 82, 84, 85, 86, 87, 88, 89, 90, 91, 92, 93, 94, 96, 98, 99, 100, 101, 102, 103, 104, 105, 106, 107, 108, 109, 110, 111, 112, 113, 114, 115, 116, 117, 119, 120, 121, 122, 123, 124, 125, 126, 127, 128, 129, 130, 131, 133, 134, 135, 136, 137, 138, 139, 140, 141, 142, 143, 144, 145, 146, 147, 148, 149, 150, 151, 153, 155, 157, 158, 159, 161, 162, 164, 165, 166, 167, 168, 169, 171, 172, 173, 174, 175, 176, 177, 178, 179, 180, 181, 182, 183, 184, 185, 186, 188, 189, 190, 191, 192, 193, 194, 195, 196, 197, 198, 200, 202, 203, 204, 205, 206, 207, 208, 209, 210, 211, 212, 213, 214, 217, 218, 219, 220
Monaghan, L. 28
monarchical episcopate 36
Montgomery, G. 33, 34
Montgomery, J. 33, 34
Moorhead, D. 83, 84
Morris, J. 15
Müller-Fahrenholz, G. 120
mysticism 9
myth(s) 87, 88, 89, 91, 116, 218

Napier, J. 199
National Deaf Church Conference 35
Neill, S. 60
neuropsychology 169
New Frontiers International 3
non-language 34
non-linguistic information 1
non-verbal signals 47
note taking 33

Oliver, M. 14
Olson, R.E. 62, 119, 120

ontological hope 147, 148, 179
ontology 50, 52, 58, 65, 75, 91, 108, 121, 128, 129, 130, 134, 141, 145, 159, 161, 168, 180, 181, 183, 195, 198, 206, 207
openness xviii, xix, xxi, 21, 63, 104, 105, 106, 107, 108, 112, 113, 116, 144, 148, 153, 161, 164, 166, 174, 189, 192, 193, 195, 212, 213, 215, 219
oppression 3, 8, 10, 14, 15, 16, 18, 19, 21, 23,45, 56, 69, 79, 82, 90, 113, 114, 149, 184, 205, 211, 217, 219
oralism 16, 17
Orthodox churches 105
Orthodox theologians 109
orthodoxy 142
orthopraxis 138, 142
Otto, R.E. 77
Ouspensky, L. 155

panentheism 62, 75
Pannenberg, W. 100, 101, 129, 130
pantheism 123
paradigm(s) 50, 65, 91, 101, 146, 151, 165, 166, 200
paradigm shift 7, 18, 75
parousia 121, 131, 139, 140, 142
Parratt, D. 22, 23
participation 185
paternalism 18, 56, 114, 217
Pentecostal churches 3, 105
Pentecostalists 3
perceptual defence 53
perichoresis 76, 82, 83, 99, 101, 115, 121, 123, 136, 159, 162, 218
Persinger, M. 47, 48
perspective xvii, 19, 133, 134, 138, 143, 196, 198
philosophy 99
Phoenix, S. 33
Pinker, S. 44, 47, 89, 167
Pinnock, C.H. 48, 49, 50

Plato 41, 73
pneumatology 75
politics 14, 55
postmodernism 100
poverty 10, 128
power xviii, xix, 13, 45, 46, 55, 79, 203, 217
praxis 61, 141, 212, 213
prejudice 19
primal experiences 58
process 83
process theology 129, 211, 212, 213
psychology 16, 17, 51, 99

Rahner, K. 120, 128
Rationalism 60
reality 93
reconciliation 83, 104, 110, 125, 139, 142, 147, 159, 185, 210
redemption 82, 83, 91, 122, 127, 142, 159, 185
relational ecclesiology 76
relational/relationality xvii, xviii, 85, 146
relationship(s) xvii, xviii, xix, xx, xxi, 1, 4, 7, 8, 9, 13, 19, 20, 33, 34, 37, 38, 39, 40, 43, 45, 49, 55, 56, 57, 58, 59, 62, 63, 64, 66, 71, 72, 75, 76, 79, 80, 81, 83, 84, 85, 90, 91, 93, 96, 97, 101, 111, 112, 113, 115, 116, 117, 127, 131, 134, 136, 137, 143, 149, 157, 159, 164, 166, 168, 170, 172, 176, 178, 181, 183, 184, 192, 193, 194, 195, 196, 197, 198, 202, 204, 205, 206, 207, 208, 209, 210, 213, 214, 215, 217, 218, 219
revelation 74, 93, 94, 141, 146, 152, 160, 171
Ridgeway, S. 31
ritual(s) 70, 71, 72, 73
Roman Catholic Church 2, 26, 27, 28, 36, 37, 154

Roman Catholics 38
Romanticism 60

Sabellianism 128
Sacks, O. 66, 67
sacraments 139, 153
Salvation Army 10, 140
salvation 8, 31, 59, 60, 82, 91, 168
salvation history 76, 102, 120
Schiller, F 196
Schleiermacher, F.D.E. 123, 128
Schweitzer, A. 60
Scripture/Word of God 39, 43, 48, 49, 50, 58, 68, 69, 70, 84, 86, 113, 115, 125, 133, 143, 147, 148, 153, 155, 156, 159, 160, 163, 168, 169, 173, 178, 205, 207
sect-type 189
Shanghai (Chinese) signs 25
Shrine, R. 27, 30
sign(s) 48, 50, 67, 81, 90, 93, 156, 161, 170, 171, 179, 180, 217
Sign Supported English 26, 40
sign language xvii, 1, 7, 16, 17, 23, 24, 25, 26, 28, 30, 31, 32, 33, 35, 36, 39, 40, 43, 45, 46, 47, 51, 53, 55, 56, 81, 84, 90, 91, 94, 113, 114, 115, 143, 154, 163, 164, 170, 178, 181, 194, 211, 217, 218
sign-metaphors xviii
signers 171
Singapore Sign Language 25
socialisation 98
society xviii, 2, 7, 9, 10, 11, 12, 13, 14, 21, 44, 45, 57, 78, 79, 80, 85, 87, 91, 100, 105, 106, 124, 125, 140, 148, 150, 154, 166, 167, 168, 194, 202, 217, 220
socio-linguistics 6
sociology 99
Sölle, D. 211
special revelation 67

Index 235

Spring Harvest 3
Stoneleigh Bible Week 3
storytelling 69, 70, 90, 217
subjection xxi, 79
subordination 205
suffering xviii, 5, 7, 38, 90, 128, 135, 136, 140, 147, 150, 160, 179, 193, 210
Sugden, C.M.N. 45
Sutton-Spence, R. 25, 69
symbolic representations 146
symbolism 73, 150, 156, 180, 181, 218
symbols 24, 49, 50, 51, 55, 57, 58, 93, 94, 107, 108, 134, 143, 146, 151, 152, 153, 154, 155, 156, 157, 158, 160, 161, 168, 170, 171, 172, 178, 179, 180, 182, 218
synonymy 162

Taub, S.F. 171
Theodore the Studite 156
Thiselton, A.C. 100, 101, 102, 115
Thompson, J. 85
Tipping, B. 22, 23
tradition 3, 156, 169, 205
Travis, S.H. 131
Trinity/trinitarianism xix, 4, 13, 38, 59, 62, 75, 76, 80, 84, 85, 90, 91, 100, 101, 102, 108, 109, 110, 112, 113, 115, 116, 120, 121, 129, 130, 136, 137, 133, 145, 146, 147, 160, 161, 162, 164, 174, 175, 176, 178, 181, 187, 195, 198, 206, 207, 208, 209, 214, 218, 219
Tripp, J. 152
truth 93
Turner, D. 201
types 93

Vatican II 154
visually motivated 25
vocabulary 162
Volf, M. 86, 206
Von Rad, G. 130
Vygotsky, L.S. 66, 67

Walton, R.C. 188, 189
Weir, M. 18, 20
Wells, D. 198
Western culture 15
Woll, B. 5, 6, 22, 24, 25, 32, 42, 56, 69, 94
Woodward, J. 5
worldview(s) 58, 73, 74, 91, 138, 147
worship 150

Young, A.W. 169, 170
Being as Communion (Crestwood, New York: St. Vladimir's Seminary Press, 1993)

Paternoster Biblical and Theological Monographs
(All titles uniform with this volume)

Joseph Abraham
Eve: Accused or Acquitted?
A Reconsideration of Feminist Readings of the Creation Narrative Texts in Genesis 1–3
Two contrary views dominate contemporary feminist biblical scholarship. One finds in the Bible an unequivocal equality between the sexes from the very creation of humanity, whilst the other sees the biblical text as irredeemably patriarchal and androcentric. Dr. Abraham enters into dialogue with both camps as well as introducing his own method of approach. An invaluable tool for anyone who is interested in this contemporary debate.
2002 / ISBN 0-85364-971-5 / xxiv + 272pp

Paul Barker
The Triumph of Grace in Deuteronomy
This book is a textual and theological analysis of the interaction between the sin and faithlessness of Israel and the grace of Yahweh in response, looking especially at Deuteronomy chapters 1–3, 8–10 and 29–30. The author argues that the grace of Yahweh is determinative for the ongoing relationship between Yahweh and Israel and that Deuteronomy anticipates and fully expects Israel to be faithless.
2004 / ISBN 1-84227-226-8

Emil Bartos
Deification in Eastern Orthodox Theology
An Evaluation and Critique of the Theology of Dumitru Staniloae
Bartos studies a fundamental yet neglected aspect of Orthodox theology: deification. By examining the doctrines of anthropology, christology, soteriology and ecclesiology as they relate to deification, he provides an important contribution to contemporary dialogue between Eastern and Western theologians.
1999 / ISBN 0-85364-956-1 / xii + 370pp

Jonathan F. Bayes
The Weakness of the Law
God's Law and the Christian in New Testament Perspective
A study of the four New Testament books which refer to the law as weak (Acts, Romans, Galatians, Hebrews) leads to a defence of the third use in the Reformed debate about the law in the life of the believer.
2000 / ISBN 0-85364-957-X / xii + 244pp

Mark Bonnington
The Antioch Episode of Galatians 2:11-14 in Historical and Cultural Context

The Galatians 2 'incident' in Antioch over table-fellowship suggests significant disagreement between the leading apostles. This book analyses the background to the disagreement by locating the incident within the dynamics of social interaction between Jews and Gentiles. It proposes a new way of understanding the relationship between the individuals and issues involved.

2004 / ISBN 1-84227-050-8

Mark Bredin
Jesus, Revolutionary of Peace
A Nonviolent Christology in the Book of Revelation

This book aims to demonstrate that the figure of Jesus in the Book of Revelation can best be understood as an active nonviolent revolutionary.

2003 / ISBN 1-84227-153-9 / xviii + 260pp

James Bruce
Prophecy, Miracles, Angels *and* Heavenly Light?
'De virtutibus': The Eschatology, Pneumatology and Missiology of Adomnán's Life of Columba

This book surveys approaches to the marvellous in hagiography, providing the first critique of Plummer's hypothesis of Irish saga origin. It then analyses the uniquely systematized phenomena in the *Life of Columba* from Adomnán's seventh-century theological perspective, identifying the coming of the eschatological Kingdom as the key to understanding.

2004 / ISBN 1-84227-227-6

Colin J. Bulley
The Priesthood of Some Believers
Developments from the General to the Special Priesthood in the Christian Literature of the First Three Centuries

The first in-depth treatment of early Christian texts on the priesthood of all believers shows that the developing priesthood of the ordained related closely to the division between laity and clergy and had deleterious effects on the practice of the general priesthood.

2000 / ISBN 1-84227-034-6 / xii + 336pp

Iain D. Campbell
Fixing the Indemnity
The Life and Work of George Adam Smith
When Old Testament scholar George Adam Smith (1856–1942) delivered the Lyman Beecher lectures at Yale University in 1899 he confidently declared that 'modern criticism has won its war against traditional theories. It only remains to fix the amount of the indemnity.' In this biography, Iain D. Campbell assesses Smith's critical approach to the Old Testament and evaluates its consequences, showing that Smith's life and work still raises questions about the relationship between biblical scholarship and evangelical faith.
2004 / ISBN 1-84227-228-4

Daniel J-S Chae
Paul as Apostle to the Gentiles
His Apostolic Self-awareness and its Influence on the Soteriological Argument in Romans
Opposing 'the post-Holocaust interpretation of Romans', Daniel Chae competently demonstrates that Paul argues for the equality of Jew and Gentile in Romans. Chae's fresh exegetical interpretation is academically outstanding and spiritually encouraging.
1997 / ISBN 0-85364-829-8 / xiv + 378pp

Luke L. Cheung
The Genre, Composition and Hermeneutics of the Epistle of James
The present work examines the employment of the wisdom genre with a certain compositional structure and the interpretation of the law through the Jesus' tradition of the double love command by the author of the Epistle of James to serve his purpose in promoting perfection and warning against doubleness among the eschatologically renewed people of God in the Diaspora.
2003 / ISBN 1-84227-062-1 / xvi + 372pp

Andrew C. Clark
Parallel Lives
The Relation of Paul to the Apostles in the Lucan Perspective
This study of the Peter-Paul parallels in Acts argues that their purpose was to emphasize the themes of continuity in salvation history and the unity of the Jewish and Gentile missions. New light is shed on Luke's literary techniques, partly through a comparison with Plutarch.
2001 / 1-84227-035-4 / xviii + 386pp

Andrew D. Clarke
Secular and Christian Leadership in Corinth
A Socio-Historical and Exegetical Study of 1 Corinthians 1–6
This volume is an investigation into the leadership structures and dynamics of first-century Roman Corinth. These are compared with the practice of leadership in the Corinthian Christian community which are reflected in 1 Corinthians 1–6, and contrasted with Paul's own principles of Christian leadership.
2004 / ISBN 1-84227-229-2 / xii + 188pp

Sylvia I. Collinson
Making Disciples
The Significance of Jesus' Educational Strategy for Today's Church
This study examines the biblical practice of discipling, formulates a definition, and makes comparisons with modern models of education. A recommendation is made for greater attention to its practice today.
2004 / ISBN 1-84227-116-4

Stephen M. Dunning
The Crisis and the Quest
A Kierkegaardian Reading of Charles Williams
Employing Kierkegaardian categories and analysis, this study investigates both the central crisis in Charles Williams's authorship between hermetism and Christianity (Kierkegaard's Religions A and B), and the quest to resolve this crisis, a quest that ultimately presses the bounds of orthodoxy.
2000 / ISBN 0-85364-985-5 / xxiv + 254pp

Keith Ferdinando
The Triumph of Christ in African Perspective
A Study of Demonology and Redemption in the African Context
The book explores the implications of the gospel for traditional African fears of occult aggression. It analyses such traditional approaches to suffering and biblical responses to fears of demonic evil, concluding with an evaluation of African beliefs from the perspective of the gospel.
1999 / ISBN 0-85364-830-1 / xviii + 450pp

Stephen Finamore
God, Order and Chaos
René Girard and the Apocalypse
Readers are often disturbed by the images of destruction in the book of Revelation and unsure why they are unleashed after the exaltation of Jesus. This book examines past approaches to these texts and uses René Girard's theories to revive some old ideas and propose some new ones.
2004 / ISBN 1-84227-197-0

Andrew Goddard
Living the Word, Resisting the World
The Life and Thought of Jacques Ellul
This work offers a definitive study of both the life and thought of the French Reformed thinker Jacques Ellul (1912-1994). It will prove an indispensable resource for those interested in this influential theologian and sociologist and for Christian ethics and political thought generally.
2002 / ISBN 1-84227-053-2 / xxiv + 378pp

Ruth Gouldbourne
The Flesh and the Feminine
Gender and Theology in the Writings of Caspar Schwenckfeld
Caspar Schwenckfeld and his movement exemplify one of the radical communities of the sixteenth century. Challenging theological and liturgical norms, they also found themselves challenging social and particularly gender assumptions. In this book, the issues of the relationship between radical theology and the understanding of gender are considered.
2004 / ISBN 1-84227-048-6

Scott J. Hafemann
Suffering and Ministry in the Spirit
Paul's Defence of His Ministry in II Corinthians 2:14–3:3
Shedding new light on the way Paul defended his apostleship, the author offers a careful, detailed study of 2 Corinthians 2:14–3:3 linked with other key passages throughout 1 and 2 Corinthians. Demonstrating the unity and coherence of Paul's argument in this passage, the author shows that Paul's suffering served as the vehicle for revealing God's power and glory through the Spirit.
2000 / ISBN 0-85364-967-7 / xiv + 262pp

Roger Hitching
The Church and Deaf People
A Study of Identity, Communication and Relationships with Special Reference to the Ecclesiology of Jürgen Moltmann
In *The Church and Deaf People* Roger Hitching sensitively examines the history and present experience of deaf people and finds similarities between aspects of sign language and Moltmann's theological method that 'open up' new ways of understanding theological concepts.
2003 / ISBN 1-84227-222-5 / xxii + 236pp

John G. Kelly
One God, One People
*The Differentiated Unity of the People of God
in the Theology of Jürgen Moltmann*
The author expounds and critiques Moltmann's doctrine of God and highlights the systematic connections between it and Moltmann's influential discussion of Israel. He then proposes a fresh approach to Jewish-Christian relations building on Moltmann's work using insights from Habermas and Rawls.
2004 / ISBN 0-85346-969-3

Mark F.W. Lovatt
Confronting the Will-to-Power
A Reconsideration of the Theology of Reinhold Niebuhr
Confronting the Will-to-Power is an analysis of the theology of Reinhold Niebuhr, arguing that his work is an attempt to identify, and provide a practical theological answer to, the existence and nature of human evil.
2001 / ISBN 1-84227-054-0 / xviii + 216pp

Neil B. MacDonald
Karl Barth and the Strange New World within the Bible
Barth, Wittgenstein, and the Metadilemmas of the Enlightenment
Barth's discovery of the strange new world within the Bible is examined in the context of Kant, Hume, Overbeck, and, most importantly, Wittgenstein. MacDonald covers some fundamental issues in theology today: epistemology, the final form of the text and biblical truth-claims.
2000 / ISBN 0-85364-970-7 / xxvi + 374pp

Douglas S. McComisky
Lukan Theology in the Light of the Gospel's Literary Structure
Luke's Gospel was purposefully written with theology embedded in its patterned literary structure. A critical analysis of this cyclical structure provides new windows into Luke's interpretation of the individual pericopes comprising the gospel and illuminates several of his theological interests.
2004 / ISBN 1-84227-148-2

Gillian McCulloch
The Deconstruction of Dualism in Theology
With Reference to Ecofeminist Theology and New Age Spirituality
This book challenges eco-theological anti-dualism in Christian theology, arguing that dualism has a twofold function in Christian religious discourse. Firstly, it enables us to express the discontinuities and divisions that are part of the process of reality. Secondly, dualistic language allows us to express the mysteries of divine transcendence/immanence and the survival of the soul without collapsing into monism and materialism, both of which are problematic for Christian epistemology.
2002 / ISBN 1-84227-044-3 / xii + 282pp

Leslie McCurdy
Attributes and Atonement
The Holy Love of God in the Theology of P.T. Forsyth
Attributes and Atonement is an intriguing full-length study of P.T. Forsyth's doctrine of the cross as it relates particularly to God's holy love. It includes an unparalleled bibliography of both primary and secondary material relating to Forsyth.
1999 / ISBN 0-85364-833-6 / xiv + 328pp

Nozomu Miyahira
Towards a Theology of the Concord of God
A Japanese Perspective on the Trinity
This book introduces a new Japanese theology and a unique Trinitarian formula based on the Japanese intellectual climate: three betweennesses and one concord. It also presents a new interpretation of the Trinity, a co-subordinationism, which is in line with orthodox Trinitarianism; each single person of the Trinity is eternally and equally subordinate (or serviceable) to the other persons, so that they retain the mutual dynamic equality.
2000 / ISBN 0-85364-863-8 / xiv + 256pp

Stephen Motyer
Your Father the Devil?
A New Approach to John and 'The Jews'
Who are 'the Jews' in John's Gospel? Defending John against the charge of anti-semitism, Motyer argues that, far from demonizing the Jews, the Gospel seeks to present Jesus as 'Good News for Jews' in a late first century setting.
1997 / ISBN 0-85364-832-8 / xiv + 260pp

Eddy José Muskus
The Origins and Early Development of Liberation Theology in Latin America
With Particular Reference to Gustavo Gutiérrez

This work challenges the fundamental premise of Liberation Theology, 'opting for the poor', and its claim that Christ is found in them. It also argues that Liberation Theology emerged as a direct result of the failure of the Roman Catholic Church in Latin America.

2002 / ISBN 0-85364-974-X / xiv + 296pp

Esther Ng
Reconstructing Christian Origins?
The Feminist Theology of Elizabeth Schüssler Fiorenza: An Evaluation

In a detailed evaluation, the author challenges Elizabeth Schüssler Fiorenza's reconstruction of early Christian origins and her underlying presuppositions. The author also presents her own views on women's roles both then and now.

2002 / ISBN 1-84227-055-9 / xxiv + 468pp

Robin Parry
Old Testament Story and Christian Ethics
The Rape of Dinah as a Case Study

What is the role of story in ethics and, more particularly, what is the role of Old Testament story in Christian ethics? This book, drawing on the work of contemporary philosophers, argues that narrative is crucial in the ethical shaping of people and, drawing on the work of contemporary Old Testament scholars, that story plays a key role in Old Testament ethics. Parry then argues that when situated in canonical context Old Testament stories can be reappropriated by Christian readers in their own ethical formation. The shocking story of the rape of Dinah and the massacre of the Shechemites provides a fascinating case study for exploring the parameters within which Christian ethical appropriations of Old Testament stories can live.

2004 / ISBN 1-84227-210-1

Ian Paul
Power to See the World Anew
The Value of Paul Ricoeur's Hermeneutic of Metaphor in Interpreting the Symbolism of Revelation 12 and 13
This book is a study of the hermeneutics of metaphor of Paul Ricoeur, one of the most important writers on hermeneutics and metaphor of the last century. It sets out the key points of his theory, important criticisms of his work, and how his approach, modified in the light of these criticisms, offers a methodological framework for reading apocalyptic texts.
2004 / ISBN 1-84227-056-7

David Powys
'Hell': A Hard Look at a Hard Question
The Fate of the Unrighteous in New Testament Thought
This comprehensive treatment seeks to unlock the original meaning of terms and phrases long thought to support the traditional doctrine of hell. It concludes that there is an alternative – one which is more biblical, and which can positively revive the rationale for Christian mission.
1997 / ISBN 0-85364-831-X / xxii + 478pp

Anna Robbins
Methods in the Madness
Diversity in Twentieth-Century Christian Social Ethics
The author compares the ethical methods of Walter Rauschenbusch, Reinhold Niebuhr and others. She argues that unless Christians are clear about the ways that theology and philosophy are expressed practically they may lose the ability to discuss social ethics across contexts, let alone reach effective agreements.
2004 / ISBN 1-84227-211-X

Ed Rybarczyk
Beyond Salvation
Eastern Orthodoxy and Classical Pentecostalism on becoming like Christ
At first glance eastern Orthodoxy and Classical Pentecostalism seem quite distinct. This groundbreaking study shows that they share much in common, especially as it concerns the experiential elements of following Christ. Both traditions assert that authentic Christianity transcends the wooden categories of modernism.
2003 / ISBN 1-84227-144-X / xxiii + 379pp

Signe Sandsmark
Is World View Neutral Education Possible and Desirable?
A Christian Response to Liberal Arguments
(Published jointly with The Stapleford Centre)
This book discusses reasons for belief in world view neutrality, and argues that 'neutral' education will have a hidden, but strong world view influence. It discusses the place for Christian education in the common school.
2000 / ISBN 0-85364-973-1 / xiv + 182pp

Rosalind Selby
The Comical Doctrine
Can a Gospel Convey Truth?
This book argues that the Gospel breaks through postmodernity's critique of truth and the referential possibilities of textuality and its gift of grace. With a rigorous, philosophical challenge to modernist and postmodernist assumptions, it offers an alternative epistemology to all who would still read with faith *and* with academic credibility.
2004 / ISBN 1-84227-212-8

Hazel Sherman
Reading Zechariah
The Allegorical Tradition of Biblical Interpretation through the Commentaries of Didymus the Blind and Theodore of Mopsuestia
A close reading of the commentary on Zechariah by Didymus the Blind alongside that of Theodore of Mopsuestia suggests that popular categorising of Antiochene and Alexandrian biblical exegesis as 'historical' or 'allegorical' is inadequate and misleading.
2004 / ISBN 1-84227-213-6

Andrew Sloane
On Being a Christian in the Academy
Nicholas Wolterstorff and the Practice of Christian Scholarship
An exposition and critical appraisal of Nicholas Wolterstorff's epistemology in the light of the philosophy of science, and an application of his thought to the practice of Christian scholarship.
2003 / ISBN 1-84227-058-3 / xvi + 274pp

Daniel Strange
The Possibility of Salvation Among the Unevangelised
An Analysis of Inclusivism in Recent Evangelical Theology
For evangelical theologians the 'fate of the unevangelised' impinges upon fundamental tenets of evangelical identity. The position known as 'inclusivism', defined by the belief that the unevangelised can be ontologically saved by Christ whilst being epistemologically unaware of him, has been defended most vigorously by the Canadian evangelical Clark H. Pinnock. Through a detailed analysis and critique of Pinnock's work, this book examines a cluster of issues surrounding the unevangelised and its implications for christology, soteriology and the doctrine of revelation.
2002 / ISBN 1-84227-047-8 / xviii + 362pp

G. Michael Thomas
The Extent of the Atonement
A Dilemma for Reformed Theology from Calvin to the Consensus
This is a study of the way Reformed theology addressed the question, 'Did Christ die for all, or for the elect only?', commencing with John Calvin, and including debates with Lutheranism, the Synod of Dort and the teaching of Moïse Amyraut.
1997 / ISBN 0-85364-828-X / x + 278pp

Mark D. Thompson
A Sure Ground on which to Stand
The Relation of Authority and Interpretive Method in
Luther's Approach to Scripture
The best interpreter of Luther is Luther himself. Unfortunately many modern studies have superimposed contemporary agendas upon this sixteenth-century Reformer's writings. This fresh study examines Luther's own words to find an explanation for his robust confidence in the Scriptures, a confidence that generated the famous 'stand' at Worms in 1521.
2003 / ISBN 1-84227-145-8 / xvi + 322pp

Graham Tomlin
The Power of the Cross
Theology and the Death of Christ in Paul, Luther and Pascal
This book explores the theology of the cross in St Paul, Luther and Pascal. It offers new perspectives on the theology of each, and some implications for the nature of power, apologetics, theology and church life in a postmodern context.
1999 / ISBN 0-85364-984-7 / xiv + 344pp

Kevin Walton
Thou Traveller Unknown
The Presence and Absence of God in the Jacob Narrative
The author offers a fresh reading of the story of Jacob in the book of Genesis through the paradox of divine presence and absence. The work also seeks to make a contribution to Pentateuchal studies by bringing together a close reading of the final text with historical critical insights, doing justice to the text's historical depth, final form and canonical status.
2003 / ISBN 1-84227-059-1 / xvi + 238pp

Graham J. Watts
Revelation and the Spirit
A Comparative Study of the Relationship between the Doctrine of Revelation and Pneumatology in the Theology of Eberhard Jüngel and of Wolfhart Pannenberg
The relationship between revelation and pneumatology is relatively unexplored. This approach offers a fresh angle on two important twentieth century theologians and raises pneumatological questions which are theologically crucial and relevant to mission in a post modern culture.
2003 / ISBN 1-84227-104-0 / xxii + 232pp

Alistair Wilson
When Will These Things Happen?
A Study of Jesus as Judge in Matthew 21–25
This study seeks to allow Matthew's carefully constructed presentation of Jesus to be given full weight in the modern evaluation of Jesus' eschatology. Careful analysis of the text of Matthew 21–25 reveals Jesus to be standing firmly in the Jewish prophetic and wisdom traditions as he proclaims and enacts imminent judgement on the Jewish authorities then boldly claims the central role in the final and universal judgement.
2004 / ISBN 1-84227-146-6 / xvi + 292pp

Lindsay Wilson
Joseph Wise and Otherwise
The Intersection of Covenant and Wisdom in Genesis 37–50
This book offers a careful literary reading of Genesis 37–50 that argues that the Joseph story contains both strong covenant themes and many wisdom-like elements. The connections between the two helps to explore how covenant and wisdom might intersect in an integrated biblical theology.
2004 / ISBN 1-84227-140-7

Nigel G. Wright
Disavowing Constantine
*Mission, Church and the Social Order in the Theologies of
John Howard Yoder and Jürgen Moltmann*
This book is a timely restatement of a radical theology of church and state in the Anabaptist and Baptist tradition. Dr Wright constructs his argument in dialogue and debate with Yoder and Moltmann, major contributors to a free church perspective.
2000 / ISBN 0-85364-978-2 / xvi + 252pp

Stephen I. Wright
The Voice of Jesus
Studies in the Interpretation of Six Gospel Parables
This literary study considers how the 'voice' of Jesus has been heard in different periods of parable interpretation, and how the categories of figure and trope may help us towards a sensitive reading of the parables today.
2000 / ISBN 0-85364-975-8 / xiv + 280pp

The Paternoster Press
PO Box 300,
Carlisle,
Cumbria CA3 0QS,
United Kingdom
Web: www.paternoster-publishing.com